The Cambuslang Revival

The Cambuslang Revival

THE SCOTTISH EVANGELICAL REVIVAL
OF THE EIGHTEENTH CENTURY

Arthur Fawcett

THE BANNER OF TRUTH TRUST

THE BANNER OF TRUTH TRUST
3 *Murrayfield Road, Edinburgh* EH12 6EL
P.O. Box 621, *Carlisle, Pennsylvania* 17013, *U.S.A.*

*

© *Arthur Fawcett* 1971
First published 1971
Reprinted 1996

ISBN 0 85151 702 1

*

Printed in Finland by WSOY

ACKNOWLEDGMENTS

It is not given to many to be allowed to do as they please with
the means to do so provided; so my thanks are due, and
given gladly, to the University of Glasgow which appointed me
to a three years' tenure of the Faulds Fellowship, to the
Senatus of the Faculty of Divinity in that University which
recommended me for this honour, and especially to my super-
visor and friend, Professor John Foster (then in the Chair of
Ecclesiastical History) who was ever percipient, interested and
encouraging.

During these years of continuous research and reading,
great help came from three outstanding Glasgow librarians,
the salt of the academic earth, to whom I owe an incalculable
debt, viz. Dr. W. R. Cunningham of the University, the Revd.
James Mackintosh of Trinity College, and Mr. John Dunlop of
the Mitchell Library. They received my thanks when they
were here, and I regret that they are no longer alive to read
this tribute.

Educational and ecclesiastical authorities have always been
helpful. New College, in the University of Edinburgh, allowed
me a protracted loan of the M'Culloch manuscripts, and the
Principal has given me permission to reproduce some of the
contents as illustrations; the Presbyteries of Glasgow and
Hamilton gave me free access to their records, and the Kirk
Sessions of Cambuslang and Kilsyth did likewise. I am grate-
ful to the latter Court for permission to use illustrations from
their records. To all of these I should like to pay tribute for
their invaluable and trusting co-operation.

A man's true treasure is his friends and, by this token, I am wealthy indeed. Many have given generous aid such as the loan of a portable typewriter from which I seemed inseparable; reading, typing, checking and the like have been done in odd minutes and in strange and widespread places. I am especially indebted to Mrs. Jean Couser who, in spite of a busy life, found time to do most of the typing, to Mr. Thomas Clark of Cambuslang who went to great trouble to supply the interesting photographs of Cambuslang, to Mr. S. M. Houghton, M.A., who performed admirably the task of indexing, and to my daughter, Mrs. Hazel Jolly, who read the typescript and made many valuable suggestions. My friends will recognise themselves here; they know, I am sure, how much I owe to them.

Having been mildly irritated by the bowdlerizing attempts of various editors to improve original texts, I have taken special care to preserve quotations exactly, with all the colourful variety of spelling, grammar, capital letters and so on. The reader can, I hope, easily make any modernisation that may be necessary.

ARTHUR FAWCETT

ABBREVIATIONS

M'C. Mss: 'Examination of persons under Spiritual Concern at Cambuslang, during the Revival in 1741–2; By the Revd William MacCulloch, Minister at Cambuslang.' 2 vols Mss *pp* 1–615; 1–680

K.S.R: Kirk Session Records

Pres. Recs: Presbytery Records

Fasti: *Fasti Ecclesiae Scoticanae, ed* Hew Scott, 1915

Anal: *Analecta, or Materials for a History of Remarkable Providences* &c. Robert Wodrow (Maitland Club edition 1842)

D.N.B: *Dictionary of National Biography* 1885–1901 *eds*

S.C.H.S: *Records of the Scottish Church History Society*

Edin. Christ. Instr: *The Edinburgh Christian Instructor*

A day of the ministration of the Spirit would bring many rare and rich blessings along with it; such as discoveries of the Redeemer's glory, convictions of the evil and vileness of sin, many crowns of victory and triumph to Christ, great additions to his friends and followers. Then gospel-light would shine clear, saving knowledge increase, ignorance and error vanish, riches of free grace would be displayed, and Satan be bound up. Then ministers and ordinances would be lively, secure sinners would be awakened, dead souls would live, hard hearts would be melted, strong lusts subdued, and many sons and daughters born to God. Such a day would heal divisions, cement breaches, make us all of one heart and mind, and bring down heaven to earth. This would redress our grievances, remove our complaints, and unite Christ's scattered flock. It would make true religion and holy persons to be in esteem, vice to be in disgrace, and iniquity as ashamed to hide its face. Then sabbaths and communions would be days of heaven. Prayer and praise, spiritual converse, talking of Christ and redeeming love, would be our chiefest delight. O then, pray for such a time.

JOHN WILLISON
The Balm of Gilead, 1742

CONTENTS

INTRODUCTORY

Of the past five centuries of church history in Scotland, the eighteenth has been the most neglected. Each of the others has its own colourful and particular interest. The sixteenth is dominated by the purposeful activities of John Knox and Andrew Melville, who cleared away much rubbish and toiled to lay the foundations of a new national church. The struggle against royal theories of divine right and the attempted imposition of an unwelcome episcopacy, with armed violence, Covenants and additions to the noble army of martyrs, filled the seventeenth century. The nineteenth resounded with the uncompromising demand for the spiritual independence of the Church of Scotland, with Thomas Chalmers and the long procession of disruption ministers deserting the General Assembly in 1843, followed by a spate of condemnation and recrimination.

The few historians who have examined the religious life and thought of the eighteenth century speak no smooth words. With characteristic vehemence, Thomas Carlyle apostrophised it as 'the age of lying, of sham, the fraudulent, bankrupt century, the reign of Beelzebub, the peculiar age of cant'. Principal Tulloch says of the Church of Scotland in this century that 'she failed to realise the greatness of her mission as a National Church', and yet, says Professor Masson, 'the eighteenth century was somehow the birth-time of the most splendid men of all sorts that Scotland has yet given to the world'.[1] It was the age of such leaders as William Carstares, William Robertson and John Erskine – of such doughty contenders for the claims of the indi-

1 Masson, D.: *Memoirs of Two Cities. p* 183.

vidual conscience as Ebenezer and Ralph Erskine, Thomas Gillespie and thousands of unremembered common people. Principal John Cairns made this century one of his own special studies, and concluded: 'There is an impression in many quarters that the eighteenth century was barren and exhausted. This is the view of Mr Carlyle, often stated by him with something like denunciation ... I cannot follow him here; there was much that was shallow and artificial, doomed to a just end – but the century was also, in many directions, one of new beginnings.'[2]

New beginnings! In all walks of Scottish life that was true. The political situation brought about by the Union of England and Scotland in 1707 had opened the door to great economic advantages for the northern kingdom. The prosperous tobacco lords walked securely on the broad paving stones near Glasgow Cross; new manufactures were being introduced and developed; improving landlords, such as Lord Kilkerran in Ayrshire and Grant of Monymusk, were revolutionising agriculture. Contact with the south had brought into Scotland a multitude of new social habits, of varying worth. The century was on the move.

Religious life and thought existed within this developing situation, affected by the process of change and making their own contribution towards it. The first three decades of the eighteenth century were to see the growth of deep divisions within the established church, and then secession from it.

Throughout Europe this was the Age of Reason, and scepticism and the chilling winds of the Enlightenment were lowering the spiritual temperature in every land. Churchmen, such as Bishop Butler in England, were discouraged almost to despair: 'It is come, I know not how, to be taken for granted by many persons that Christianity is not so much a subject for enquiry, but that it is now at length discovered to be fictitious.' Religion was at a low ebb, but the tide was soon to turn. In Scotland there was the rise of Moderatism, stressing the religion of taste and feeling, the cult of Good Manners, of, first and last, polish. Presbyterianism had to be shown as a religion fit for gentlemen.

Bishop Söderblom, in his Gifford Lectures for 1931, points out

2 Cairns, J.: *Unbelief in the Eighteenth Century. p* 283.

2

that 'the yearning for salvation and the sense of God's nearness break forth at certain epochs simultaneously with over-mastering power and with effects that are felt centuries and millenniums later'. Adducing further evidence for this proposition from the century of St Francis, Aquinas, Dante and the Gothic cathedrals, he goes on: 'No one may prescribe laws and ways to the Eternal Spirit ... there flashes forth, now and then, as it were, a gleam from the world beyond ... It is as if the Eternal at certain periods visited the race more actively and perceptibly than at others. From secret sources there well up clearness and certainty ... the prophet is a manifestation of God's activity.'[3]

The eighteenth century was also the age of revivals, the era of Jonathan Edwards, George Whitefield, Howell Harris and the two Wesleys, who confronted the frosty indifference of the nominal religion of that day with the zealous ardour of their dedication. Not the philosophical reasonings of Bishop Butler but the fruits of evangelistic field-preaching saved the day for religion.

This was no easy enterprise for these open-air apostles, with their message of regeneration. The fastidious John Wesley had a great struggle with his desire for correctness before he ventured to 'become more vile' and preach in this irregular fashion out-of-doors. Perhaps the most detested word in the religious vocabulary of the day was 'enthusiasm' and it is on record that Dr Drummond, when Archbishop of York, advised Mr Conyers, a clergyman within his jurisdiction, that he, 'would be better employed preaching the morality of Socrates than canting about the new birth'.[4] Against this we may set Horace Walpole's comment on the archbishop: 'He was much addicted to the bottle.'

When Goethe saw the French success at the Battle of Valmy in 1792, he perceived that this raw citizen army 'had captured the real secret of power, which is never a function of mechanism, but always an ardour of the soul'. Amid all the tensions and exasperations of this first half of the eighteenth century, an 'ardour of the soul' burned in an unprepossessing parish minister

3 Söderblom, N.: *The Living God.* pp 232–3.
4 Birrell, A.: *Res Judicatae. p* 16; *D.N.B.* vol xvi *pp* 38–40.

in the West of Scotland, and warmed others through him. That small flame kindled into a blaze, changed the course of the history of the Church of Scotland, and became one of the inspirations of the modern missionary movement.

At the actual time, this movement aroused bitter controversy, the echoes of which have barely died away. One of the leading Scottish historians in the nineteenth century wrote: 'In a southern parish church called Cambuslang, there had arisen one of those strange and melancholy exhibitions called religious revivals, with which, fortunately, Scotland has been but rarely and but casually visited. The "Cambuslang Wark", heretofore presided over by Mr McCulloch, the minister of the parish, exhibited the usual phenomena of such orgies – the profuse fits of weeping and trembling, the endemic epilepsies and faintings, the contortions and howls, with terrible symptoms of contrition emitted by old obdurate sinners awakened with a sudden lightning-flash to all the horrors of their condition.

'But another and more potent spirit was invoked when Whitefield joined the reverend local leader and his cluster of zealous country divines. The spiritual tempest was worked up to its wildest climax, when, in an encampment of tents on the hillside, Whitefield, at the head of a band of clergy, held, day after day, a festival, which might be called awful, but scarcely solemn.'[5] Fortunately for truth, we are not shut up to the bias of Burton and this extraordinary farrago of misrepresentation, for we have an amazing amount of information about those days, both manuscript and printed, and these bear witness to an extremely high sense of responsibility for accurate and detailed reporting among those ministers, chiefly William M'Culloch of Cambuslang and James Robe of Kilsyth, who gathered together and set down the facts.

It might be helpful to say a little about some of these sources,

5 Burton, J. Hill: *The History of Scotland*. vol viii *pp* 413–4. This is an extraordinary farrago of misrepresentation from so eminent an historian. Burton becomes less formidable and authoritative when one notes his ignorance of the 'tents', which were structures of wood and canvas, similar to a military sentry-box in appearance, for sheltering the preachers when out of doors.

and especially the manuscripts associated with Cambuslang. In 1742, the very year in which the revival began at that place, the minister there began to compile a written record of the testimonies of many who had come under its influence. He reported in 1751 that 'they gave me very particular accounts of God's dealings with their souls, in their first awakenings and outgates, with their following soul-exercises . . . distresses, deliverances, and comforts'. This was done also in 1743 and 1744, 'and some of them also continued these accounts to [17]48'.

M'Culloch goes on: 'I set down very many of these from their mouths, always in their own sense, and very much also in their own words: and many of these accounts have appear'd to competent judges to whom they have been shewn, and who have perus'd them with care, to be very rational and scriptural, and worthy to see the light: which perhaps may be done hereafter.'[6]

It is highly probable that M'Culloch was encouraged to undertake this formidable task by his older colleague and friend the Rev James Robe of Kilsyth, who had made this type of record about his own community. In the Preface to his book, *A Faithful Narrative of the Extraordinary Work of the Spirit of God at Kilsyth &c*, Robe laments the absence of adequate information about earlier revivals. 'The Ommission of our worthy Forefathers to transmit to Posterity a full and Circumstantial account of the Conversion of 500 by one Sermon at the Kirk of *Shots* in the Year 1630 . . . I have heard much complained of and Lamented'.[7] He describes his own method thus: 'I have kept a book, wherein from Day to Day, I wrote down whatever was most Material in the Exercise of the Distrest. This may appear an unsupportable

6 Robe, J.: *Kilsyth Narrative*. (1789 edition) *pp* 312. On 5 December 1743, Lord Grange wrote to M'Culloch concerning 'Yours of 18 Nov. last. . . . I well remember that night we walked together from Mr Robe's to the town of Kilsyth, and the house we stopt at. . . . I have much the greater concern for the success of your book because I am fully of your opinion, that instances in fact of the power and influence of the Holy Ghost by the gospel on the hearts and lives of men is needful to convince the world of the truth of Christianity. . . . And such are the subject of your book.' (*Edinburgh Christian Instructor 1838. p* 68.)
7 *Ibid. p* 62.

Labour at first view, especially where the Number of the Dist-
rest are so many. Yet I found it to be very easy, it saved much
Time to me. An Index I kept, brought me soon to the part of the
Book, where the Person's Case was recorded. I had then a full
View of their Case, as it was when they were first with me: I saw
what Progress their Convictions had made, and knew where I
was to begin with them, without examining their Case every
Time from the very beginning anew.'[8]

Many of these personal case-histories set down by Robe were
printed by him during the years 1742–1744, but M'Culloch's
half-hesitant suggestion about publishing the accounts he had
gathered did not materialise for over a hundred years. In 1845,
under the aegis of the Free Church of Scotland, there was published *The Revivals of the Eighteenth Century, particularly at Cambuslang, &c.*, by the Rev D. Macfarlan, DD, of Renfrew; on the title
page it is stated that the book was 'compiled from Original
Manuscripts and Contemporary Publications'.

The manuscripts spoken of were chiefly two volumes of these
case-histories compiled by M'Culloch at Cambuslang, and presented by his grand-daughter, Mrs Coutts, to the Free Church
Library in 1844. In his book Dr Macfarlan gives extracts from
twenty-three out of a total of one hundred and six cases, not
hesitating to change the pithy vernacular of the originals into
a somewhat more unctuous and far less graphic style. At times
the Victorian preacher obscures the terse directness of rustic
ploughman, weaver, and the like! Dr Macfarlan's primary
motive in publishing the book seems to have been hortatory, an
attempt to quicken religious expectation within the newly born
Free Church, rather than to offer an objective historical assessment. His omissions are significant.

The M'Culloch manuscripts consist of two small quarto volumes bound in calf. The first volume contains forty-six cases and
a report set out in dialogue form of an interview between two of
the converts from Cambuslang and the two Secession leaders,
Ebenezer Erskine and James Fisher. It has 615 pages; individual
names are all concealed by initials, and at the end there is an
index of sixty-one names, from A.B. to C.H., with a few bio-

8 *Ibid. p* 102.

graphical details. The greater part of the handwriting is uniform, probably that of M'Culloch himself.

Volume two comprises sixty cases, written in different handwritings, with various degrees of legibility. It has 680 pages, and an index numbered from one to eighty-eight of 'those ministers and others who were useful'; thus Wh – d is always mentioned in the body of the text as (12), and M'Culloch as (26). There may have been certain spiritual satisfactions in this passion for anonymity, but it adds considerably to the complications of the historian's task.

It is obvious that paper was provided for the various men and women to tell their own stories, within the framework of some kind of questionnaire, and eight pages or a multiple of this number were given to each person. Some, with words and letters crammed together, used up all the paper provided, and then asked for more; others, less able or voluble, could tell their complete tale on four, or even three, pages.

After these had been rewritten, and the names changed into numbers, along with other alterations deemed necessary, they were sent to the 'competent judges' spoken of by M'Culloch. Undoubtedly, in most of the cases, Dr Alexander Webster of Edinburgh was the first to make comment and suggest deletions; probably Thomas Gillespie of Carnock, later to be the founder of the Relief Church, was next, to be followed by John Willison of Dundee and James Ogilvie of Aberdeen. These four men were outstanding ministers of the Church of Scotland, noted for zeal and wisdom, observers of, and participants in, the awakening at Cambuslang.

The accounts are of thirty-five men and seventy-one women; seven men and thirty-one women being twenty years of age or under, and eighteen men and twenty-seven women aged from twenty-one to thirty years. Many trades and classes are represented (with a preponderance of shoemakers) – young married gentlewomen and ex-soldier colliers, baillies and packmen's daughters – and they come from widely scattered places, such as Kilmarnock, Greenock, Cardross, Carmunnock, Shotts and Lesmahagow.

Within the simplicity of these manuscript pages, with their naïve stories, is contained a wealth of information about the social and religious backgrounds from which the converts came, with details about education and habits, popular superstitions, customs and worship. Although M'Culloch never achieved his heart's desire in publishing them as a book, he built better than he knew when he preserved for us these accounts.

I

The Religious Situation in Scotland

The 'Glorious Revolution' of 1688 marked an epoch for the established church in Scotland; the Stuarts, infatuated with their theories of Divine Right, and insisting upon 'No Bishop, no King', had gone, and with very little stir. The inevitable coercions and intolerances bound up with their concept of kingship went with them, and men felt that they could breathe freely again. Before sailing from Holland to seek his new kingdom, William of Orange had sent a Declaration to Scotland, offering to protect civil liberty and the Protestant religion.

William himself desired a religious settlement that would serve to bind together England and Scotland as closely as was possible. In the northern kingdom he wished to retain episcopacy, but modified to include presbyterianism. His own native Holland had been the home of free thought in the seventeenth century; thither had come Descartes, Spinoza, Arminius and the followers of Socinus, driven out from Poland, with a medley of varying sects and persecuted exiles. Toleration had become a political necessity in order to achieve state security and prosperity.

This scheme of comprehension proved abortive – Scotland had suffered too much and too recently – and so presbyterianism was established again, but with a difference. The Covenants were tacitly ignored, and excommunication was relieved of its civil penalties. It was enacted that the 'first meeting of the General Assembly was to be at Edinburgh the third Thursday of October next to come'. But who was to constitute that body?

There were serious objections to any proposal to hand over ecclesiastical government to the whole body of clergy in the

9

kingdom. Lord Crawford, putting one point of view, wrote that it was taking a great risk to give equal authority to conforming and nonconforming ministers alike, since prelacy had been abolished. He goes on: 'Can it be imagined we shall have Presbytery established, or that government continued, when the management is in the hands of men of different, if not opposite principles, but being three to one for number, would certainly in a short time cast out such as were not of a piece with them?'[1] Such a decision would have been to fly in the face of history and forfeit what had been gained by 'our late sufferers'.

On the other hand, what of the uncompromising adherents of the good old way, those into whose soul the iron had entered in recent bitter days? Would they not be disposed to extreme measures if they were entrusted with effective power?

Parliament decided eventually that only those who had been 'outed' for nonconformity since 1661 should exercise authority – sixty were left out of the ejected four hundred – and that they should have the power to co-opt such ministers and elders as they thought fit. As the time of Assembly drew near, prominent noblemen, such as the Earl of Crawford and others, wrote urgent letters to the leading ministers, pleading for restraint and caution.

On 16 October 1690, after an interval of thirty-seven years, the General Assembly met, and His Majesty's Commissioner, Lord Carmichael, presented the royal message, short but succinct, its chief emphasis being 'We expect that your management shall be such as we shall have no reason to repent of what we have done. A calm and peaceable procedure will be no less pleasing to us than it becometh you. We never could be of the mind that violence was suited to the advancing of true religion; nor do we intend that our authority shall ever be a tool to the irregular passions of any party. Moderation is what religion enjoins, neighbouring Churches expect from, and we recommend to you.'[2]

1 Cunningham, J.: *The Church History of Scotland.* ii p 287.
2 *Acts of the General Assembly.* p 222 (published by Church Law Society).

It was an impressive body of 163 men that met in St Giles' Church; men were there who had carried gun and sword at Rullion Green and Bothwell Bridge fighting for their faith; men who bore branded on their bodies the marks of the rack and the thumbscrew, and who could tell of the horrors of such loathsome dungeons as Dunnottar and the Bass Rock; men on whose heads the government . . . had set a price.[3] There, back again from Holland, was the saintly Thomas Hog of Kiltearn; there too was Henry Erskine, father of Ebenezer and Ralph, exile and fugitive for his unyielding courage. Chief among them all, *primus inter pares*, was that greatest of churchmen serving Scotland, William Carstares, diplomat and disciple, his thumbs marked by the torturing screws. Although not actually a member of the Assembly, he exerted great influence behind the scenes.

Principle and policy alike dictated to William III that the many former Episcopalians of the days before 1688 must be, if at all possible, retained within the national church. Three hundred curates had been 'rabbled' out of their manses and parishes in the first flush of presbyterian victory. He could not afford to have so large a number driven into dissent and starvation, thrown willy-nilly into the machinations of Jacobite intrigues. It was, therefore, laid down that those who took the oath of loyalty to the government and submitted to presbyterian polity, should be secured in their livings, and admitted to the courts of the Church.

Thus there emerged a heterogeneous mixture of covenanting ministers who had bravely borne hardships, and of prelatic clergy, 'vicars of Bray', whose convictions about episcopacy were not sufficiently strong to induce them to abandon their livings. From these earliest days there was a serious cleavage within the national church, a dichotomy which was to widen and separate the two groups even more as the years went by.

Gilbert Burnet, bishop and historian, described in caustic terms the ministers who replaced the ejected Presbyterians after the Restoration: they were 'generally very mean and despicable in all respects. They were the worst preachers I ever heard:

3 Smellie, A.: *Men of the Covenant. p* 508.

they were ignorant to a reproach; and many of them were openly vicious. They were a disgrace to their orders, and the sacred functions; and were indeed the dreg and refuse of the northern parts. Those of them who arose above contempt or scandal, were men of such violent tempers, that they were as much hated as the others were despised. This was the fatal beginning of restoring Episcopacy in Scotland.'[4] Some of these men, who had been put into the priest's office for a piece of bread, were among the ministers who stayed on within the established church after 1690.

Yet another Episcopalian, Sir Walter Scott, no great lover of the covenanting tradition, put into the mouth of David Deans what many were feeling: 'Out upon your General Assembly and the back o' my hand to your Court o' Session! What is the ane but a waefu' bunch o' cauldrife professors and ministers, that sate bien and warm when the persecuted remnant were warstling wi' hunger, and cauld, and fear of death, and danger of fire and sword, upon wet brae-sides, peat-haggs and flow-mosses, and that now creep out of their holes, like blue-bottle flees in a blink of sunshine to take the pu'pits and places of better folk – of them that witnessed, and testified, and fought, and endured pit, prison-house, and transportation beyond seas? A bonny bike there's o' them.'

James Hog of Carnock, exiled in Holland during the days of persecution, but now returned to take his place as one of the most zealous evangelical leaders in Scotland, tells of his astonishment and disappointment in his colleagues: 'We came to be crowded with a set of new presbyterians, who had gone all the lengths of complians in the late times. They, with others who had sheltered under the indulgences of the last reigns . . . had, notwithstanding, a mighty influence in these days. Our temporary Presbyterians and sundry old persecutors who swayed with the times, were much caressed.'

These men sought with all their power to ensconce themselves in the leading courts of the Church, and never failed to be at the General Assemblies, although Hog maintains that 'they

4 Burnet, G.: *History of My Own Time* (ed O. Airey). i *p* 275.

utterly neglected inferior courts, and took no inspection of the congregations to which they belonged . . . Thus old sufferers came to be borne down.'[5] The old and the new were set for conflict, and clash was inevitable.

Lamartine once summed up the contemporary situation in his native land in the phrase, 'La France s'ennuie'; if Scotland was not bored, she was at least tired of the incessant controversies which had filled the seventeenth century with angry words and violent blows. Respite was needed so that the national life could develop, and it was tacitly agreed by most that the stormy chapter should stay closed.

New opportunities were opening up for trade and commerce, and men preferred to divert their energies towards material progress rather than to controversy about the niceties of ecclesiastic government. Reaction had followed religious strife. Religion no longer constituted the warp and woof of the people, but became one of many diverse strands. The age of secular pre-eminence was dawning. The new generation did not appreciate sufficiently how great had been the price paid and the gains achieved in the tumult of the Church's war; by deeds done, sufferings endured and principles hammered out on the anvil of controversy, great victories had been won for the cause of liberty, both civil and religious.

A marked change had come over the intellectual atmosphere also. In 1689, John Locke, one of the greatest English names in philosophy, wrote the first of his four famous letters on toleration, the *Epistola de Tolerantia*, at Gouda in Holland. This was a powerful argument for the right of separate religious groups to have freedom of worship, undeterred by civil penalties, and was a continuance of the cogent pleas of Locke's own teacher, that great Puritan divine, John Owen. It was rapidly translated into Dutch, French and English; the close ties between Holland and Scotland must have made the book known in the latter kingdom, where many could not help but be impressed by the philosopher's enlightened pleading.

This new spirit of toleration found a welcome from many in

5 Hog, J.: *Memoir* (*Edin. Christian Instr. 1838. p* 454).

Scotland on the ground of its expediency. This was noted by James Hog. 'The heavy yoke of persecution by a chain of wonders was now taken off, and hereby many were inclined to easy courses; and an excessive aversion from what they apprehended might be irritating, and bring us into trouble, proved a snare . . . our settlement was in a weak and infant state, and our adversaries were many and strong; hence, such methods were thought advisable, that we might not too much provoke them.'[6]

It was merely a peace of exhaustion and, although prudence demanded compliance and compromise to ensure stability in church and state, many regarded the *status quo* as merely an instalment.

This uneasy truce of the first decade of the Revolution Settlement was not to last; the age-long separation between progressives and conservatives was soon made plain, especially since no outward pressures were compelling unity. The century which followed was to see the competing claims of the inviolability of the individual conscience set over against the overriding authority of the supreme court of the established church. The contending parties were each so right – and, alas, so wrong!

Political issues tended to widen these divisions. At the Union of the two kingdoms of England and Scotland in 1707, although the bells of St Giles' in Edinburgh played, 'Why should I be sad on My Wedding Day?' and Chancellor Seafield noted 'Now there's ane end of ane auld sang', for many it was a day of mourning rather than of joy. Many pulpits resounded with angry condemnation of this unholy alliance with the prelatical neighbour across the Border, and under the eloquent peroration of James Clark,[7] 'Therefore be up and valiant for the City of God', the people of Glasgow threatened the authorities and actually took possession of the city for some days. In 1712, there followed the Oath of Abjuration by which all ministers

6 *Ibid. p* 456.
7 James Clark, Minister of the Tron Parish Church, Glasgow, from 1702–1723. *Fasti.* iii *p* 474.

were compelled to swear that they 'would support, maintain, and defend the succession of the Crown . . . as settled by the English Parliament'. Many of the Presbyterian ministers had covenanted to abolish unscriptural episcopacy; but could they do this, if they swore to protect it in the very Crown? Tremendous controversy was aroused, especially in the West of Scotland, and at least one-third of the Scottish clergy refused to take the prescribed Oath.[8]

Once again the disruptive forces that lead to schism were set loose, and there were many searchings of heart. Thomas Halyburton, professor of divinity at St Andrews in 1712, was asked on his death-bed for his opinion about the Oath, and he replied that the peace of the church was the all-important matter[9] – 'with respect to the difference that is likely to ensue among ministers, with the greatest earnestness I say, My dear brethren, difference is a hot thing. There must be condescension, forbearance and tenderness; we must not fly at the ball. . . . Follow peace. Peace is worth much. I would not have a hand in wounding the church of Scotland for a world.'[10] In his last sickness, Halyburton dictated a note to his family: 'Whereas we have a prospect of divided times . . . beware of interesting yourselves in that difference or entertaining prejudices against ministers upon the one hand or the other. There will be faithful ministers on both sides, and on either hand they will act according to their light sincerely.'[11]

Old established beliefs, hallowed by tradition, were no longer sacrosanct. Elizabeth Mure of Caldwell (1714–95) speaks in her diary of the remarkable change in manners with the casting off of many restraints that was to follow as a result of this increasing intercourse between England and Scotland.

8 'Perhaps no subscription in the long history of the Church was ever the cause of such abounding bitterness' (Boston, T.: *Memoirs, ed* G. H. Morrison. *p* xxiv)

9 Thomas Halyburton, professor of divinity at St Andrews in 1710. Died in 1712, aged thirty-eight. Known as the 'holy Halyburton'. *Memoirs*, conjointly published by George Whitefield and John Wesley in 1739. (*Wesley Bibliography*. R. Green. *p* 13.)

10 *Memoirs of Halyburton. p* 238.

11 *Ibid. p* 255.

Young people met together in clubs and 'there they pulled to pieces the manners of those that differed from them; every thing was matter of conversation: Religion, Morals, Love, Friendship, Good manners, Dress . . . The subjects were all new and all entertaining.'[12] From many sources, we learn of the amazing growth of these clubs. Robert Wodrow, minister of Eastwood, writing in 1724, expresses deep anxiety about the news concerning the young divinity students in Glasgow. Some years earlier he had known personally of seventy-two meetings for prayer in Glasgow, 'and these now . . . are sunk to four or five'.[13] The young ministers and students of divinity were 'falling in with the English fashionable way of preaching . . . and love to call grace virtue . . . which differs much from our good old way in this Church'.[14] In October 1724, Mr Wallace of Moffat, later one of the leading Moderate ministers in Edinburgh, 'made a noise' by his sermon on 'Faith without works is dead'. The following year, Mr Telfer of Hawick caused another furore at Glasgow. Wodrow, after noting that ministers such as Mr Wishart copied their sermons from Tillotson, adds drily, 'Mr T—'s sermons are thought to be his oun make, and loose generall, incoherent discourses, with some turns out of Shaftsburry, the Tatlers and Spectators, and such odd common-places for Ministers!'[15]

Students are ever prone to speculation and opposing the *status quo*, and such affirmations as those of Mr John Millar, son of Wodrow's friend and neighbour, the Rev Robert Millar of Paisley, that there was 'a set of young men coming up that would shake off the shakles of their education' . . . and he hoped 'some of them in a few years would stand before Judicatorys, and make glorious appearances for truth' sound familiar enough today, though they distressed Wodrow greatly. The latter diagnosed the problem as arising from the absence of the divinity professor from their unfettered discussions. 'The *origo*

12 Scottish Diaries 1746–1846. *pp* 43, 72, 76.
13 *Anal.* iii *pp* 129–30.
14 *Ibid.* iii *p* 155.
15 *Ibid.* iii *pp* 167, 240.

mali is suffering these rau, unripe youths, to medle with what they are unequall to, without a preses (*ie* a chairman) to keep them right; which was never alloued in my father's time.'[16]

Wodrow's father was the first professor of divinity after the Revolution Settlement;[17] he was followed by John Simson, whose novel speculations and shuffling, vacillating explanations fevered his students and made him for a long time face charges of heresy in the church courts.[18] In 1729 the General Assembly suspended Simson *sine die* and this sentence was continued until his death in 1740. Wodrow comments that 'Mr Simson draws his salary, and the youth are without a teacher'.[19] With such unsettling teaching, and eventually little teaching at all in theology for almost twelve years, things were far from well for the students of divinity in Glasgow. Of them Wodrow notes yet again: 'there is nothing like meetings for prayer . . . and many meet in other clubs, and for drinking'.[20] 'Jupiter' Carlyle in his memoirs, limns a picture of convivial life as a student in Glasgow, anticipating Thomas Carlyle's outburst on him as 'that pot-walloping Sadducee'. It was one of Simson's students who was appointed professor of philosophy in the University of Glasgow, and by his teaching, which crowded his class room with eager students, he became the 'father of Moderatism' in the Church of Scotland. Francis Hutcheson set out to 'put a new face upon theology in Scotland.'[21] Doctrinal exposition was not encouraged, nor was there to be any stirring appeal to conscience; instead, the Christian

16 *Ibid.* iii *pp* 179, 181.

17 *Divinity Professors &c.* Reid, H.M.B. *pp* 171–203.

18 'Mr Simson, a hotch-potch or bagful of Arian, Arminian, Socinian, Pelagian, old condemn'd damnable errors, infecting the youth, giving ground to fear it will spread further and leaven moe . . . he may justly be called the most wylie and subtile fox that ever Satan let loose into Christ's vineyard in Scotland since the Reformation.' (Walker, P.: *Six Saints &c.* i *pp* 149, 167.)

19 Wodrow *Correspondence.* iii *pp* 467, 469.

20 *Anal.* iii *p* 514.

21 Letter of Hutcheson 31 May 1742, quoted J. M'Cosh *The Scottish Theology p* 64. *Vide* Wodrow's query at the appointment in December 1729. 'What influence his teaching here may have, time will discover.' *Anal.* iv *p* 99.

religion was set forward as a system of the highest morality, offering some hope of an immortality of bliss, but providing no pardon to the poor sinner anxious about the past.[22] The new teaching took full account of ignorance but had little sense of sin; it did not offer enough![23]

Just as this Moderate section of the Church was coming under new moulding influences, so the more evangelical group also was undergoing a process of change. A new note could be heard in their preaching; something warmer and more welcoming. Awed by the Calvinist conception of the divine sovereignty, with its emphasis on election and predestination, for some the faith had hardened off into fatalism. There were many who questioned this theology, and especially the Episcopalians, who were strongly Arminian in Scotland. Duncan Innes, an Edinburgh shoe-maker who had left the Church of Scotland to become an Episcopalian, wrote several polemics on this subject. So, in 1742, one of the reasons for his decision to leave the church of his fathers was his rejection of the 'absolute, unconditional, irreversible and eternal Decree of Election of some, and Reprobation of the rest and far greatest Part of Mankind'. He averred that this doctrine served only 'to fill the Heads of some with groundless and presumptuous Hopes, fancying themselves to be among the Number of that happy *Few* . . . it is equally destructive to such as may have a melancholy Turn of Mind . . . by instigating them to despair of GOD's paternal Goodness, as not being among the Number of the Elect'. This scheme of salvation is like 'that of a *State-Lottery* where there are a great many Blanks, but very few

22 M'Cosh, J.: *The Scottish Theology.* p 64.
23 When Hutcheson preached for his father, the minister of Armagh who was sick, all the congregation except three persons left the service before the sermon ended. One of them told his father, 'Your silly loon, Frank, has fashed a' the congregation wi' his idle cackle: for he has been babbling this oor aboot a gude and benevolent God, and that the sauls o' the Heathens themsels will gang to heeven, if they follow the light of their ain consciences. Not a word does the daf boy ken, speer, or say, abou the gude, auld, comfortable doctrine of election, reprobation, original sin and faith. Hoot, mon, awa' wi' sic a fellow.' Stuart, J.: *Historical Memoirs of the City of Armagh.* pp 488–9.

prizes; where every one *must* venture, but only a certain Number can be successful . . .'. Innes goes on: 'I shall only beg the favour of you . . . how you'll reconcile your *Election and Reprobation Scheme* with these tender and passionate Calls and Invitations of our blessed SAVIOUR.'[24] In a later pamphlet, he sets out to find the number of the Beast, given in Revelation 13.18 as 'Six hundred, Threescore and Six'. Counting all the words in the Solemn League and Covenant, he sees that they add up to 666 and the problem is solved. Or almost, for he sums up: 'Now this is but a Conjecture, but then it is as reasonable a Conjecture as any other that was ever offered.'[25]

This doctrinal emphasis which so annoyed Innes was undergoing modification. In 1645, at the time of the Westminster Assembly, a book was published in London entitled *The Marrow of Modern Divinity*, consisting chiefly of extracts from the writings of Reformed theologians, such as Calvin, Beza, Luther, Reynolds, Hooker, Goodwin and others who were at that time considered modern. Its aim was to show the complete freeness of the gospel offer of salvation, and to lead the guilty sinner straight to the Saviour's mercy. It was written by E.F., often assumed to be a Gloucester gentleman, Edward Fisher, although the evidence for this is by no means conclusive.[26] Within three years seven editions of the book were issued; at the beginning of the eighteenth century it began its notable influence in Scotland.[27]

Thomas Boston, although dissatisfied with his personal religious experience, was ordained to the charge of Simprin, Berwickshire, in 1699. He began an eager search for something better, and gives an account of his discovery. 'Meanwhile, being still on the scent, as I was sitting one day in a house at

24 *A letter from a Layman to a Lay Deacon of the Kirk of Scotland, Containing the Reasons for his dissenting from the* PRESBYTERIAN, *and joining the* EPISCOPAL *Communion &c.* MDCCXLII. *A Defence and Vindication of his Action by D——I—— p* i (Rosebery Pamphlets, Nat. Lib. of Scotland). *pp* i, 6, 8, 9.

25 *The Sequel of a Letter from a Layman &c. p* 26 (1750).

26 *Vide: The Marrow of Modern Divinity.* ed C. G. M'Crie, *pp* xvi–xix for a discussion on this point.

27 Samuel Rutherford may have read the book when in London and some copies had certainly reached Scotland.

Simprin, I espied above the window-head two little old books;
which, when I had taken down, I found entitled, the one *The
Marrow of Modern Divinity* ... These I reckon had been brought
home from England by the master of the house, a soldier in the
time of the civil wars ...'. Boston brought the book away, and
eventually purchased it for himself. 'I rejoiced in it, as a light
which the Lord had seasonably struck up to me in my darkness.'[28] This spark was soon to kindle a mighty flame in the
land. Boston's advocacy of the book to his ministerial friends
set them searching eagerly for copies, and in 1718 the *Marrow*
was reprinted with a preface by James Hog of Carnock.

It has been pointed out that the ruling conception of the
theology of the seventeenth century was of God as Sovereign,
rather than Father. The doctrine of the *Marrow* was to serve as
a bridge between the belief that strengthened men to bear
persecution in dangerous days and a more tender creed.[29]
The doctrine of the *Marrow* was Calvinism, not universalism as
its opponents were constantly asserting, for although it was in
the main the original teaching of the great Genevan, it seemed
to be something more than was often taught.

Puzzled about the range of the redemptive work of Christ,
Boston read in the *Marrow* that Jesus Christ had commissioned
his disciples to preach the gospel to every creature, 'that is, go
and tell every man without exception that here is good news
for him, Christ is dead for him, and if he will take Him and
accept of His righteousness he shall have Him'. When Neo-
phytus, one of the allegorical characters in the book, asks
whether such boldness would not really display pride and presumption, the *Marrow* makes Evangelista reply: 'To come to
Christ by believing that He will accept of you, justify and save
you freely by His grace, according to His gracious promise, this
is neither pride nor presumption. For Christ having tendered
and offered it to you freely, believe it, man, it is a true humility
of heart to take what Christ offereth you.'[30]

28 *Memoirs of Thomas Boston*, ed G. H. Morrison. p 169.
29 Henderson, H. F.: *Religious Controversies.* p 21.
30 *The Marrow &c.*, ed C. G. M'Crie. pp 112-3, p 122.

Boston, in his sermon 'Christ gifted to sinners', asks to whom Christ is given and answers: 'to mankind sinners indefinitely. It is not to the elect only but to sinners indefinitely . . . sinners of the race of Adam without exception, whatever they have been, whatever they are.' Quoting John 3.16, he adds, 'You see here it goes as wide as the world, the world of men. And he said, Go ye preach to every creature.' Again, in another sermon, 'Christ the Saviour of the World', he declares, 'If you are not one of the devil-kind, but of sinful mankind, it was for you . . . is not this love?'

J. Walker, writing of the theology of this period, notes that 'Boston and the Marrow men, first of all among our divines, entered fully into the missionary spirit of the Bible; were able to see that Calvinistic doctrine was not inconsistent with world-conquering aspirations and efforts'.[31] It was this faith that sustained Thomas Boston, 'the unforgettable' as he has been well styled, and constrained him to pour out his whole life for his eighty-three parishioners in Simprin, and later, his flock at Ettrick. From Boston there issued a stream of influence that was to have tremendous consequences. This was the faith of the two Erskines also. It was Ebenezer who stood up in the synod of Fife when some were denying that salvation was for all mankind and said: 'Moderator, Our Lord Jesus says of himself, My Father giveth you the true bread from heaven. This he uttered to a promiscuous multitude; and let me see the man who dares to affirm that he said wrong.'[32]

The influence of Martin Luther is very obvious in the *Marrow of Modern Divinity*.[33] He is ranked as equal with Calvin – 'So that we may assuredly conclude with Luther . . . indeed, as Calvin saith'[34] – and in the first section of the book, Luther is cited forty-six times, more than twice as often as Calvin. Luther's *Commentary on Galatians* was among the first parcel of books received by Boston, and remembered with gratitude;

31 Walker, J.: *Theology &c. p* 60.
32 Fraser, D.: *Life of Eben. Erskine. p* 242.
33 Art. 'Influence of Martin Luther on Scottish Theology in the Eighteenth Century' H. Watt. *S.C.H.S.* vi *pp* 147–60.
34 *Marrow, ed* C. G. M'Crie. *pp* 63–4.

such outstanding Christian leaders as Fraser of Brea and Adam Gib were helped by this same book.

Another example of this Lutheran impetus in the revival movements of the eighteenth century may be quoted of John Wesley: '24 May 1738 – In the evening I went very unwillingly to a society in Aldersgate Street, where one was reading Luther's Preface to the Epistle to the Romans. About a quarter before nine . . . I felt my heart strangely warmed. I felt I did trust in Christ, Christ alone, for salvation; and an assurance was given me that He had taken away *my* sins, even *mine*, and saved *me* from the law of sin and death.'

Among the Laing Mss Div ii (471) in the University of Edinburgh there are some of the sermons of Robert Jardine, minister of Lochmaben (1732–49).[35] On 10 July 1737 he notes: 'We had twelve Tables, 82 at every Table, but 30 at the last. In all about 930. Preached Jno. xxi.15.' We have the manuscript of this communion sermon:

'What is your motive to Love? Do ye love him for himself or only for his benefits? To love him only for these is a mean self-love, like the multitude in John 6 which followed Christ for loaves, and like some marriages among men, where not the person but the portion is the object of affection.

'Do ye love Christ wholly? Is everything in the blessed J[esus] desireable and amiable to you? . . . Do you love him not only as your prophet and teacher, as your sacrifice and advocate but as your L[ord] . . . I have a message from my L[ord], my M[aster] to you, to every one of you, even to tell you, that the great Lord of heaven and earth hath an only begotten Son to whom he has given all power in h. and E . . . this glorious one is willing to enter into a mar[riage] Covt. with the blackest and vilest sinner . . . and all he seeks is your love and affection and that you'll give him your hearts.

'I ask you in his name, will ye love him or not? Can ye find in your ht. to refuse so reasonable a demand? Mind, it is his cause I'm pleading for him. I ask your love. Slight, despise me

35 Father of Dr John Jardine, who became one of the most prominent ministers in Edinburgh and one of the royal chaplains.

his unworthy servt. as you will, but O do not despise him. Revile, contemn me as you please but only give Christ your hearts and I have got my errand. Love him and I have gained my design.

'Lastly, what reason can ye give why ye will not Love him? What can ye object against him? Testify your love to him by sitting down at his table . . . it will blow up in thy heart a triumphant flame of love to a crucified Jesus.' This sentiment anticipates the pleadings of Robert Cunningham, the prize-fighting butcher, turned evangelist, in the 1859 Revival: 'What ails ye at Christ?'

There were, however, some who objected violently to this new emphasis and, in 1720, the General Assembly passed an Act, naming the *Marrow of Modern Divinity* as being contrary to the Holy Scriptures, the Confession of Faith and the Cate-chisms, and all ministers were prohibited from recommending it by preaching or by printing and were instructed to warn their parishioners not to read or use it.[36] This sweeping condem-nation was challenged at once, and a representation was drawn up requesting that the Act be revoked. This document was signed by twelve men, known as 'The Marrow Men' or jestingly as 'The Twelve Apostles'; in 1721 they refused cate-gorically to accept the decision of the Assembly, in spite of rebuke and admonition from the Moderator. Deposition might have followed this defiance but for the intervention of govern-ment, who were apprehensive about invasion.

The Marrow Men trembled on the very brink of secession, but that step was made incredibly difficult by the historic assertion that there was but one kirk in Scotland. James Durham, who was beloved of all the earnest-minded Presby-terians for his courage – had he not defied Oliver Cromwell to his face? – and for his piety, had successfully healed a serious breach in the church during the seventeenth century by such vehement pleadings: 'Never did men run to quench fire in a City, lest all should be destroyed, with more diligence than men

36 A full account may be found in the *Edin. Chr. Inst.* in an article by Thomas M'Crie. 1831–2.

ought to bestir themselves to quench this in the Church. Never did mariners use more speed to stop a leak in a ship, lest all should be drowned, than Ministers especially, and all Christian men, should haste to stop this beginning of the breaking-in of these waters of strife, lest thereby the whole Church be over-whelmed.'[37]

Ninian Niving, preaching in December 1729, points out that 'we have been tossing and tumbling these many years in a poor shattered vessel, and no storms of persecution from without have been able to overwhelm us', but laments that 'we, contrary to all the motions of Grace, fall a quarrelling among ourselves, and are in danger of perishing every moment, thro' a vain contention, Who shall sit at the Helm?' After noting the passion for self-vindication by the two contending parties, he declares that the quarrels and divisions are completely un-necessary. 'The spirit of contention runs so high and yet the matter in dispute is so very small. So very small, that to forgive, and to forget, seem to be the only things that are wanting in order to a perfect peace and full reconcilement.'[38] Nevertheless, although there was no open schism at this time, victimisation and discrimination followed the intransigence of the supporters of the Marrow doctrine. Their leading protagonists were hampered when they sought to move to other parishes; Ebenezer Erskine's projected translation from Portmoak to Kirkcaldy in 1725 was refused because it would have augmented his influence in the church; Boston wished to move on account of his poor health, and all seemed well 'till I fell under their displeasure in the affair of the Marrow, which I reckon to have staked me down in Etterick'.[39]

Harsh treatment was administered to candidates for the ministry who were suspected of similar leanings. Wodrow, who was far from approving of the Marrow men and their doctrine,

37 Durham, J.: *The Dying Man's* TESTAMENT *to the Church of Scotland, or a Treatise concerning Scandal*. Edin. 1659. *p* 313. Durham died at thirty-six years of age.
38 Niving, N.: *Considerations in the Time of Adversity* (Rosebery Pamphlets). *pp* 11, 19.
39 Fraser, D.: *Life & Diary of Eben. Erskine. pp* 320–6.

tells of one, John Craige, chosen unanimously by the parish of Kinross to be their minister. It was reported that he 'favoured the Marrow', so Principal Haddow and Mr A. Anderson had a committee appointed from the Synod of Fife to join the presbytery in examining him. They formed twenty queries from the Marrow and gave Craige only until that afternoon to answer them. All were answered except the last, 'whether he approved of the act of Assembly against the Marrow'. He asked to be excused this and owned it to be the deed of the church, but the Committee insisted on an express answer in writing. Begging them not to insist, 'he inclined to have been silent but he declared, according to his present light, he was of the sentiments of the Representers and was content to stand and fall with them. This was what they wanted.' They then voted to 'Stop his trials . . . a most imprudent and unhappy step'. Ralph Erskine says: 'whenever any student or candidate was supposed to be tinctured with the Marrow, that is with a Gospel spirit . . . there was no quarter for such; queries upon queries were formed to discourage them, and stop their way, either of their being entered upon trials or ordained unto churches . . . many pious youths . . . had the door of entrance into the ministry quite barred against them'.[40]

Matters came to a head over an Act passed by the General Assembly in 1731 which provided that in exercising the *ius devolutum*, Protestant heritors and elders were to 'elect', instead of to 'name and propose', a minister, and the congregation, as embodied in the heads of families, came into the process only in order to concur.[41]

This was a return to the procedure of 1690, and Ebenezer Erskine led the opposition against it. On 16 May 1732 he spoke in the Assembly: 'I know of no ecclesiastical authority under

40 Erskine, R.: *Faith no Fancy.* A similar official imprimatur was evidenced in the case of Howell Harris, a truly apostolic figure, in Wales. Whitefield, his friend, says that Harris was twice refused admission to holy orders on the pretence that he was not of age. 'He is now above 25 years of age. . . . Above a month ago he offered himself again, but was put off' (Tyerman, L.: *Life of George Whitefield.* i p 188).

41 Campbell, A. J.: *Two Centuries of the Church of Scotland.* p 53.

heaven, but what is derived from Christ, the exalted King of Zion. . . . His authority as a King, is the alone foundation of all church government and discipline.'[42] On 10 October of that year, he preached as Moderator of the Synod of Perth and Stirling on 'The Stone rejected by the Builders'; he spoke strongly against this 'new wound given to the prerogative of Christ and the privileges of His subjects'.[43] This so annoyed his brethren that they judged him deserving of a formal rebuke. Supported by three other ministers, Erskine appealed to the General Assembly of 1733. Angered by the tone of this protest, that body ordered the four brethren to withdraw this appeal and, upon their refusing, the Commission of Assembly first suspended and then excluded them from their ministerial functions. On 5 December of that same year, the four brethren, Ebenezer Erskine of Stirling, Alexander Moncrieff of Abernethy, William Wilson of Perth and James Fisher of Kinclaven, met at Gairney Bridge and formed the Associate Presbytery, closing their first Testimony with the words: 'And we hereby appeal to the first free, faithful and reforming General Assembly of the Church of Scotland.' There were many who felt that the General Assembly had gone too far, and for six years attempts were made to heal the breach. The sentence of suspension was repealed; the offending Act of 1731 was also repealed – but all to no purpose. The seceders had evidently determined to separate unless they could secure far-reaching measures of reform. Finally, on 15 May 1740, Ebenezer Erskine and his colleagues, now eight in number, were solemnly deposed.

If the seceders had anticipated that such of their colleagues as John Willison of Dundee (one of those sent by the General Assembly in 1734 to petition Parliament in London for the removal of the grievance of Patronage, but, to his sorrow, without success) and John Currie of Kinglassie, who had supported their efforts to remedy grievances, would join with them, they were disappointed. It was different with the laity. From all parts of the country, groups of people, especially

42 Fraser, D.: *Life and Diary of E. Erskine.* p 358.
43 Erskine, E.: *Works.* ed D. Fraser. i p 472.

members of the many societies for prayer, wrote asking for 'sermon'.[44] The demand for a more spiritual ministry was far greater than could be supplied. Inside the established church there remained a small group who were in the church but not of it. They supported the aims of the seceders, but conceived it sinful to become schismatics. Henry Davidson of Galashiels and his friend and neighbour, Gabriel Wilson of Maxton, both Marrow men and close friends of Thomas Boston, never again dispensed the Lord's Supper in their congregations after the Secession. They formed a small group of supporters, akin to the Independents, and for over twenty years observed the sacrament with them.[45]

Around the year 1740 the situation was indeed critical for the Church of Scotland. Within it was a new and growing generation of ministers who were more concerned about culture than conversions – a group of 'Senecan' clergy who spoke of their Covenanting forbears with contempt and amusement. At the time of the controversy over Professor Simson, an anonymous writer compiled an unpublished 'Letter to a Reverend Clergyman in Scotland', a minister with scruples about the confession and formulae of the church. 'You ought not for this to divulge your private opinions and be deposed for your pains. Think with the Wise but Talk with the Vulgar . . . print books without prefixing your names . . . by the use of a little banter in your conversation, you may ridicule the errors in vogue . . . And who knows but ere twenty years you may have a majority even in a General Assembly and then you may venture to act above board . . . Above all, do not contradict the Received Doctrines in your sermons. You will defeat them better by letting them fall into Desuetude . . . do not foolishly expose [yourselves] to sufferings thro an unwise boldness in a good cause.'[46] Outside the established church, there had existed for

---

44 McKelvie, W.: *Annals and Statistics of the U. P. Church.* (Edin. 1873) *pp* 2–4.
45 Memoir: *Letters to Christian Friends by the late Henry Davidson* (1811).
46 *Laing Mss.* ii *p* 620. Robert Wallace, whom we have already noted for his Moderate sympathies, had this manuscript in his possession and commented 29 December 1767: 'Here are many acute and just sentiments . . . written by a wise and prudent man.'

fifty years the extremist Cameronians, but their appeal was very limited. Now there was this other attraction: an active, popular group of ministers of earnest evangelical spirit, the first seceders from the Church of Scotland (although they maintained that they were only withdrawing from 'the prevailing party'), who answered a very real need and widespread demand. Their success was considerable. Within a quarter of a century, it was estimated, in the Schism Overture of 1766, that there were 120 meeting-houses with 100,000 members in the country.[47] The issue would have been very different indeed had it not been for the revival that broke out in the parish of Cambuslang in 1742. It was this event, and the associated movements that spread over Scotland, that rallied other evangelical ministers of the national Kirk and inspired the hesitating laity to stay within the borders of the national church and serve her by the will of God. It was, once more, the story of a little leaven which permeated the church of the future.

47 Morren, N.: *Annals &c*, 1752–66. *p* 307 *ff*.

2

M'Culloch Comes to Cambuslang

On 26 January 1731, Mr Henderson, the minister of Blantyre, reported to the Presbytery of Hamilton that he had carried out its instructions to him 'to conveen the Paroch of Kambuslang and try Their inclinations with respect to a Settlement'. He told his brethren 'that a great many had declared their inclinations to have Mr M'Culloch to be Their Minister'. After hearing a deputation from that parish, most of whom concurred, it was decided to call a meeting at that place, 'for Electing and Subscribing a Call to one to be Their Minister, and that upon Thursday the 18th of Febry Next'.[1] On Thursday April 29, he was duly received by the parish of Cambuslang as their minister.

Thus was brought to an end the long-drawn-out struggle by the people of Cambuslang against the principal heritor in the parish, his grace the Duke of Hamilton; after six years they had secured their claim to have no minister but one of their own choosing. The previous minister, the Rev Archibald Hamilton, had been unwell and unfit for his duties for several years before his death in 1724. An assistant had been employed by him from October 1721 and, on 3 September 1723, Hamilton intimated to the heritors and session that he was willing, upon their choice of a good and well-qualified person, to demit his charge, and to quit one half of his stipend to the one who should succeed him. While negotiations were proceeding for a suitable man, the valetudinarian minister died.

On 30 March 1725 the Presbytery records state: 'Compeired Thomas Hutton Writer in Hamilton and signified My Lord

1 Hamilton Pres. Recs.

Duke Hamilton's inclinations with respect to the Settlement of Kambuslang'. The heritors and elders from that place presented a petition, requesting the Presbytery to 'deal with his Grace ... to concur with them for a comfortable settlement of the Paroch'. Two ministers interviewed the ducal patron but reported on 22 February 1726, that 'he declared Himself firm to His first choice of Mr Thomas Findlater to be Minister of Kambuslang'.[2]

Thomas Findlater was the son of the minister of Hamilton, who had become the centre of a controversy in the church courts about this time. In October 1725 Wodrow mentions this 'unhappy affair of Mr Findlater at Hamilton, his scandal of adulterous carriage breaks out'.[3] A year later the people who had offered to provide evidence against him withdrew their charges 'which they say came from the Duke's [of Hamilton] gratifying them about some lime'.[4] The great majority of Findlater's session maintained that he had not visited his parish for at least eighteen years, and his open Sabbath-breaking was notorious.[5]

Whatever truth there was in these complaints, the parish of Cambuslang was resolute in refusing to have his son to be their minister, even with the fullest backing from the patron. Deadlock resulted. In July 1728 the Duke of Hamilton gave the parish of Cambuslang 'a peremptory answer, that he would give no other to them than Mr Findlater's son, his Minister. The people have withstood him these five or six years, and will never come in to him ... I knou not a parish in the West of Scotland in such a taking as Cambuslang and Hamiltoun, Cambuslang has been on the matter, vaccant these fourteen years; and I am told ther is not one under sixteen years who ever has been catechised. ... Promises have been made for Mr M'Culloch, the people's choice, and matters are still staved off.'[6] This state of impasse went on for yet another two years, and no way out of it was found until Mr Findlater, the unwanted presentee to Cambus-

2 *Ibid.*
3 *Anal.* iii *p* 237.
4 *Ibid.* iii *p* 334.
5 *Ibid.* iv *p* 5.
6 *Ibid.* iv *p* 5.

lang, was forced upon the parish of West Linton, in the Synod of Lothian, in January 1731. This could be achieved only by sending out a posse of soldiers who took six or eight of the parishioners as prisoners to Edinburgh.[7] Wodrow comments sadly: 'This is turning a common thing. . . . Our troubles are grouing as to settlements . . . I am affrayed, if things continou at the rate they are, Presbitry and Ministers loss the affections of the common people by thir setlments . . . and when we loss the inclinations of the people, we are not much to lean to the affections of the noblmen and gentlmen, men whom we now strive to please.' How prophetic were these forebodings!

Although this meant loss for West Linton, it brought gain to Cambuslang, for in that same month of Findlater's forced induction, the Duke of Hamilton gave his consent to the proposal that M'Culloch should be invited to become minister at Cambuslang.[8] So, in spite of opposition by the most influential resident heritor in the parish of Cambuslang, *viz* Hamilton of Westburn (an antagonism kept up for more than twenty years), William M'Culloch at forty years of age was ushered in to his first charge, the charge where he was to close his days forty years later. The earliest description of the rural parish to which, after a long waiting, William M'Culloch was inducted is that of Mr Hamilton of Wishaw, 'an Antiquary of no little fame'. He writes in the first decade of the eighteenth century: 'Cambuslang . . . lyeth upon the south-west syde of the river of Clyde. . . . It is a pleasant and fertile soill, with a good salmond fishing . . . the lands of Greenlees . . . where there is coal considerable. There is also in . . . the lands of Coatts, Chapel and Moriston . . . good coal.'[9]

Dr James Meek, successor to M'Culloch as minister of Cambuslang (1774–97), supplied the description of the parish for the *First Statistical Account of Scotland* in 1793, in which he compares local conditions in 1750 and 1790, and thus furnishes an excellent picture of the community about mid-century. The

7 Small, Robert: *History of the U.P. Church.* i *p* 563.
8 *Anal.* iv *p* 188.
9 Hamilton, Wm.: *Description of the Sheriffdom of Lanark.* xii *pp* 19, 23.

kirk, he notes, 'is 5 miles S.E. from Glasgow and 6 miles W. from Hamilton', standing in a district of beautiful scenery, with a number of hills and valleys and fertile land. From the top of the 'hill of Dichmont, there is certainly one of the finest inland prospects in Scotland'. The pellucid Clyde flowed from the upper ward of Lanarkshire, passing through the extensive woods and plantations near Hamilton, and bounded the parish for almost three miles. It was from 200 to 250 feet wide, but was easily forded. Quite a number of those who came to Cambuslang during 1742 spoke of walking over the river.[10]

The main road, busy with travellers and trade, passed through the parish from east to west; it was 'narrow and rough, scarcely passable with carts in the summer, and in the winter so deep in mud as to be hardly passable with horses'.[11] In 1753, legislation was enacted to improve the deplorable state of this road, described in the *Glasgow Burgh Records* as 'very dangerous to travellers'.[12] Although the property of the parish was divided among eleven heritors, two-thirds of it belonged to the only non-resident heritor, his grace the Duke of Hamilton, who also received the produce of considerable coal-workings.

The population numbered less than a thousand people, with about two hundred separate families,[13] and these were engaged

10 *Old Statistical Account* (ed Sir John Sinclair 1793). v *pp* 242–3. Of this period and district, Janet Hamilton sets down her grandfather's memories that 'salmon were then so plentiful in the Clyde and were so much used as an article of food in the farmers' houses in its vicinity that servants made it a part of their hiring stipulations that they should not be required to eat salmon more than once a day'. Janet Hamilton: *Poems of Purpose Etc. p* 177.
11 *Old Statistical Account.* v *p* 253.
12 'the road leading from the village of Gorbals to a place called the Chapel of Cambuslang, in the county of Lanerk much frequented by travellers, of great consequence to the commerce of the Country, and the convenient marching of His Majesty's troops, and the foresaid roads, by the deepness of the soil in some places, and the narrowness and ruggedness of the road in others, are in many places become impassable in winter for wheel carriages and horses, and very dangerous for travellers'. Authority was vested in trustees with power to levy tolls. 26 George II. C.28 (quoted in *Glasgow Burgh Records* 1739, 1759. vi *p* 590).
13 The census taken by Dr Webster in 1755 reported 934 persons in the parish.

mainly in agriculture and the expanding industries of coal-mining and weaving.

Most of the farms were worked on the run-rig system, with wasteful baulks between the various ridges, full of stones and bushes. As yet there were very few enclosures. Such feudal customs still obtained as the obligation of a tenant 'to lead his landlord's coals, and give him some days' work in seed time and harvest'. Wheat and potatoes were not planted in the open fields until about 1760.

Although the greater part of the inhabitants were employed in farming, there were many colliers and weavers. The coal seams were many feet deep at the river, out-cropping to the surface almost a mile and a half away. There were no pumping facilities and so coal had to be wrought when wet, the work being 'laborious, hazardous and disagreeable.'[14] Added to the hardships of their toil was the further degradation of slavery. Until 1799, all colliers and salters in Scotland belonged to the owner of the workings where they laboured, passing along with any other property to the new owner. Wives, daughters and sons continued in this humiliating condition, forming a separate and avoided group, with language and habits all their own.[15] Some of them were compelled to wear brass collars around their necks as the badge of their servitude. There were many such people in Cambuslang, yet even this despised community came within the reach of the church's activities, and we have reports of the conversions of 'Mary Lap, daughter of George Lap, Collier . . . and of David Logan, an old soldier, now a collier in Cambuslang'. One of the elders in the session was John Arbuckle 'coal hewer in Coles'.

The other main industry in the parish was the weaving of holland or fine linen, begun about 1730: the weavers bought the yarn, wove it into cloth, bleached this cloth and carried it to market.[16] There are frequent references to young women reading their Bibles whilst 'at the wheel'. It was in such a place and

14 *Old Statistical Account.* VI. *pp* 252, 257.
15 Erskine, J.: *An Institute of the Law of Scotland.* Book 1. ch vii *pp* 2, 61.
16 *Old Statistical Account.* V. *p* 258.

within such a community that the new minister began his life-work in 1731. It is now time to look at his own background and try to envisage the influences which were moulding his early days.

William M'Culloch was born in 1691 at Whithorn, in the countryside hallowed by the famous Candida Casa of St Ninian; his father was the parish schoolmaster, who had once lived in Anwoth (where saintly Samuel Rutherford was minister) but in later years he moved to Wigtown.[17] Of William M'Culloch's own childhood, we have only meagre information; his son, in a Memoir prefixed to a posthumous volume of his father's sermons, tells us that 'he received the rudiments of his education from his father, who perceiving his studious disposition, sent him to the Universities of Edinburgh and Glasgow.'[18]

There can, however, be no doubt that the early years spent in remote and rebellious Galloway left their stamp upon the studious youth, whose adult disposition was ever 'to look too farr into things'. All around him were evidences for his eyes to see and experiences for his ears to hear of his local countrymen, who had resisted episcopacy to financial ruin and martyr graves. Only six years before M'Culloch's birth, David Grahame, brother of the infamous Claverhouse, reported to the Scottish Privy Council that 'there were as many elephants and crocodiles in Galloway as loyal and orderly persons'.[19]

'Kirkcudbright and Wigtonshire were the Jerusalem and Judea of the Covenant', wrote Andrew Symson, editor of the *Register of the Synod of Galloway* from October 1664 to April 1671, and his records make plain the resistance of ministers and people to the episcopal regime. Letters of Banishment were put into execution against many of the former ministers who were still dwelling in the diocese.[20] 'Several ministers within the Presbytry of Kirkcoudbright are defective of Sessions by and through

17 *Anal.* iii *pp* 132, 134.
18 M'Culloch, W.; *Sermons on Several Subjects.* (Memoir by Robert M'Culloch.)
19 Agnew, A.: *History of the Hereditary Sheriffs of Galloway. p* 425.
20 *Register of the Synod of Galloway from October 1664 to April 1671* (ed A. Symson). *pp* 34, 37, 49.

the unwillingness of their parishioners to joyne with them.'[21] And Symson himself, a man of learning, ability and kindly disposition, complained that his own congregation had dwindled to one, and even this man lost his life by a fall from a horse in March 1682. In a 'funeral Elegie' to this friend, Symson mourns:

> He, HE alone, WERE my parishioners,
> Yea, and my constant hearers! Oh! that I
> Had pow'r to eternize his memory . . .[22]

William M'Culloch, when a boy, must often have listened to stories in his home that both chilled and thrilled his heart. The decade before his birth was crammed with memorable incident. On 19 January 1682, John Grahame of Claverhouse was appointed Sheriff of Wigtown, and the next month outlined his policy to his superiors: 'I will threaten much, but forbear severe execution for a while.'[23] But he soon began, with ruthless efficiency, to apply his policy of 'thorough'. From the beginning of 1685, conditions became almost intolerable for the people of Galloway, who were treated with all the severity that might have been expected had they been rebels in arms. Soldiers, the riff-raff of the people, were billeted throughout the countryside and searched homes and such open-air refuges as the mountain-cave or forest-shelter, seeking to discover and destroy the covenanters. Suspicion spread over the district like a pestilence and normal intercourse of man with man was brought to an end. Says William Mackenzie, the historian of Galloway: 'Multitudes were murdered every month, without the tedious formality of a trial; for *inter arma silent leges*. Hanging, shooting, drowning, torturing, and cutting off the ears were works of constant recurrence. Some were sent to Jamaica and sold as slaves, whilst others were immured in unwholesome dungeons, where watchful soldiers stood in endless succession to keep them from sleeping. The highway and the desert, the fruitful field, and the barren moor, were alike subject to danger.'[24]

21 *Ibid. p* 55.   22 Agnew, A.: *ut supra. p* 407.   23 *Ibid. p* 392.
24 Mackenzie, W.: *The History of Galloway*. ii *pp* 261, 262.

Field-preaching was punishable with death, and the sentence had to be carried out within three hours after judgment; at the drum-head courts martial which served as tribunals to enforce church attendance, the possession of a Bible was accepted as direct evidence of the owner's nonconformity.[25] On 23 January 1685, James Dun and five other men of the parish of Minnigaff, about eight miles from Wigtown, were surprised by a party of soldiers whilst engaged in prayer and shot out of hand.[26] Less than four months later, 'Margaret M'Lachland of Kirkinner paroch, a woman of sixty-three years of age . . . was taken off her knees in prayer and carried to prison.' A young girl of eighteen, Margaret Wilson, who had been hiding in the mountains with her younger brother and sister, was also taken at the same time. The judges 'sentenced them to be tyed to palisadoes fixed in the sand, within the flood mark of the sea, and there to stand till the flood overflowed them and drowned them'. So reads the session record of Penninghame.

This sentence was carried out on Wigtown sands on 11 May 1685. There can be little doubt that William M'Culloch must have met many who saw this judicial murder, for, as one eyewitness averred, 'the hail sands war covered wi' cluds o' folk, a' gathered into clusters here and there, offering up prayers for the two women while they were being put down'.[27] One of the Kirkcowan elders, Gilbert Milroy, could have told of the days when he fled from the parish and his wife was tortured by lighted matches placed between her fingers. He only escaped having his ears cut off because the surgeon passed him by as a dying man, and then he was shipped in fetters to Jamaica and sold into slavery, until the events of 1688 restored him to liberty and home.[28]

The young boy's mind must have been filled with such harrowing stories; there were also tales of the adventures of the field-preachers. John Welsh of Irongray, the great-grandson of John Knox and 'the first of the field-preachers,'[29] preached at

25 Agnew, A.: *ut supra. p* 396.
26 Mackenzie, W.: *ut supra. p* 265.
27 Agnew, A.: *ut supra. p* 431.
28 Mackenzie, W.: *ut supra. pp* 278–9.
29 *Fasti.* ii *p* 287.

New Luce in Wigtownshire before he fled to London after the battle of Bothwell Bridge in 1679. That strange mystic, Alexander Peden, the most celebrated of them all, was a minister of that same parish of New Luce (1659–86).[30] In his outdoor preaching one day, Peden encouraged his harried parishioners, 'A poor believer gets never a bonnier blink of Jesus Christ than when the cross lies heaviest between his shoulders'.[31] The wistful, ardent James Renwick, the last of the martyrs, executed in February 1688 at twenty-five years of age, was a native of Moniaive in Dumfriesshire.[32]

Not only were evil men resisted in the south-west of Scotland – evil spirits were defied. Not far from M'Culloch's home was the parish of Kirkcolm, haunted by the ghost of Galdenoch, who set the thatch on fire, 'washed grannie in the burn, and laid her on the dyke to dry', and resisted all efforts at exorcism by neighbouring clergymen. But the stentorian Alexander Marshall, minister of Kirkcolm (1700–43), pitted his mighty lungs against the ghost and sang the psalm-tune Bangor throughout the whole night until 'an unearthly voice, husky and weak–whined, "Roar awa, Marshall, I can roar nae mair"'. Thus, runs the tale, did the minister triumph and secure peace for his flock.[33] Such an exploit ran round the countryside. There were other stories that could only be whispered. In 1698, the seven-year-old son of the schoolmaster at Whithorn would doubtless hear of the burning near Kirkcudbright of Elspeth M'Ewen, the witch.[34]

On all sides there were places made sacred by hallowed names: Anwoth, ever associated with the seraphic Rutherford, and Stranraer, scene of the labours of the saintly John Livingstone, to whose communion occasions and evening devotions boat loads of worshippers rowed across from Ireland. Not all the struggles were past history, however, for there were living leaders, extremists and rebels against church authority, who were active in Galloway as M'Culloch grew up. John Hepburn,

30 *Ibid.* ii p 345.
31 Johnstone, J.: *Alexander Peden, the Prophet of the Covenant.* p 207.
32 Mackenzie, W.: *ut supra.* p 290.
33 Agnew, A.: *ut supra.* pp 457–60.
34 Mackenzie, W.: *ut supra.* pp 342–3. Appendix, 37–40.

minister of Urr in Dumfriesshire (1680–1723) was the inspiration of a large number of scattered Hebronite societies who met for prayer and fellowship.[35] Nearer than Urr was the parish of Balmaghie in Kirkcudbrightshire, with one of its preachers John Macmillan who stayed in the district to minister to the Cameronian societies until 1727.[36]

All around M'Culloch were the living influences of the warring present and the recent past. On all sides were to be seen, pondered and remembered:

> Grey, recumbent tombs of the dead in desert places,
> Standing stones on the vacant wine-red moor,
> Hills of sheep, and the howes of the silent vanished races,
> And winds, austere and pure.

And he would have well understood the wistful words of another Scot of a later date, sick and exiled in distant Samoa:

> Be it granted me to behold you again in dying,
> Hills of home! and to hear again the call;
> Hear about the graves of the martyrs the peewees crying,
> And hear no more at all.

When but a boy of seven, M'Culloch began to be serious about religion, and remembered later how he was brought into further concern when about thirteen years of age under the preaching of Mr Ker, minister at Wigtown (1701–29). About this time he became a communicant.[37]

At the Universities of Edinburgh and Glasgow, he laid the foundations of sound learning, graduating from Glasgow on 26 April 1712. He was a man of uncommon abilities, excelling in languages and mathematical subjects, and had unusual skill in Hebrew.[38] For a time he taught numerous classes of young men in Glasgow, constructing his own models for the classes in astronomy and geography.[39] Dean Stanley pays his own tribute to

35 MacMillan, William: *John Hepburn and the Hebronites.*
36 Reid, H. M. B.: *A Cameronian Apostle.*
37 *Anal.* iv *p* 279.
38 Preface to M'Culloch mss. vol i.
39 M'Culloch, W.: *Sermons &c.* Memoir.

M'Culloch's gifts and disposition when he asserts that 'he was no wild fanatic, but a learned, unostentatious scholar, a slow, cautious and prudent parish minister'.[40]

Despite his above-average scholarship, however, he had little gift for the pulpit. His own son writes that 'he was not a very ready speaker; though eminent for learning and piety, he was not eloquent . . . his manner was slow and cautious, very different from that of popular orators'.[41] He was given the nickname of a 'yill or Ale-minister' for, when he rose to speak, many of the audience left to quench their thirst in the public house.[42]

He was licensed to preach the gospel by the Presbytery of Wigtown in 1722, and lived mainly with Mr Hamilton of Aitkenhead, Cathcart, where he served as chaplain and tutor. This was a familiar and convenient arrangement whereby probationers supported themselves whilst waiting for a call to minister in some parish.[43] In 1723, Mr Paul Hamilton, a planter and church official in Carolina, came to Glasgow, seeking for two ministers who would be willing to labour in that state. At first there was great difficulty in finding anyone, and on 6 February 1724 M'Culloch offered himself for this overseas work, but two candidates, John Deans and William Maxwell, had already been ordained for this ministry and so he was not accepted.[44] The Presbytery of Glasgow was unwilling to ordain him in the absence of any definite vacancy in Carolina, in spite of his great inclination to go abroad. Seven years later, M'Culloch spoke of this episode to Robert Wodrow who commented that 'he was made very much to question matters, and came to a peremptory resolution to leave the country, and go wher he was not knouen'. When, however, M'Culloch opened the Bible at the first chapter of Jonah, he was dumbfounded and abandoned his purpose. [His only son Robert lived as a merchant in

40 Stanley, A. P.: *The Church of Scotland. p* 137.
41 M'Culloch, W.: *Sermons &c. pp* 15–16.
42 *New Statistical Account.* vi *p* 426.
43 Thomas Boston was with the Bruces of Kennet; Leechman with the Mures of Caldwell.
44 *Anal.* iii *pp* 131, 132; Glasgow Pres. Recs. 22, 23 January, 6 February, 1724.

D   39

America before returning to Scotland to study for the ministry[45]].

In the following year, 1725, M'Culloch was singled out for honour. Thomas Crawford of Crawfordsburn had endowed a yearly sermon to be preached by a probationer named by the ministers of Glasgow. This discourse, 'A Sermon against the Idolatrous Worship of the Church of Rome, Preach'd in the New-Church of Glasgow, the Fifth of November 1725', was the only one published by M'Culloch himself, and was 'done entirely in Compliance with the Unanimous Desire of the General Session of this City; without which all Private Sollicitations of Friends had been to no Effect'.

Printed by Robert Sanders of Glasgow, the sermon, consisting of forty-eight printed pages, had for its text, 'Then Jesus answered and said Get thee hence, Satan; for it is written, Thou shalt worship the Lord thy God, and him only shalt thou serve' (Matthew 4.10). M'Culloch began by drawing attention to the 'Popish Pretender, sitting under the Pope's nose at Rome, who does not want [lack] his Powerful Friends abroad, and . . . too many Well-wishers among our selves, and our unhappy Divisions, Parties and Factions have not a little strengthned that Interest'.[46]

The tone of the sermon is extremely moderate, in view of the times, and without biting invective. The fine distinctions made between *latria* and *dulia* are discussed, and extensive quotation made from prominent Roman Catholic writers, Bellarmine, Cajetan, Thomas Aquinas and others, with several lengthy excerpts from the Council of Trent. In truly modern style, he argues from philology: "'Tis true indeed, the word ONLY is not in the Hebrew Text from whence our Saviour cites this Law . . . But the order of the words in the Original requires this Addition . . . that the Reader may be appriz'd of this peculiar force. Accordingly, not only the *Seventy* but the *Vul-*

---

45 *Anal.* iv p 279. M'Culloch's only son Robert turned first to the mercantile profession and went to America where he lived for a short time before returning to Scotland to complete his suspended studies in divinity. So writes his daughter (*Memoirs &c of Mrs Coutts. p* 10).

46 M'Culloch, W.: *A Sermon against Idolatrous Worship &c. p* 3.

gar Latin read the words there, as our Saviour does here.'[47]

After lamenting that 'many Disputes and Controversies among Protestants have been managed with undue Heat and over-eager Contention,' he comes to a conclusion that is character-istic of the man, in its appeal to reality in practice. In the last paragraph he warns his hearers that, although they might detest popish idolatry, they should also take heed 'they be not involv'd in another sort of Idolatry, no less ruining and destructive to the Soul. A Man may renounce Romish idolatry and may seemingly have a great deal of Zeal for Gospel Purity, and be often talking of the Pattern in the Mount, and yet *if he have the World set in his Heart, if he say to Gold, Thou art my Hope, and to fine Gold, Thou art my Confidence; if he trust in uncertain Riches, and not in the Living God,* he is as rank an Idolater as the *Papists* that worship Saints and Angels: nay, as the Pagan that bows to Stocks and Stones.'[48]

One is left to wonder what the captains of industry and the leaders of the city's life, 'the princes of the Plainstones' with their scarlet cloaks and gold-headed canes, growing richer every day by the lucrative tobacco trade[49] and other industries, thought of the peroration. It does reveal in the preacher utter sincerity and courage, one who could speak the truth, and speak it in love.

It may well be that this printed sermon drew the attention of the parish of Cambuslang towards the preacher, for on 8 April 1726 the Presbytery of Hamilton noted that 'the Paroch of Kambuslang . . . having applyed for a hearing of Mr M'Culloch Chaplain to Aitkenhead . . . did invite the sd. Mr M'Culloch to preach before Them at yr next meeting att Hamilton and to bring His Testimonials with him.'[50]

Five years later, after being a probationer for nine years, M'Culloch found himself at the threshold of his life's work as minister of Cambuslang. He could never have foreseen, nor could any have predicted, what were to be the fruits of this long-deferred task.

47 *Ibid. p* 34.
48 *Ibid. p* 47.
49 Strang, J.: *Glasgow and its Clubs. pp* 40–1.
50 Hamilton Pres. Recs.

3
Problems of the Parish

When the new minister entered upon his duties in the parish, it was in the face of formidable difficulties. We have already seen how the feeble health of his predecessor had led to widespread neglect of the spiritual interests of the people, and the bickering preceding M'Culloch's settlement, which had antagonised his leading heritor, was followed by continuing friction.

For the first three years he did not dispense the sacrament of the Lord's Supper in the parish and, when the Presbytery investigated this matter, his defence was that in 1731 he had not sufficient elders; in the following year, he deemed it necessary to instruct his flock and to get to know them better; in 1733, he was sick. One writer suggests that 'his excuse reads rather lamely',[1] but we do know from his session records that in 1733 he suffered from a 'sore Rheumatic fever', and two years later a committee of masons and wrights reported about the state of the manse at Cambuslang that it 'needed the Low floor next to the kitchen pavemented, and the windows needed storm-shutters to keep out rain'.[2] The neglected state of the parish must have had a depressing effect upon him and there is a very full record of how, four months after his ordination, he unburdened himself to Wodrow, the minister of Eastwood, whose 'inquisitive mind, percipient eye and fellow-feeling for all that is human' have so enriched our knowledge of his times. Tortured by doubts about his own fitness for the sacred office, he sought out his senior colleague in August 1731.

1 Brown, J. T.: *Cambuslang &c. p* 46.
2 *Hamilton Pres. Recs.* 12 November 1735.

'He asked me whither I thought it warrantable and laufull ... for a Minister who knew he was not called of God, and who was nothing but a hollou hypocrite, to demitt his Ministry, and give way to another, who might be usefull? He opened his mind very fully to me.' The main problem was that 'since his ordination, he has been preaching on Conversion, and the nature of it ... and nou he thinks he is perfectly a stranger to this great work'.

Wodrow 'presumed to say he had more of a call to the Ministry than severalls had atteaned to; and I took him to be of a thinking, melancholy disposition, and ready to dip too farr into things' and pointed out to the troubled enquirer that it was thoughtful, studious persons who were chiefly haunted by doubts.

In his pastoral duties, M'Culloch had been compelled to examine his own experience. 'He is also much damped in conversation with his people, and their telling him experiences he has been a stranger to ... I hope the Lord has good to do by Mr M'Culloch and is training him to be usefull.'[3]

It is easy to sneer at the 'miracle-mongering minister of Eastwood' and to dismiss him, as the prejudiced Henry Grey Graham does, as 'an inquisitive, garrulous, credulous man whose ears were erect at every tale of wonder';[4] but, is there not something almost prophetic about this opinion on so unpromising an evangelist, whose success Wodrow never saw?

Nor can we doubt the wisdom of Wodrow's advice to his troubled colleague, who was suffering from 'a violent pain in his hind-head with the rack of thought and contrary tydes. I advised him to riding-exercise ... but that, it seems, he much declines and gives himself too much to thought and solitude.'

Five years after his ordination, M'Culloch married Janet Dinwoodie, daughter of a Glasgow merchant;[5] William Hamil-

3 *Anal.* iv *pp* 279–81.
4 Graham, H. G.: *Social Life of Scotland &c. p* 347. For an unbiased appreciation of Wodrow *vide* articles by W. J. Couper (*Records S.C.H.S.* iii *pp* 112–34; v *pp* 238–50).
5 In the Register for the Widows' Fund, Presbytery of Glasgow, she is known as Janet Dinwoodie. M'Culloch was admitted as a Burgess and

ton, son of the former minister of Cambuslang, and minister of Douglas in the Presbytery of Lanark (1721–69), was married to Christian, also a daughter of Robert Dinwoodie. Hamilton was to be one of the band of ministers who helped his brother-in-law during the revival days. The parish of Cambuslang had had a long connection with evangelical religion, and the new minister would find in the records of the kirk session and the history of the parish much to remind him of the price paid by both ministers and people in former days. On all sides, he would meet the very namesakes and direct descendants of these sufferers for the truth.

There was the bold John Howison, minister of Cambuslang (1580–1618), a champion of the popular cause who, when moderator of the presbytery, preached in Glasgow Cathedral in June 1582. At the behest of the provost, he was dragged from the pulpit, 'smote on the face, pulled by the beard, one of his teeth beat out, and put in the tolbuith lyke as a theefe by the provost, and bailies and their complices'.[6] Two years later, preaching this time in Blackfriars, Edinburgh, he attacked the 'Tulchan' bishops and affirmed: 'There is ane heid of the kirk made; there being nae heid but Jesus Christ, nor cannot be'. Then, warming to his subject . . . 'For my ain part I ken I will be noted, I regard not. What can the king get of me but my heid and my bluid?'[7] For his outspokenness he was imprisoned in Falkland Palace. So bold a man could not fail to mould his parishioners, amongst whom he was to die in 1618. Nor did his reputation depend entirely upon fearless polemic. Under his dour boldness was a kindly heart. He founded the first public school in Cambuslang; in 1613 he endowed a bursary in the University of Glasgow to help needy students, which still continues the work he thus began.

Upon the shelves in M'Culloch's library we may be sure

---

gild brother of Glasgow on 14 September 1744. (*Glasgow Burgh Records.* vi *p* 184.)

6 Brown, J. T.: *ut supra. p* 22.

7 Original in MS State Paper Office, Accusation of Howison (quoted Brown. *p* 26. *Fasti.* iii *pp* 234–6).

there was a copy of *The Fulfilling of Scripture*, published in Rotterdam by a former minister of the parish, Robert Fleming. He had come to Cambuslang in 1653 as a sickly youth of twenty-three, and was one of the many ministers 'outed' in 1662 for refusing to abjure the Covenant. Conventicle preacher, prisoner and exile, he was 'a devout and pious man . . . full of love and of a peaceable temper'.[8] The Episcopalian minister who took Fleming's place, David Cunningham, found the parish in an almost continuous state of uproar and during his incumbency (1666–88) there are no minutes of any meeting of session.[9] The era of persecution had begun and, in 1662, two of the leading parishioners were fined £600 and £1,000 Scots, and one of these, Gabriel Hamilton of Westburn, was committed to prison in 1676 and fined 1,000 merks 'for keeping conventicles'. He was still in prison seven years later.

Two of Fleming's elders were brought to account. In 1664 John Corsbie (or Crosbie) in Easter-cotes was driven from his home for refusing to assist the new minister in cases of discipline. Robert Hamilton in Spittal in 1666 was 'put to the horn', *ie* outlawed, and his house searched and spoiled.[10] At the first meeting of session after the re-establishment of presbyterian church government, 15 June 1690, these two were named as elders.[11] With them is one John Arbuckle, a name associated with the eldership of Cambuslang for over a hundred years.

In 1687, fifty men and two officers of Athol's Highland Host were billeted on John Corsbie for eight days and twenty-two men on James Jackson (another name found in the list of elders in 1742). In 1679, more soldiers were settled at Cambuslang for five weeks and levied £861 from the parish.

M'Culloch's ministry began among a people who had had direct and, in some cases, personal experiences of suffering for their faith. This long-continued resistance to civil and ecclesiastical tyranny brought some less desirable consequences in its

8 *Fasti.* iii *p* 237; W. Stevens: *History of the Scots Kirk, Rotterdam. p* 113.
9 Wilson, J. A.: *History of Cambuslang. p* 85.
10 Wodrow, Robert: *History of the Sufferings* Etc. ii *p* 3.
11 Quoted Wilson: *ut supra. p* 88.

train, and a legacy of extremism was left to trouble the life of the parish. The ministry of M'Culloch's immediate predecessor, Archibald Hamilton, would do little to discourage this spirit.

The flames of ecclesiastical controversy, which had been damped down a little during the reign of William III, blazed out again in the closing days of his successor Anne, owing to the imposition of the Abjuration Oath in 1712. We noticed earlier how this measure became a source of violent discord throughout the land.

Robert Wodrow was a declared non-juror, and wrote on 5 November 1712 that it would be sinful for him to take the oath; he was honest enough to say that he dared not go to the length of condemning his brethren who thought otherwise. 'I firmly believe them men of conscience, and of the same principles with me, and many of them live and lie much nearer God than I do. . . . If you think me lax and latitudinarian, I cannot help it. *O scientia charitas!*'[12]

But he does express strong dissatisfaction with the somewhat irresponsible conduct of many who, like himself, refused the Oath, and especially mentions the minister of Cambuslang. The last day for subscribing the Oath was 28 October 1712, but on 30 October Hamilton read out from his pulpit the reasons for which he could not take it. 'This makes some noise here, and I wish had been foreborne',[13] writes Wodrow, who conjectures that this will be misconstrued as an attempt to curry favour with the people. 'I am informed some of his hearers were much satisfied.'[14]

There were at work in the west of Scotland more inflammatory influences than Mr Hamilton. Mr Addison (or Adamson), a Perthshire catechist, came into the Hamilton Presbytery in April 1713. Preaching upon the blind man who came to Christ and cast away his garments, he told his audience what garments they ought to cast away. He 'began with the garment of the Union, that of the Patronages, that of the Tolleration,

12 Wodrow: *Correspondence.* i p 330; also i p 340 *fn.*
13 *Ibid.* i pp 339–40.
14 *Ibid.* i p 350.

that of the Oath of Abjuration! These are his common topicks, and render him very popular.'[15]

This peripatetic enthusiast created a sensation in the west. He refused to take collections gathered for him, apart from as much as was needed to get a new suit of clothes. At Kilbride, Addison declared: 'that as among the twelve Disciples there was one Judas, soe nou among twelve Ministers there could be found eleven Devils! he cryes out against the Revolution as built upon a heap of dirt'. Almost two years later, July 1714, we learn that 'Mr Adamson is raging like a madman in his sermon, in Hamiltoun, Lanerk and Air Presbytery. . . . He is soe violent, he cannot continou long.'[16] Eventually this 'wild work in the bounds of Glasgow and Hamilton . . nauseous stuff'[17] was brought to an end when Addison refused to appear before a commission of the Assembly, and turned Independent.

The fanaticism of Addison and the impetuosity of Hamilton had its own peculiar appeal to the ultra-Covenanting faction, with their almost anarchic defiance of authority. In 1720, a 'Protest and Testimony' was handed in to the session of Cambuslang by Hugh Cumin. He inveighed against 'all defections contrary to the Word of God and our Covenant engagements, National and Solemn League and Covenant' and protested about the character of some 'scandalous persons' who had been made officers in the kirk. If things were rectified, Cumin concluded: 'I promise to hear the Gospel in this place, as witness my hand at Coates the twentieth of April 1720.'

Hugh Cumin became an elder at Cambuslang, and was honoured as Presbytery elder in 1733 and 1737; he was to be a storm-centre for several years. It was Cumin, and other extremists in M'Culloch's session, who eventually brought about a crisis that culminated in 1739 in an open breach. Couper, writing in his *Scottish Revivals*, says: 'It is now impossible to discover what was the subject of dispute or to follow the proceedings taken. About 1745, when a better day had dawned,

15 *Anal.* i *pp* 242–3.
16 *Anal.* ii *pp* 244, 263, 285.
17 Wodrow: *ut supra.* i *p* 529.

the session considered that it would not "answer any valuable purpose of edification to transmit to posterity the remembrance of that unhappy breach" and destroyed all the papers connected with the matter, especially as "all partys . . . signified their desire that it might be buried in oblivion".'

Fortunately for the historian, the session was unable to mutilate the records of the Presbytery of Hamilton, and within its pages there is a very full account of these events. If we bring to view again what these good men wished to obliterate, it will serve to make even plainer something of M'Culloch's problems with his strong-minded leaders, and also show what a reconciling power was inherent in the revival of 1742.

On 26 February 1740, John Bar, Presbytery elder for Cambuslang, gave in to the Presbytery of Hamilton a 'Petition and Complaint against His Brethren Elders of the sd. Paroch'. After asserting that he had behaved inoffensively towards all men since his ordination as an elder at Cambuslang seven years before, Bar tells how he visited the kirk at Mearns on Sacrament Sunday, 27 May 1739.

We take up Bar's own story as told to the Presbytery of Hamilton: 'Upon the Thursday following being the fast day preceeding the sacrament in Cambuslang my Brethren Elders being mett in Session charged my being att Mearns as an high misdemenour, a breach of office, a Crime worthy of Censure and declared Their resolution of deserting Their office if I should officiate . . . Upon the Sabbath when the Minister desired the Elders to do Their duty, They refused and keept their seats till I, conscious of no crime worthy of such treatment, purely for the peace of the Congregation and Decency on such occasions left the Church and went to the Tent to the great grief of my mind and scorn of many beholders.'[18]

The petitioner then went on to tell of his long search for some 'happy expedient' to bring peace – and almost nine months had passed since his being boycotted at the Sacrament – yet all to no purpose, for 'no concession by me, pains by others or length of time can prevail, but on the contrary by some pretended

18 Hamilton Pres. Recs.

sentence or supposition of a sentence of my Brethren, I am either Deposed or suspended from my office by Them without ever the least conviction of a Crime'. Bar, therefore, laid his case before the Presbytery, asking that he might suffer suitable punishment if adjudged criminal and 'if innocent, I may be acquit and my innocency appear and I do Protest that this my complaint does not flow from any resentment or Divisive Design'.

Certain elders from Cambuslang were cited to the next meeting of Presbytery, *viz* Archibald Couper, Hugh Cumin, Archibald Fyfe, John Strang and Andrew Fyfe. On 10 April 1740 these men gave in their written reply, complaining that John Bar 'refused to give a satisfying answer' when asked whether he had been at Mearns. His going there was 'Invading the Elder's office' – he had helped to gather the collection for the poor – and by doing so he had given offence to the congregation and session at Cambuslang.

Immediately after this complaint, apparently so trivial, the elders revealed stronger objections: 'Therefore We desire the Presbytery may let us see that Patronage is agreeable to the word of God or else we can not in conscience Joyn with John Bar Psal. 74, 5, 6 but now they have broken down the Carved work with axes and hammers', and they go on to declare that they had been denied a free voice in the session at Cambuslang. Apparently, at the sacrament when the breach became evident, M'Culloch had called on the ministers present, Mr Connell of East Kilbride and Mr Henderson of Blantyre, to bear witness should any elder draw back through needless scruples. 'Therefore he', goes on the written reply, 'reckoning that to be needless scruples which others reckon matter of conscience We let the Presbytery know that we are not wearied of our Master's service but Lament we cannot exercise government in God's house. We could keep Session with our Neighbour ministers if the Presbytery appointed one to Moderate with us.'

After a long discussion with the elders, who persisted in the same mind, the Presbytery unanimously asserted the innocence of John Bar and declared that M'Culloch should administer a 'Very Particular Rebuke' to the elders who were 'introducing various dissorders and confusions in this church, contrary to the Spirit of peace, holyness and Love'. But the obdurate elders 'refused to submit to the Rebuke and Appealed to the Tribunal of Christ'.

The kirk session, including John Bar, was appointed to meet on Thursday, 8 May, but M'Culloch had to report that only John Bar and James Jackson had attended, and the latter had said that 'in his own mind he had no difficulty as to His sitting in Session with John Bar yet being afraid of the Clamour of the People of the Paroch he declined to sit in Session with him at this time'. Evidently there were rigorists in the congregation as well as in the session. On 24 June the Presbytery deposed the objecting and recalcitrant elders from their office.

On 29 July 1740 a long paper was brought to the Presbytery by Archibald Couper on behalf of the deposed elders; he asked permission for it to be read and inserted in the records, which was done. In it they speak of 'the affair betwixt Mr M'Culloch and us and also betwixt John Bar and us' and complain that the Presbytery had ignored their previous request 'to let us see that Patronage is agreeable to the Word of God'.

Reference is made to the resistance shown by the parish to the proposed settlement of Mr Findlater, the binding obligation of the Confession of Faith and to both the National Covenant and the Solemn League and Covenant. Any deviation from these would be a betrayal 'of our late sufferers and even to any at present whether Ministers or Christians that are setting up for Reformation Principles. If we should go in with the guizers of the time as they now occurr to us we must necessarily go contrary to our own light and likewayes to both publick and private Engagements . . . Therefore we desire through Grace to own all our Covenanted Principles and Especially Christ's Headship in His own House and we reckon whatever invasions be made by any Judicatory upon His Kingly office must be Void and Null in itself.'

After this there is reference to the defections of the times and the denial of the presbyterian principles . . . 'so that we being driven to this extremity by Ecclesiastical oppression and considering that so many honest Ministers are Deposed for owning the same Reformation Principles we cannot think that those Decisions can possibly agree with the Word of God and our approven standards'.

In the final paragraph of this lengthy justification, they deny and defy the prerogatives of the Presbytery as a superior court. 'We further Protest that this unwarrantable sentence shall no wayes alienate our office and Character as Elders and office-bearers in the Church of Christ . . . and we have as full liberty and Power to exercise the same when called thereto as if no such sentence had been passed, and that our office and Character shall no more come under the Cognizance and inspection of the Presbytery untill They come to own Reformation Principles . . . we hereby Decline Them as not acting as a Lawfull and Right constitute Court of Christ the alone King and Head of His own Church . . . and we hereby may Apply or Appeal unto the first Lawfull and Right constitute Court of Christ for redress . . . *Sic Subts.*

Archibald Couper   How Cummin   Archibald Fyfe
James Turnbull   I.S. (John Strang?)   Andrew Fyfe.'

In the following year, 1741, there was no elder appointed to Presbytery from Cambuslang, but on 22 April 1742, after the revival began at that place, there came before the Presbytery 'Archibald Fyfe . . . and professed his Dissatisfaction with what he had done'. Both M'Culloch and the Laird of Westburn sent letters pleading for him, and the sentence of deposition was accordingly removed.

Embodied within the 'reasons of Protest, Declinature and Appeal' given by the deposed elders, are further evidences of another of the problems facing M'Culloch. The reference to 'Ecclesiastical Oppression' and that 'so many honest Ministers are Deposed for owning the same Reformation Principles' points directly to the controversy around the Secession of 1733. Here are the very echoes of Ebenezer Erskine's famous sermon at Stirling. The Seceding Brethren, now eight in number, had been solemnly deposed by the General Assembly on 15 May 1740, only two months before the protest of the Cambuslang elders. Adherents to their cause were already meeting in Glasgow.

At first there was no fixed place of assembly in that city for those who sought fellowship with the seceders. One venue is designated Rochesay, the property of William Letham of the Barony parish; others are Bogton, near Cathcart; Balscragrie, the modern Balshagray; Petershill in the Springburn district and Dildue, now Daldowie. These places are named in the minutes of those societies for prayer which were later to form the first Secession church in Glasgow.[19]

In June 1739, a sympathiser, 'William Thomson, Esq., of Corshill in the parish of Cathcart', offered the lease of a piece of ground where public worship might be regularly held, and a session was formally constituted in February 1740. To this spot there travelled continually many members of the Cambuslang congregation. The three daughters of the elder already noted in Bar's case, James Jackson, were all in the habit of going to 'hear the North Country Ministers at Corsehill' of whom they 'had a great opinion'. Another young woman, Mary Mitchell, went to hear the seceders 'because I saw Many others going'. This must have given M'Culloch[20] some anxious thought; yet, in spite of the problems facing him, the disruptiveness of extremists and the counter-attractions of the seceders, there were also many things to warm his heart. It was during the first decade of M'Culloch's ministry that the fresh winds of revival began to blow in several countries, in some measure providing an answer to the indifference begotten of that age of light without love.

At Freehold, New Jersey, there began an awakening in 1730: this was 'the first place in the East-Jersey to be settled with a gospel ministry' and 'this was owing . . . under GOD to some Scots People, that came to it, among whom there was none so

19 *Historical Sketch, Greyfriars Church. p* 28.
20 M'C. Mss. vol i *p* 94.

painful in this blessed Undertaking as one Walter Ker; who in the Year 1685 for his faithful and conscientious Adherence to GOD and his Truth as professed by the Church of Scotland, was there apprehended, and sent into this Country, under a Sentence of perpetual Banishment . . . He is yet alive (October 11, 1744) . . . being in his 88th Year'.[21] In 1734 there followed the Great Awakening at Northampton under the leadership of Jonathan Edwards.

From about 1730, Wales heard and sang the new music of the gospel as brought by men like Griffith Jones, and from 1735 by Daniel Rowland, Howell Harris and Howell Davis. George Whitefield was, as he wrote in his Diary, 'brought into the Knowledge of His free grace' about Whitsun 1735 and soon began his apostolic labours. John Wesley's heart was strangely warmed on 24 May 1738.

There was a breaking-out of new life in many places; a spiritual springtide. News of these unusual events was carried far and wide by printed pamphlets, and never was there such an age for voluminous letter-writing. It is not easy to trace any definite connection between these movements and the little community in Cambuslang, and yet there is something infectious about such happenings, and earnest men must have longed and prayed for some new throbbing of power within their own sphere.

We have hinted at the probability of Robert Fleming's book, *The Fulfilling of Scripture*, being in the manse at Cambuslang; in it there was much to inspire, with its record of previous similar spiritual awakenings. In its pages M'Culloch would read of 'that large measure of the Spirit, and outletting thereof which did convincingly follow the Gospel and ministry of the word in these last times . . . no lesse than in the first planting of the Christian church'.[22] Fleming was writing in 1669.

First he tells of events about the year 1625, during days of

---

21 Letter in *The Christian History* written by Rev Wm Tennent, *ed* T. Prince 1744. *pp* 298–9. *Vide Register of the Privy Council of Scotland.* vol xi (third series) 1685–6 *ed* H. Paton, *p* 173, for edict of banishment.
22 Fleming, R.: *Fulfilling &c. p* 241.

persecution, which 'by the prophane rabble of that time was called the Stewarton Sickness'. At 'Irwine and Stewarton', under the ministry of Mr Dickson, 'many were choaked and taken by the heart ... that in hearing of the word, they have been made to fall over ... who after proved most solid and lively Christians'. Many then alive recalled that 'few Sabbaths did passe without some evidently converted'.

How the heart of the earnest pastor at Cambuslang must have stirred as he read on: 'and truely, this great spring tide which I may so call of the Gospel, was not of a short time, but for some yeares continuance, yea thus like a spreading moor-burn, the power of Godliness did advance from one place to another'![23]

Fleming then goes on to tell of 'that solemn Communion at the Kirk of the Shots, June 20 1630, at which time there was so convincing an appearance of God, and downpouring of the Spirit ... that it was known, which I can speak on sure ground, near 500 had at that time a discernable change wrought on them, of whom most proved lively Christians afterward. It was the sowing of a seed through Clidesdeal [ie Clydesdale], so as many of the most eminent Christians in that countrey, could date either their conversion, or some remarkable confirmation in their case from that day'.[24] The account of John Livingston's reluctance to preach, the many hundreds spending the whole night in prayer, and the testimony of Livingston that success was mainly due 'in getting his heart brought into the right disposition' must have made a powerful appeal to one of M'Culloch's temperament.

This account by Fleming of the fruitfulness of the 'out-lettings at Stewarton and Shotts' was also corroborated by a contemporary of M'Culloch, Patrick Walker (1666–1745), the 'Cameronian pedlar', the packman writer of vivid simple prose. In his book, *Six Saints of the Covenant*, he quotes his friend, George Barclay, a Covenanting preacher, as saying that 'above all places in Scotland, he found the greatest gale upon his

23 *Ibid. p* 243.
24 *Ibid. p* 244.

spirite upon the water of Clide: which he attributed much to the plentiful successful prayers of some of the old Christians, and their offspring, who got a merciful cast of free grace, when casts were a dealing at the Kirk of Shotts, the 20th of June 1630, which perfumed and gave a scent to the overward of Clidesdale above all other places, but, alas! is now much gone'.[25]

All M'Culloch's own experience would lead him to endorse this judgment of Walker's, for Cambuslang itself was in Clydesdale and had its own witnesses to the continuity of that work of a hundred years earlier. His brooding, earnest spirit would have accepted Walker's verdict, set forth in the Preface to his *Life of Peden*, 'being perswaded that if ever the Lord pity this weather-beaten Sardis, Laodicean Church, and send forth a thaw-wind, and spring-tide day of the gospel, to thaw the frozen face of affairs, as was at Stewartoun, and spread through the west of Scotland as muir-burn . . . a hundred years since, and at the kirk of Shots five years thereafter . . . many other things that now are wersh [Scots, insipid] and unsavoury, will come in request again'.[26]

One thing at least was certain; in these former classic examples of powerful movements of the Spirit, prayer was central in each situation. Fleming had instanced John Welsh, associated with M'Culloch's own native south-west, as giving eight hours out of every twenty-four to prayer, spending days and nights in fasting and intercession. 'It was his use on the coldest winter nights, to rise for prayer . . . he hath been found lying on the ground weeping, and wrestling with the Lord . . . once, overcharged with grief, he told his wife he had that to presse him which she had not, the soules of 3000 to answer for, whilest he knew not how it was with many of them'.[27]

This was one step that could be taken by both minister and congregation, and so we are not surprised to learn that societies for prayer began to be revived in Cambuslang.

25 Walker, P.: *Six Saints &c.* vol i *p* 337.
26 *Ibid.* vol i *pp* 41–2.
27 Fleming, R.: *Fulfilling &c.* *p* 250.

M'Culloch himself remembered in 1751 that 'in 1731, when I came to this parish, there were 3 of these meetings in it. In 1742, they encreased to a dozen or more'.[28]

It is time for us to investigate these societies for prayer, to see their composition and practice, and to make some assessment of their place in the revival of 1742.

28 *Kilsyth Narrative. p* 316.

4
The Societies for Prayer

The renaissance emphasis on the value of the individual was taken over by Luther and other Reformation leaders in the sixteenth century, giving strength to the doctrine of the priesthood of all believers – 'the one great religious principle which lies at the basis of the whole Reformation movement', as Principal Lindsay once said in his *History of the Reformation*.[1]

Luther himself, breaking with the ecclesiastical hierarchy of his day, found strength in, and gave help to, the laity. Says the historian of the Reformation, quoting Luther: 'All believing laymen "are worthy to appear before God, to pray for others, to teach each other mutually the things that are of God". Even in the celebration of the holiest rites, there was no distinction . . . At the Eucharist . . . "we all kneel beside him (our priest or minister) and around him, men and women, young and old, master and servant, mistress and maid, all holy priests together . . . We are there in our priestly dignity".'[2] Luther proposed to establish religious societies throughout Germany, consisting of small groups of believers, enrolled by name and meeting for prayer, reading the Scriptures, administering the sacraments and engaging in works of charity. No elaborate liturgy was laid down, but Christian laymen with 'short and proper means' directed 'all in common to the Word and prayer and charity'. The aim was to nourish inward religion.

In the following century, when Lutheran orthodoxy had

1 Lindsay, T. M.: *History of the Reformation.* i *p* 444.
2 *Ibid.* i *pp* 443–4.

ossified into a narrow formalism, Philip Jakob Spener (1635–1705) called his congregation in 1669 to seek after a righteousness greater than that of mere conformity to the commonly accepted external pattern. Soon large numbers of his people were meeting in small groups in various private homes to discuss practical religion. They were the *'ecclesiolae in ecclesia'*.[3]

In his *Pia Desideria* which appeared at Frankfort in 1675, Spener advocated the earnest study of the Bible and the co-operation of laymen in the spiritual guidance of the congregation as means to the reviving of religion. Largely a lay movement, this new school of 'pietists' established their influence in the newly-founded university of Halle, established in 1694, to which one of their leaders, Francke, was appointed as professor of theology. Thousands of students flocked there from all parts: pietism became the dominant force in German religious life. Francke promoted in Halle ragged schools and orphanages, which were much later to inspire George Müller to a similar venture in Bristol; to Halle, the king of Denmark sent men to be trained as missionaries, and the great work at Tranquebar in India began in 1706; the Moravian leader, Zinzendorf, who organised the *Unitas Fratrum* in 1727, was Spener's godson and pupil. When the two Wesley brothers sailed for Georgia in October 1735, there were twenty-six Moravians from the *Unitas Fratrum* on board, whose courage in time of storm impressed John Wesley greatly. On 6 November he began to read a new book, the *Pietas Hallensis* by A. H. Francke.[4]

Similar movements to that in Germany were taking place in other European countries, and especially in Holland, which had provided asylum for so many religious refugees in the latter half of the seventeenth century. One group of exiled ministers met weekly for prayer, and included Mr Howe, famous for his intercessions. About 1686, at one of these gatherings, it was Mr Howe's turn to pray; he did so with such fervour 'that the sweet haled doun. Mrs Hou his wife, knouing his manner, and that it would not divert him, in the time of it, stepped to him

3 *Vide.* McGiffert, A. C.: *Protestant Thought before Kant. pp* 155–62.
4 *The Journal of John Wesley* (ed Curnock). i *p* 116.

gently, took off his wigg, and with her napkin dryed the sweet, and put on his wigg again'.[5] James Hog, later of Carnock, writing in his memoirs under the name of *Philomathes*, tells of his studies at one of the Dutch universities, and of meeting with those who 'conversed together about the great salvation, and poured out their hearts unto the Lord in prayer with one accord'.[6] As a tutor in a noble family there, he associated with 'excellent ones of the earth' who 'met in societies . . . several of considerable quality'.[7]

Religious societies, meeting for prayer and Bible reading, were also to be found in England during the seventeenth century. When Robert Baillie was in London for the Westminster Assembly, he wrote home to Scotland on 10 August 1645: 'Truely the godly here are a praying people',[8] and he notes that many met often in private houses. Writing in 1724, about eighty years later, Wodrow speaks of the news from his friend Mr Kemp who lived in London. There 'he joyned in a privat fellouship-meeting, who conveened every Munday, about six of the clock, and spent some hours in prayer and conference, where he was much refreshed. He adds, that ther are multitudes of these meetings, both of young men and elder persons in London.'[9]

In 1727, Wodrow recorded with sorrow that his friend John Stirling, Principal of Glasgow University, had died; for seventeen years, they had ridden together three times each year to Assemblies and Commissions in Edinburgh.[10] In the library of the University of Glasgow there is a slim volume, *An Account of the Rise and Progress of the Religious Societies in the City of London* by Josiah Woodward, DD, Minister of Poplar, 3rd Edition, printed in 1701. It is a very full and exact account of the remarkable growth of societies for prayer in London. Written in ink on the title-page is '*Ex Libris Bibliotheca civitatis Glasg:*

5 *Anal.* iii *p* 303.
6 *Memoir of James Hog* (*ed* Bruce) 1798. *p* 10.
7 *Ibid. p* 22.
8 *The Letters & Journal of Robert Baillie* (*ed* D. Laing). ii *p* 305.
9 *Anal.* iii *p* 371.
10 *Ibid.* iii *pp* 444–6.

Empt prop Acced sumpt 1702 Jo: Stirling Principle'. Was this little book ever in the pocket, or saddle-bag, of the Principal of the University as he jogged along with Wodrow to do the business of the church in the capital?

These societies of which Woodward wrote began in London about 1678, although there were some in other places 'who knew nothing of these London-Societies'. Similar groups had brought great benefits to the 'Sister-Kingdoms of Scotland and Ireland'. 'Dr Frank, Professor of Divinity in the City of Hall in Saxony', had written on 21 January 1700 to inform Woodward that his book had been translated into German, and that encouraging news was to hand from France, Switzerland, and the Rhineland.[11]

The inspirer of this development in London was Dr Anthony Horneck (1641–97), who came from Heidelberg to England about 1661, and was appointed preacher at the Savoy. Some young men who were disturbed by his preaching discussed the matter with him, and drew up some rules of conduct 'whereby Poor Families have been reliev'd, some Poor People set into a way of Trade, sundry Prisoners set at Liberty, some Poor Scholars furthered at the University, and several Orphans maintain'd'.[12]

During the reign of James II they paid for public prayers to be said at St Clement Danes every evening and, when persecution became more intense, rather than endanger their friends, 'they adjourn'd to some Publicke-House where they could have a Room to themselves; and under the Pretext of spending a Shilling or two, they conferr'd seriously together as formerly'. Evangelistic in spirit, they resolved to try and bring one friend each to their various meetings, and Woodward records that there were forty distinct groups at the time of writing.[13]

Some criticised this development as the beginning of yet another sect, but every member of the societies had to confess

11 Woodward, J.: *Account of the Rise of the Religious Societies*. pp 4, 6, 7–9.
(*Vide* also an excellent modern study, *Voluntary Religious Societies 1520–1799*. F. W. B. Bullock, 1963.)
12 *Ibid.* pp 23–4.
13 *Ibid.* pp 28–9, 40.

himself of the Church of England, frequent communion was obligatory upon them, nothing was permitted without the express consent of their minister and they had the blessing of the Bishop of London. They were active supporters of the 'Honourable Society for Propagating Christian Knowledge ... setting up about 40 Schools in this City and Suburbs ... where over a thousand children were taught freely'. Hearing of 'The Reverend Doctor Bray's pious Intentions of improving the Knowledge and Practice of the Gospel in our Plantations' they had 'readily contributed One Hundred Pounds'.[14]

Similar societies had been set up in Oxford and Cambridge;[15] about twenty years later, the two Wesley brothers were at Oxford, where the 'Methodist' society was started. Whilst admitting the deep influence exerted by Henry Scougal of Aberdeen upon John and Charles Wesley, it is probably going too far to assert, as D. Butler does, that 'in spirit and conception, the Oxford Club owed its inspiration to Henry Scougal, and the early origin of Methodism is to be found in the northern university town'.[16] As we have seen, such societies were already in vogue at Oxford before the Methodist undergraduates arrived there.

In a recent study of Samuel Walker and the eighteenth-century revival movement in Cornwall, G. C. B. Davies has revealed how much this work was inspired by prayer societies on the pattern described by Woodward. At Truro the minister himself took charge of a group of mature Christians and taught them first; then they acted as lay-leaders to teach others in companies of five to eight persons. John Martyn, father of the famous missionary, Henry Martyn, was a member of Walker's society.[17]

When Principal Stirling read of the work of these societies in London, he would have no difficulty in recognising their kinship to a parallel movement in Scotland.

The Lollards of Kyle had met in groups towards the end of

14 *Ibid. pp* 94-5.   15 *Ibid. p* 46.
16 Butler, D.: *Henry Scougal and the Oxford Methodists. p* 142.
17 Davies, G. C. B.: *The Cornish Evangelicals 1735-1760. passim.*

the fifteenth century to read a vernacular edition of Wycliffe's translation of the Bible, made by Murdoch Nisbet. Later, copies of Tyndale's translation were smuggled into Scotland by merchants trading chiefly from Leith, and read at dead of night in private houses.[18] John Knox discloses how real was the value of such small groups meeting together for fellowship. Writing in 1558, he declared that despite the tyranny of 'the Papisticall Kirk . . . the knowledge of God did wonderouslie increase within this realme, partlie by reading, partlie by brotherlye conferance, which in those dangerouse dayis was used to the comforte of many'.[19]

In 1556, Knox was called to Geneva to pastor the church there; from the Continent he wrote a letter, '7 of July, 1557', to be circulated in the places where he had preached. First he pointed out that 'the use of Godis hailie (ie holy) word' was as necessary for them as nourishment and sunshine. . . . 'And thairfoir, deir brethrene, yf that you luke for a lyfe to cum, of necessitie it is that ye exercise yourselves in the buke of the Lord your God. Lat na day slip over without sum comfort ressavit fra the mouth of God.'[20] Family prayers are enjoined at least once a day for 'within your awn housis ye are bishopis and kingis, your wyffis, children, and familie ar your bishoprik and charge . . . thairfoir, I say, ye must mak thame partakeris in reading, exhortation, and in making commoun prayeris'. He then goes on to speak of his wish for weekly 'assemblies of brethren' and offers several practical instructions. After opening in prayer and invoking the help of the Holy Spirit, let 'sum place of scripture be planelie and distinctlie red . . . whilk endit, gif any brother have exhortation, interpretatioun, or dout, lat him not feir to speik and move the same, sa that he do it with moderatioun, either to edifie or be edifeit . . . Multiplicatioun of wordis, perplext interpretatioun and wilfulnes in reasonyng is to be avoydit at all tymes.'[21]

18 *The Life of John Knox*, ed T. M'Crie. *p* 16.
19 Knox, J.: *Works* (*ed* Laing). i *p* 61.
20 This letter is printed in full in *The Life of Knox*, ed T. M'Crie. *pp* 349–52.
21 *Ibid. pp* 350–1.

In that Book of Common Order, commonly known as John Knox's Liturgy, under the heading 'Interpretation of the Scriptures', it is laid down: 'Every week once the Congregation assemble to hear some place of the Scriptures orderly expounded. . . . at the which time it is lawful for every man to speak or enquire, as God shall move his heart and the text minister occasion, so it be without pertinacity or disdain, as one that rather seeketh to profit than to contend.'[22] Even at this larger meeting of the congregation, the same aims were to be served as in the smaller groups.

During the bitter struggle to establish the first Reformation in Scotland, the leaders announced in 1558: 'It is thought necessare, that doctrin, preacheing, and interpretatioun of Scriptures be had and used privatlie in qwyet houssis, without great conventionis of the people tharto.'[23] In that same year, Knox, facing opposition from the Queen Regent and the prelates, began to seek for some remedy, and decided 'that the Brethren in everie toune at certain tymes should assemble togidder, to Commoun Prayeris, to Exercise and Reading of the Scripturis'.

This method proved to be so successful that within a few months elders were appointed to guide these groups for 'at that tyme we had na publict ministeris on the worde; onlie did certane zelous men . . . exhorte thare brethrein, according to the giftes and graces granted unto thame'. Knox singles out five by name for special mention, and 'these early and zealous friends of the Reformation, who undertook the office of Exhorters, were all laymen, with perhaps the exception of Robert Hamilton'.[24]

Thus, from its earliest days, the reformed church in Scotland drew strength and inspiration from meetings for fellowship, which included prayer and Bible study, where all might contribute, if they were so minded, and where laymen of tried gifts taught with acceptance. If we have dwelt at some length on the

22 *Book of Common Order: John Knox's Liturgy* (*ed* Sprott). *p* 19.
23 Knox: *Works.* i *pp* 275–6.
24 *Ibid. pp* 299–300. *fn* 2.

influence of John Knox, both in precept and practice, it is because his shadow falls across the whole course of Scotland's religious development.

In the troubled years of the seventeenth century, the small group served as a mainstay in time of stress. Thomas Hog was born in Ross-shire in 1628, and was later venerated as Hog of Kiltearn, a saintly man who prayed '*tanta reverentia, ut si Deo, et tanta fiducia, ut si amico*'[25] ('with as much reverence as if he were speaking to God, and with as much boldness as if he had been speaking to his friend'). It was under his inspiration that the ecclesiastically unofficial, but religiously recognised, order of evangelical laymen (the 'Men') came into being.[26] It was whilst Hog was a student at the University of Aberdeen, boarding in a private house, that he joined in worship daily with his fellow-boarders. One of these was a probationer for the ministry and acted as leader. 'After reading a portion of Scripture, he used to propose questions and difficulties to the rest from what they had read . . . He frequented praying societies'.[27]

Henry Scougal (1650–78), the saintly Professor of Theology in King's College, Aberdeen, memorialised in the University Chapel, where he lies buried, as *caeli avidus et caelo maturus* (eager for heaven and ripe for heaven), had a somewhat similar experience to that of Hog. Scougal in his early days was made constant president among his fellow-students at their private meetings for prayer.[28] Fervent presbyterian and pious episcopalian were at one here.

A similar development to that in the north-east was also taking place in the south of Scotland. Praying societies became an expression of popular religion and a stimulus to it. There were some leaders of the church who sought to prevent them, fearing Independency, but the support of Samuel Rutherford, Robert Blair, David Dickson and John Livingstone prevented

---

25 *Memoirs of Mrs Wm Veitch, Mr Thomas Hog, &c. p* 88.
26 *Vide* McInnes, C.: *Evangelical Movements &c. pp* 211 *ff.*
27 *Memoirs of Mrs Wm Veitch, Mr Thomas Hog &c. pp* 71–2.
28 Scougal: *Life of God &c.* (ed 1747). *p* 274.

the Assembly of 1639 from taking too severe measures against 'religious exercise in families'.

During the persecutions of the later Stuarts, the small groups meeting for prayer played a noble part in sustaining faith and courage. Religion was compelled more and more to become personal and inward. Alexander Peden, preaching in the open air at Glenluce in 1682, declared: 'He is not worth his room in Scotland that prayeth not the half of his time . . . O sirs! ye must pray ploughing, harrowing, and shearing, ay and at all your labour.' At another similar occasion he said: 'Sirs, I'll tell you where the Kirk of God is – wherever there is a praying lad or lass at a dyke-side in Scotland.'

For many these were the oracles of God, and the popular heroes were the men who practised this preaching. The reputation of such ministers as Peter Kid, imprisoned on the Bass Rock in the Firth of Forth for sixteen months,[29] has been handed down in the epitaph carved in the churchyard at Carluke:

> A faithful, holy pastor here lies hid,
> One of a thousand, – Mr Peter Kid;
> Firm as a stone, but of a heart contrite,
> A wrestling, praying, weeping Israelite.

John Welsh of Irongray wrote his pamphlet *Fifty and Two DIRECTIONS* to advise his congregation in days of persecution.[30] In Direction xiii, he urges that the time which used to be set apart for worship on the Sabbath and other days should now be devoted to worship at home: 'seeing publick Opportunities of hearing Preachings is taken away from you; lay a Law upon your selves, that what Time ye were used to spend in going to the Kirk, sitting in it, and going home, that ye spend that Time betwixt God and you in secret, and in your Families, either in Prayer or Reading the Scriptures, or Book of Martyrs.'[31]

29 *Fasti.* iii *p* 285.
30 Reprinted at Glasgow 'by Alexander Miller and Sold in his Shop opposite to the well Salt Mercat' *c* 1740.
31 *Ibid. p* 24.

Many of these societies that passed through the fires of persecution followed the lead of Cameron, Cargill and Renwick, to become the 'United Societies' as the intransigent Cameronians were pleased to call themselves. These persisted into the days of the Revolution Settlement of 1689, and refused to merge their identity in a church that had not sworn the Covenants.

But there were many other less extreme groups who chose to remain within the established church, holding their regular meetings in private houses on weekdays. Of them it has been finely said: 'It is not hard to picture the men and their meetings. A lonely thatched cot on the moor, reached by miry roads and uncertain paths – the long trudge through the darkness, with hearts lifted up at the sight of the distant yellow light which marked their destination – the grizzled men, bowed with the weariness of unending labour, and the strong, silent women, still wearing the plaids which had sheltered them from the rawness of the night air – the humble furniture, and the dim light of the cottage, and the reverence which sat on every face and shewed itself at every word and in every gesture. When they met, they hardly greeted, and when they parted it was with the dryest words of farewell. For strangers they would have even a scantier welcome. They had not met for social amenities. The business which brought them from distant homes was prayer and the searching of Scripture and the discussion of the points of pure doctrine. Their theology was Calvinism, tempered by the tenderness of the theology of the Marrow, and their aim was personal holiness.'[32]

Many of the prayer societies must have conformed to this description, but it is far too sweeping a generalisation. Every kind of social class was to be found within them. Wodrow says of the Presbytery meeting in November 1729 that 'we agreed that Ministers should meet for prayer, with their Sessions, monethly . . . we agreed to set up meetings for prayer among ourselves'.[33]

32 Article by Prof Davidson (*U.P. Magazine 1899*) *p* 253.
33 *Anal.* iv *p* 92. *Vide* The Carrick Class of Ministers (*New Stat. Acc.* v *p* 375).

In the diary of Alexander Johnstone (1723–26) we have the chronicle of this overseer of roads in east Stirlingshire. A prominent elder in Bothkennar Church, he sat in the General Assembly. On Wednesday, 3 September 1723, his entry reads: 'Met with the society for prayer, who had appointed this day from ten in the morning to six at night, to be spent in religious duties . . . The members present were Mr Michael Menzies, advocate, Mr John M'Cartney, Mr George Andrew, mert, Thos. Ellot, writter, Mr Halbert Munro, Mr Charles Logan, student of divinity and myself.' Here were men from the professions, some of the social leaders of the community.[34]

Although both sexes must have been present in some districts, the custom grew up for men to meet with men, and women with women. Further divisions are made at times between married and single persons, and there is abundant evidence of meetings of children, run by the children themselves.

During his student days at Edinburgh University, John Erskine was connected with a society meeting weekly for prayer. It consisted of about twenty members, some of them belonging to families of considerable rank.[35]

The primary business of the prayer societies was of a devotional nature, to read the Scriptures, to discuss practical doctrine and to pray. But often there were other developments; action took place at the level of aspiration. In 1731, Wodrow paid tribute to John Dundas of Philipstown, 'Clerk to this Church twenty-eight years' who was ill with jaundice, and with his name coupled that of Niccol Spence, his colleague in the management of church business. 'These two, with Sir H. Cuningham, Sir Francis Grant, afterward Lord Cullen, James Steuart, Clerk of Edinburgh, Commissar Broady, Dr Dundas, Sir Francis Pringle, Mr George Meldrum, and some others, wer members of a Praying Society . . . about 1698.[36] This privat

34 *S.C.H.S. Recs.* iv *pp* 266–72.
35 *Christian Repository* 1819. *pp* 420–5. Review of *The Life of Erskine.*
36 *Anal.* iv *p* 235. Wodrow speaks of a Manuscript Record of their weekly meetings and hopes to examine this and transmit the facts to posterity.

meeting laid the first foundation of that noble designe of reformation of manners in King William's time . . . about ten years after, they gave the first beginnings to the Society for Propagation of Christian Knouledge and Reformation of the Highlands and Islands, which has come to so great a lenth. Hou great a matter doth some times a little good fire kindle! They concerted subscriptions, they formed the charter to be expede by [the] Queen, and brought the matters to an excellent bearing; and all as a little weekly society for prayer and conference upon Christian purposes! There wer but eight or ten members, lauers . . . nou and then, some of the Ministers of Edinburgh met with them, and all they did was in concert with them, joyned with prayer.' Thus was one of Scotland's greatest educational, evangelical and missionary enterprises in the eighteenth century born!

Sometimes they took action concerning current affairs in church and state. In June 1712, Wodrow wrote: 'I find addresses propagating up and doun the country; there is one from the Societys in Kilbride, Cambuslang, Carmonock, Gorbells, and Govan, in correspondence. One from the Praying Societys in Glasgow, James Aird is at it; anothere there from Rugland [ie Rutherglen]. These two last are very plain in declaring the Oath of Abjuration contrary to our knouen principles'.[37]

If the societies were sometimes constrained to make protests about the action of government, they also rendered homely domestic ministries. Janet Hamilton, writing of the period around 1733, relates how, in cases of unusual suffering or distress, neighbours would assemble at the home of the sufferer, if this was convenient, and then, moved by strong compassion, each one would pray in turn for the one in need.[38]

In the second decade of the eighteenth century, the government of many of these societies was tightened up by the setting down of definite rules to cover the admission of members, their subsequent discipline, and guidance about topics for discussion.

37 *Anal.* ii *p* 55.
38 Hamilton, Janet: *Poems &c. p* 188.

On 29 October 1714, Ebenezer Erskine, his session clerk and fifteen others signed a list of rules drawn up to control the praying society of Portmoak in Fife. Meetings were to be held on the fifteenth and the last day of every month; a Moderator was to be chosen each half-year to take care of procedure. Privy censures, *ie* pointing out any faults to one another, usually the work of the kirk session, were instituted; reasons had to be given by members in the case of absence from the meetings, and several absences without due cause involved expulsion.

'For admission into our Society, we shall not be too strict, nor too large', says Rule 7, and so the weak in gifts were welcomed, whilst the unsound in principle and practice could be kept out.

If the numbers increased, the society was to divide into two groups. All meetings were secret and nothing was to be divulged. Rule 11 laid down: 'The members of the Society shall pray by turns, according to the alphabetical order of their names: and at every meeting three, and at most five or six, shall pray; except when Providence calls for more than ordinary wrestling.' In each meeting there was to be reading from the Scriptures and a chapter from the Confession of Faith, as subjects for discussion. Also a question of practical divinity was to be proposed for the next meeting to discuss, or a controverted point, a case of conscience or some difficult place in Scripture.[39] An almost identical set of rules was adopted by a young men's society which met at Kinesswood, and these principles were preserved by one of the members, David Pearson, of the Bruce-Logan controversy.[40]

Three years later, on 11 May 1717, a praying society was organised at St Andrews; eighty-four members signed their names to the foundation.[41] Meetings were held weekly; 'none of us shal absent or withdraw ourselves fm our meetings, except in cases of necessity' and then a stated reason was

39 Fraser, D.: *Life & Diary of Eben. Erskine. pp* 523–6.
40 *U.P. Mag. 1899. p* 253. *fn.*
41 Art. by D. Hay Fleming. 'The Praying Society of St Andrews' (*Original Secession Mag.* January 1879. *pp* 38–50).

obligatory at the next meeting. 'For keeping our society fm being pested with persons that ought not to be admitted', examination and trial were incumbent upon all who wished to join.

In the small manuscript volume of its records, there is a list of all the questions proposed by members to the society; 571 in all are enumerated. The first was: 'What advantage is to be had in, and what warrant is there for, waiting on God in fellowship meetings?' Others were: 'Q. 13 – What are the most proper means for attaining assurance? Q. 55 – What are the reasons why the petitions of God's people were more remarkably answer'd of old than now? Q. 82 – What's meant by conversion? Q. 168 – How shal a person attain to true and saving faith?' The last question was recorded in 1733.

After the Secession of 1733, the main support for the Erskines and their friends came from members of praying societies up and down the land. On 13 December 1738, a petition was signed by eighty-three persons, members of such societies in and about Glasgow, and out of this the first Secession church in Glasgow was formed on 9 February 1740.

In Buchan, the praying societies were closely organised before 1733. Each society investigated any *fama* against its members, and new members had to join the society for their own district. The meetings were often presided over by elders. The great majority of the members adhered to the seceders.[42]

In view of the invaluable support given by the societies to the Associate Presbytery, as the seceders called themselves, it is not surprising to find that body recommending the formation of such societies in one of their first Acts, 1740. In 1756 they issued a pamphlet under their imprimatur *Rules and Directions for Fellowship-meetings, By the Reverend Mr John Hepburn, Late Minister at* URR *in Galloway*. These rules were definite and even more coercive than the others we have noticed. A fixed place was prescribed, equally distant for all the members. Questions were to be proposed from the Confession of Faith or the Shorter Catechism . . . 'let no jars or needless debates get place'. Were

42 Findlay, J. T.: *Secession in the North. pp* 6–8.

this to happen, however, 'it is fit they break off, and go to prayer again'. The members submitted to an even more rigorous discipline: 'no member should take on him any public office ... nor yet go to law, without acquainting the meeting, and seeking their advice and consent'. Two or three delegates were to interview any prospective members.[43]

One of the major centres of the 1742 revival was Kilsyth, and we are fortunate in having within the records of the kirk session of that town, a complete list of rules, drawn up to govern the proposed prayer societies. 'An Overture for the Setting up of Societies in the Congregation' was read, considered and approved by the session on 5 December 1721, whereby it was 'Enacted by the session, That Societies for prayer and Christian conference be Sett up in the Congregation ...' We give them almost verbatim:

1. That praying persons of a blameless conversation be pitched upon and divided in Several Societies thorou the parish ... Accordingly the Minr gave in a list of persons, which was approven.
2. That they meet at least once in the month ... that they begin with prayer.
3. Where it can be conveniently done, a part of a psalm be sung ...
4. Then let one pray.
5. Then let them read a portion of the Lord's Word, at least one Chapter beginning at the New Testament.
6. After reading, let another pray.
7. After this, let one of the Society ask three or four questions out of Vincent's Catechism, which the Society are to be advertised of at their former Meeting to prepare to answer.
8. Upon the back of this, One of their Number having prayed, if any present desire the Advice of the Meeting anent their own Spiritual State, or anent what may be sin or duty ... let it be kindly given, and if the Society observe any thing

43 Article by Hugh Watt. 'The Praying Societies of the Early Eighteenth Century.' *Orig. Sec. Mag.* February 1934. *pp* 49–53.

exceptionable in any member, let them admonish the sd. member thereof in tenderness and love.

9. Let no curious questions be proposed that are either above the capacity of the Society, or do not tend immediately to the advancement of practical Religion . . .

10. It would also be helpfull in the way of duty to confer either now or at any other time during the meeting anent the sins of the congregation in general . . . that they may be bewailed and mourned over before the Lord.

11. That no member talk abroad any thing spoken or done in the Society.

12. That absent members give an account of the reason of their absence, which, if not sustained, are to submit themselves to the admonition of the Society . . .

13. That each Society make choise of one of their Number Monthly to Correspond with the Minrs. Society.

14. That non afterwards be admitted into these Societies without express allowance from the Minrs. Society and that non but members be allowed to be present at these Societies.[44]

One striking feature of this organisation at Kilsyth was the central place held by the minister's society, which seems to have acted as an executive, controlling all the others. There were obviously very real dangers of inquisitorial action and censoriousness. When we come to look at the revival in Kilsyth, we shall see how these societies, set up in 1721, flourished, then died away, but were quickened once more about the time of the awakening in 1742.

These prayer societies were widespread and their activities inspired Christian thought and practice. Their very vigour served to draw upon them opposition and criticism. Lord Elchies, a famous Scottish judge, writing to his estate agent on 10 January 1728, says 'I have heard a complaint that Wm. McKondachie keeps a meeting-house, forsooth! in his house, and, as I'm told, drains the Kirk pretty much; and I doubt not

44 Kilsyth. K.S.R.

it may have that effect; mankind is commonly given to novelties, and for the most part likes what is forbidden them. However you'l discharge that practice in time coming; ther must be no meeting-house in my ground; and where-ever else it is, all my tennents must keep the kirk.'[45]

Lord Elchies sought to put down the praying societies by the strong hand – religious conformity by coercion. There were others who sought by mild ridicule, or superciliousness, to damn the movement with faint praise. Dr Robert Wallace, minister of Greyfriars Church in Edinburgh, wrote a treatise *Christian piety Illustrated and certain Mistakes concerning it Detected* (now among the Laing manuscripts in the University of Edinburgh), in which he attacked enthusiasm.[46] 'Many of you are much disposed to erect your selves into little societies or fellowship meetings as they are called ... they are thought mighty usefull in advancing piety.' But he doubts 'whether it is proper ... for the young, the weak, the unexperienced to enlist themselves ... Whether it is suitable to that modesty and humility which ought to shine in their behaviour.' Even if these young people had sound and distinct notions, they are not able to express distinctly what they think. 'Their hearts are much better than their heads.' Instead of correcting one another's errors, they only confirm them; 'they raise unnecessary doubts and perplex one another'. Realising that not all the members of these societies were as unlettered and ignorant as he hinted, Wallace points out that he 'knew one of these societies which was composed of persons who meant as well and from their education and circumstances might have been presumed to know as much as most who are members of such societies att present ... I could never perceive that they increased in knowledge, on the contrary'. If anyone charged him with raillery, then all he could say was that 'you deserve it in some degree for your preeposterous gravity and engaging in prospects which are above your strength. I mean nothing

45 *Letters of Lord Elchies. p* 36. McConachy was one of the two most important tenants on the estates. *Vide p* 226.
46 Laing Mss. ii *p* 976.

but your reall advantage and to save you from the ridicule of some who will not make so many allowances for you as I can do.'

Yet, in spite of the dangers inherent in such fellowship (and the evangelical ministers well knew that these were very real) and the professional denigration of them as religious 'amateurs' by Moderates like Wallace, these groups, scattered over the country, were not without significance. Many men and women, from every rank of life, questing after personal holiness and endeavouring to watch one another's souls, did much to warm the spiritual atmosphere of the land. They were in truth preparing a highway for the Lord.

5
Books and the People

Before turning to consider the rise and development of the Cambuslang awakening in 1742, it will be worth our while to look at the intellectual influences that were shaping the opinions of ministers and people throughout the west of Scotland. What were the people reading in 1742?

There is a fairly widespread belief that the Scottish people in the eighteenth century were, in the main, illiterate; this has been fostered by the dicta of social historians like Henry G. Graham, who states that at the beginning of that century, 'the inhabitants to a vast extent were unable to read or to write'.[1] This is a gross exaggeration.

'Jupiter' Carlyle (1722–1805) informs us that he was taught to read by an old woman who kept a school. She had accomplished her task so well that one day, shut out from his father's church at Prestonpans because of the large crowd that had gathered, and finding a dozen old women also outside the door, he offered to read to them.

They lifted him on to a tombstone where, says he, 'I read very audibly to a congregation, which increased to about a score, the whole of the Song of Solomon'.[2] One wonders which created the greater stir – the colourful cadences of the ancient Hebrew love-story, or the precocious reading of the minister's six-year-old laddie! Robert Riccaltoun, another Scottish boy, born in 1691, could read the Bible distinctly before he was five years of age.[3]

1 Graham, H. G.: *Social Life of Scotland &c. p* 123.
2 Carlyle, A.: *Autobiography &c. pp* 4–5.   3 *Works of John Newton.* vi *p* 448.

But it was not only the children of the manse and ministers-to-be who were able to read. Janet Hamilton tells of her maternal grandfather, born in 1704 and orphaned early in life, who was taken to be a 'herd laddie' by a farmer in Cambus-nethan when ten years old. Already the boy had been taught to read by his father, and this was maintained by 'the pious and careful teaching of the goodwife of Carbarns, who, when the cows were driven in from the pasture at "twal-hours", for some time during the heat of the summer-day, never failed to set him a chapter or two to read from the Bible'.[4] True piety has ever been the spur towards intellectual progress.

Nor does this accomplishment of early reading seem to have been rare, as we may learn from the men and women who supplied M'Culloch with details about their histories. Thus one young lady, Anne Wylie, testifies: 'I could read the Bible by the time I was six years old',[5] and then goes on to name various books she had read, including Watson's *Body of Divinity*. Elizabeth Dykes writes: 'I was taught by my Father to read the Bible by the time I was six years of age,'[6] whilst Robert Hamilton, a young weaver from Glasgow, reports: 'When I was put to School, I inclind so much to reading that I would ofttimes have stayd of my own accord, with the Master that taught me reading, after the School was dismissed.'[7]

For those who lived in the more remote areas, often there were serious difficulties in the way of learning. Says Archibald Bell: 'I was born in the High-Lands: and My Parents living far from any place where there was a School, I was not put to it, nor could I read any till I was about fourteen years of age: and then, in time of My Apprentice-Ship, I got lessons and so came at length to learn to read the Bible.'[8]

There were others who learned to read even later: so Margaret Clark, 'Spouse to John McGlass, Day-Labourer in Givan', aged forty-two, sometimes stayed at home from church

4 Hamilton, Janet: *Poems &c. p* 180.
5 Anne Wylie: 'An Unmarried Woman of 32.' M'C. Mss. i *p* 39.
6 Elizabeth Dykes, 'sixteen years of age, from Carmyle': *Ibid.* i *p* 208.
7 Robert Hamilton, 'twenty-nine years of age': *Ibid.* ii *p* 75.
8 Archibald Bell: *Ibid.* i *p* 398.

when a young woman 'because I could not read, and I was much ashamed that I could not make use of the Bible in the Kirk, as others about me did. And therefore I set about learning to read, when I was about 18 years of age, having never learn'd to read any before that: and it was one of the Terms of my Agreement with those whom I serv'd, that I should always get a lesson every day: and by following it out in that manner, I came to be capable to read the Bible.'[9]

It is equally certain, judging from these manuscript records, that there were many who could write; there are degrees of legibility, but none is wholly indecipherable. Spelling is, however, another matter, and the widest latitude seems to have been allowed. There was some system of contractions used in setting down some of these narratives, closely analagous to modern shorthand. This should not really surprise us, for it is on record that at Portmoak many of Ebenezer Erskine's hearers took down his sermons in shorthand; the minister co-operated in that he gave public guidance to these diligent 'scribes', asking whether they were ready to begin. Later, in the Sabbath evenings, the discourses of the day were read over to friends and neighbours.[10]

After the unsettled and tumultuous days of the seventeenth century, so unpropitious for educational progress, there came with the Revolution Settlement a sincere concern for the institution of schools and libraries. An Act of Parliament in 1696 ordained 'That there be a school settled and a schoolmaster appointed in every parish not already provided ... And for that Effect, That the Heritors in every Parish meet and provide a commodious House for a school, and settle and modify a Sallary to a Schoolmaster, which shall not be under one hundred Merks, nor above Two hundred Merks, to be paid Yearly at two Terms ...'.[11]

The schoolmasters were, in the main, ill-provided for; it was far easier to legislate that heritors should make adequate

9 Margaret Clark. *Ibid.* ii *p* 447.
10 *Life & Diary of Eben. Erskine. pp* 196–7.
11 *Act of First Parliament, William III.* C. xxvi.

financial arrangements for the schoolmasters' salaries than to turn this fine ideal into actual achievement. Since the dominie had to live, it was at times necessary to augment his scanty pittance by odd means. At one school, each Candlemas, every boy had to bring a fighting-cock and a shilling. The schoolroom floor became a cockpit and the master's diet was enriched for some time by the addition of the slain combatants. If any bird sought safety in flight, it was branded as a 'fugie', fixed to a post in the schoolyard, and done to death at a halfpenny a shot. Thus was the work of education subsidised![12]

Here and there, generous-minded men were helping on this work of education by legacies and bequests. In 1723, Mr John Patrick, a merchant in London but a native of Kilsyth, made a bequest 'to the use of the school in Chapel-green or Bridgend, in the parish of Kilsyth . . . the interest of product of sixty pounds sterling . . . for the only use and benefit of poor children . . . to be educated in useful learning'.[13]

James Warden, minister of Cadder parish, left 1,000 merks in 1745 for supplying a school in his native village of Auchinairn.[14] James Stirling, minister of the Barony, Glasgow, at his death in 1736 bequeathed 3,000 merks to encourage the schools in his parish and to buy Bibles and catechisms for the poor.[15] Andrew Taite, minister of Carmunnock, who died in 1742, left £100 sterling 'to buy as many copies of Alleine's *Alarm to the Unconverted* as would give a copy to each family in the parish'.[16] About the same time, John Mill, minister at Dunrossness in the distant Shetlands, was 'procuring many copies of Crawford and Vincent's *Catechisms*' to distribute to his people.[17] One of the main leaders in this growing interest in education (a man to whom adequate tribute has yet to be paid) was James Kirkwood, the friend of Bishop Burnet and the advocate of parochial libraries.[18] Born at Dunbar in 1650, he became acquainted with the needs of the Gaelic-speaking people when he was

12 Murray, E. G.: *The Old School at Cardross.* p 15.
13 *Edin. Christian Instr.* April 1838. p 177.
14 *Fasti.* iii p 374.   15 *Ibid.* i p 393.   16 *Ibid.* iii p 379.
17 Mill, J.: *Diary 1740–1803* (S.H.S.) p 12.
18 Millar, J.: *History of Dunbar.* pp 207–9; D.N.B. xxxvi pp 225–6.

chaplain to the first Earl of Breadalbane. Moving to England, he became associated with the wealthy philanthropist, Robert Boyle, who gave him financial help in sending 'Irish' Scriptures into the Highlands. Kirkwood was the author of a tract which appeared anonymously in 1699, *An Overture for Founding and Maintaining Bibliothecks in every Paroch throughout the Kingdom.* It put forward a comprehensive scheme whereby the parish minister's books were to form the nucleus of each library, and the schoolmaster was to act as librarian. The General Assembly approved the scheme but did nothing, although in the year after Kirkwood's death it passed an Act for the establishment of a public library in every presbytery throughout the land.

From the foundations laid by Kirkwood there rose the Scottish Society for Propagating Christian Knowledge, better known as the S.S.P.C.K., which received its royal charter in 1709. Caring for schools and teachers, by 1732 it employed 109 schoolmasters. One of its experiments, under the supervision of the parish minister, was the providing and despatching of travelling libraries, which consisted of boxes containing about forty books.

In 1726, Allan Ramsay (1686–1758) founded the first regular circulating library in Scotland, but his hedonistic

> Be blythe, and let the world e'en shog
> As it thinks fit . . .

and his

> Grip fast the hours which hasty hurl,
> the morn's the morn,

(Horace's *Carpe Diem*, reissued in the Doric) were anathema to orthodox Presbyterians.

In May 1728, Wodrow complains that 'all the villanous profane and obscene books and playes printed at London by Curle and others, are gote doun... by Allan Ramsay, and lent out, for an easy price, to young boyes, servant weemen of the better sort, and gentlemen'. After some difficulty, Lord Grange persuaded the magistrates to inspect 'his book of borrouers';

they sent a deputation to examine the books, but Ramsay 'had nottice an hour before, and had withdrauen a great many of the worst, and nothing was done to purpose'.[19]

It is clear that by 1740 there was a growing hunger for reading, and the printing presses of Edinburgh and the Salt-mercat in Glasgow were kept busy turning out books and pamphlets of every possible kind. The first place in the affections of the reading public was held, unquestionably, by the Bible; its influence is to be seen on every hand, moulding and shaping habits of thought and deed. It was pre-eminent, both for ministers and congregations. And no wonder, for the Bible was inextricably intertwined with the religious development of the Scottish people from the dawn of the Reformation.

In 1670, Archbishop Leighton sent six episcopalian divines to preach in the vacant parishes in the west, and one of them, Gilbert Burnet the historian (later to be Bishop of Salisbury), gave an interesting picture of their reception. The people came to listen to them, although not in great crowds. 'We were indeed amazed to see a poor commonalty so capable to argue upon points of government, and on the bounds to be set to the power of princes in matters of religion. Upon all these topics, they had texts of Scripture at hand, and were ready with their answers to any thing that was said to them. This measure of knowledge was spread even amongst the meanest of them, their cottagers and their servants.'[20]

Throughout the dark days of persecution, the Bible was cherished as the sustainer of faith and the provider of comfort. That strange but colourful figure, Alexander Peden, pays tribute to this in one of his sermons: 'There was a poor widow in Clydesdale, as I came through ... when she was asked how she did in this ill time, "I do very well", said she, "I get more good in one verse of the Bible now than I did in it all langsyne. He hath casten me the keys of the pantry-door, and bids me take my fill".'[21] When Daniel Defoe, Dissenter, novelist and

19 *Anal.* iii *p* 515.
20 Burnet, G.: *History of My Own Time* (ed Airey). i *p* 524.
21 Johnstone, J. C.: *Alexander Peden, the Prophet &c. p* 200.

prince of reporters, accompanied the English Commissioners
to the Union in 1707, he noted with some care the attitude of
the people in Scotland at public worship. How eager the
congregations were to hear the preaching! It was 'as though
they wished to eat the words as they left the minister's mouth'.
Defoe goes on to add one thing more – 'a hint to English
hearers' – 'In a whole church full of people, not one shall be
seen without a Bible . . . if you shut your eyes when the minister
names any text of Scripture, you shall hear a little rustling
noise over the whole place, made by turning the leaves of the
Bible.'[22]

George Whitefield commented on the same thing. When he
made his first visit to Scotland, in the summer of 1741, he
preached in Ralph Erskine's meeting-house 'to a very thronged
assembly. After I had done prayer, and had named my text,
the rustling made by opening the Bibles all at once, quite
surprised me – a scene I never was witness to before.'[23]

The Bible was not only the indispensable accompaniment to
public worship; it was also read, studied and loved in private.
John Willison of Dundee, a warm friend to the revival at
Cambuslang, has summed up this attitude: 'We should look
upon it as a golden epistle, indited by the Spirit of God; we
should receive it as a love-letter from heaven, opening up God's
designs of love to our souls; we should go to it as for our daily
food and subsistence, and daily enquire in it for the will of
God . . . We should read with faith, reverence and application
to ourselves . . . and in reading every part, we should still keep
Christ in our eye, as the end, scope and substance of the whole
Scriptures.'[24]

As we might expect, there was a devout reverence for the
Bible among those converts whose stories have been preserved
by M'Culloch. Central in the almost nation-wide habit of
family prayers, the Book was often associated with the work of

22 Defoe, D.: *Memoirs of Church of Scotland* (ed Wilson, 1844 edition). *p* 355.
23 Tyerman, L.: *Life of George Whitefield*. i *p* 508.
24 Quoted in Art. 'Puritanism in Eighteenth-Century Scotland', by G. D.
Henderson. *Evangelical Quarterly*. xix No 3 *p* 221.

the day. Janet Jackson, daughter of a Cambuslang elder, tells how, in her distress, 'I . . . sate down to My Work in My Fathers House; as I spun at My Wheel, I read in My Bible upon My Knee'.[25] Another, narrating how she did this selfsame thing, adds 'which is My usual custom'.[26] James Jack was advised by a minister 'that when I was at my work, I should have My Bible beside Me, and read over the 51st Psalm (taking a verse only at a time) and put it up in a way of Ejaculatory prayer to God'.[27]

Charles Lamb, in his own whimsical fashion, made a plea for saying grace for blessings other than meals, such as when setting out for a ramble by moonlight, or meeting with friends . . . 'Why have we none for books, those spiritual repasts – a grace before Milton . . . before Shakspeare?'[28] This idea had, in fact, been anticipated more than seventy years earlier by Mary Shaw, the eighteen-year-old daughter of a ship's carpenter from Greenock; she picked up the Bible, and 'I ask'd a Blessing on what I was going to read in the Bible, that the Lord would give Me the sanctifyd use of it'.[29]

The Bible was the standard by which many puzzled en-quirers judged the strange happenings at Cambuslang. Archibald Smith, a middle-aged mason from Kilbride, heard conflicting reports and decided to make first-hand investigation. 'I put my Bible in my pocket on a week-day, saying I should see what was among them ere I came home.'[30] Sarah Gilchrist, the daughter of the schoolmaster at Cardross, Dunbartonshire, was quite sure that a Quaker spirit was possessing the people at Cambuslang, but soon altered her opinion 'seeing them make so much use of their Bibles, and looking out for places there'.[31] When concern began to increase shortly before the outbreak of the revival at Cambuslang on Thursday, 18 February 1742,

25 M'C. Mss. i p 25.
26 Ibid. i p 564. (Eliz. Brecham.)
27 Ibid. i p 500.
28 Essays of Elia. 'Grace before Meat.'
29 M'C. Mss. ii p 26.
30 Ibid. ii p 442.
31 Ibid. ii p 137.

eight or nine young people met in Jean Galbraith's house in that village and were guided by Mr Duncan, a licensed minister of the Church of Scotland, an elder, John Bar, and Ingram More, one of the lay leaders. Duncan advised those in distress 'not to read so much on other practical Books, as on the Bible', and this served as a rebuke for some who had been reading sermons and other religious books rather than the Bible.[32]

Occasionally the Bible was regarded as something in the nature of a talisman: Isobel Matthie of Kilbride was visited by a minister and would not let him take the book from her hand, saying it was 'God's holy word, I would not part with'.[33] Another, an unmarried woman of thirty-two, under scandal for some sexual offence and therefore barred from the Sacrament, read in the Bible from Isaiah 54. 'At reading these words, I felt them applyed to Me with great power, that banished all My griefs and fears, and filled Me with great joy, particularly at reading these words, Thy Maker is thy Husband, so I could not forbear kissing my Bible.'[34] (Gillespie and Webster, when editing the manuscript volumes, suggested that these two quotations be deleted). A great number of people were studying the Bible and it appears to have been read in most of its pages; from Genesis to Revelation, people quoted its words and revealed an amazing familiarity with most of the books, including much that would nowadays be considered of mainly antiquarian interest and of little value for the devotional life.

It is not possible to evaluate the tremendous significance of the metrical psalter; almost all the subjects of the revival – at least those whose stories we have – quoted from it. Again and again, it is from the remembered lines of its pages that light flashed into gloomy darkness. One young servant-girl of twenty, Jean Robe, speaks of walking twelve miles into Stirling to hear the seceders, before coming to Cambuslang. This so angered her master that he cursed her with great vehemence, 'saying

32 *Ibid.* i *p* 29.
33 *Ibid.* i *p* 525.
34 *Ibid.* i *p* 143.

We were a parcel of Mad people that went there; and we would never rest till we would get a parcel of Dragoons to scatter us'. In great depression of spirit she was about to give up hope, 'but hearing My Mistress reading the Psalms, that word she was reading beside Me, while I was spinning at the wheel

> Assuredly he shall thee save
> And give deliverance

came with such power that I was filled with joy'.[35]

John Parker, a light-hearted young man of twenty-three, delighted 'in going to fairs and markets and Weedings [sic], where young people drink and make merry with one another';[36] but he 'was made to see . . . the evil of carnal delights, of getting songs and ballads by heart and whistling and singing them over and hearing them plaid on Vials and the like, the matter of these Songs not being very chaste ofttimes, and at best but triffling . . . therefore I broke off these practices . . . got some Psalms by heart, or some parts of them, and often sung them when I was following my work . . . I found my self as much in My Element in praising God in this manner, as in whistling and singing before.'[37]

Although the Bible stood as the highest and best for the questing soul, the veritable 'holy of holies', the records nevertheless show that any man who came to Cambuslang was by no means 'a man of one book'. There was a wide range of serious theological literature that was known and used. One young woman mentions that she 'got Shepard's *Sincere Convert*, . . . Craig's *Poems*, . . . Watson's *Body of Divinity*, where he speaks of the New Creature, . . . and Vincent's *Catechism*'[38] – a formidable reading list!

One is somewhat surprised to read of Janet Reston, a young woman of twenty, going to the well to draw water and 'coming by the Tree, I could not forbear taking out Vincent's *Catechism* to read a little, because I could get no other time for reading.

35 *Ibid.* i *p* 183.
36 *Ibid.* i *p* 662.
37 *Ibid.* ii *pp* 668–9.
38 *Ibid.* i *pp* 39–75. (Anne Wylie).

Turning to 1 Peter 2.19, 20, the words filled Me with so much joy, that I could not forbear skipping for joy.'[39] Such exuberance must have been thought unseemly by the editors, for Webster, Willison and Gillespie mark this closing phrase for deletion!

The most popular works of devotion, judged by frequency of mention, were Vincent's *Catechism* – several ministers, including John Hamilton of the Barony, Glasgow, and John Mill of Dunrossness, had given copies of this book to their parishioners – Watson's *Body of Divinity*, *Life of Elizabeth Waste or West*, and, easily the favourite, Guthry's *Tryal*. William Guthrie (1620–65), a 'Scottish Traherne or Henry Vaughan' as John Buchan styled him, was one of the most attractive religious leaders of the seventeenth century. In that day of bitter theological disputation, he could publicly exhort his congregation to praise God, 'if you have noe more, for this good day, and sunshine to the lambs'.[40] Retaining an enthusiastic devotion to such field-sports as hawking, hunting and fishing, yet untiring in his evangelistic labours, he made the remote village of Fenwick (sometimes called Finnick or New Kilmarnock), where he was minister for twenty years, the spiritual centre of the west of Scotland. People went regularly from Glasgow, Hamilton and Lanark many miles to hear him, and his contemporary, John Livingston, tells us that so eager were these visitors that 'they turned the corn-field of his glebe into a little town; every one building a house for his family upon it, that they might live in the enjoyment of his ministry'.[41]

Guthrie's book, *A short Treatise of the* CHRISTIAN'S *Great Interest*, was divided into two parts and was better known by the heading of the first of these sections, 'The Trial of a Saving Interest in Christ'. In his preface he assured his readers: 'I have purposely used a most homely and plain Stile, lest . . . I should be above the Reach of the Rude and Ignorant, whose Advan-

39 *Ibid.* i *p* 542.
40 *Anal.* i *p* 137.
41 Guthrie, W.: *Christian's Great Interest*, 1828 edition (quoted by Thomas Chalmers in Prefatory Essay) *p* 43.

tage I have mainly, if not only, consulted: I have likewise studied Brevity in every Thing ... consistent with Plainness and Perspicuity; knowing that the Persons to whom I address my self herein, have neither much Money to spend upon Books, nor much Time to spare upon Reading.'[42] There is abundant evidence that such excellent aims were realised. Speaking of Guthrie's literary style, J. H. Millar asserts: 'There are no rhapsodies; his writing is clear, pleasant, almost matter-of-fact, and the use of the Scots idiom lends it a distinctive flavour.'[43] What a pity that this homely tang has been lost in the re-phrasing of the nineteenth-century edition of the book!

Although written for the common folk, the book found its way into the hands and hearts of the greatest in the land. William Carstares gave a copy to Queen Mary and 'sometime thereafter he enquired how she relished the little swatch of Scots Presbyterian writings. She said she admired it, and should never part with it while she lived.'[44] The famous divine, Dr Owen, 'pulled Guthry's *Saving Interest* out of his pocket and declared that the author "has been one of the greatest divines. I cary this still about with me. I have written folios, but that conteans more than they all!"'[45] A deputation that went to London from Scotland in 1714 and called upon Bishop Burnet reported that 'he spoke to them of Guthrie's *Saving Interest*, and told them he had reprinted it for the use of his diocese; that he reconed it one of the best books that ever was writt, and to contean a vast deal of Divinity in it, and gave every one of them a gilded copy of it'.[46] Over sixty editions of it have been printed during the years.

The common people for whom the author wrote also received the book gladly[47], and in M'Culloch's manuscripts there are many references to it. One young woman writes 'about the 12th of Feb: 1742 ... heard My Father read on Guthries tryal of a

42 Guthrie's *Tryal* &c. *p* iii (1724 edition).
43 Millar, J. H.: *Scottish Prose in the Seventeenth and Eighteenth Centuries. p* 48.
44 Walker, P.: *Six Saints &c.* i *p* 270.
45 *Anal.* i *p* 336.
46 *Anal.* iii *pp* 296–7.
47 Walker, P.: *Six Saints &c.* ii *p* 175, *n* 53.

Saving Interest in Christ, and by what was read from that book, My convictions and distress increased'.[48] John Wier, a young man of twenty-one years of age, had to face strong opposition because he was attending the services at Cambuslang. 'The Gentle man in whose ground I lived . . . threatned he would arreist our crop and turn us out of his Land if we went to Cambuslang . . . and particularly abused Mr Whitefield, calling him a Mountebank and Damn'd Rascal, who was putting all the People mad[49] . . . But reading in Guthrie's *Tryal* that "a sincere soul would go through seas of blood, or if it were through hell at the nearest to be at Christ", I thought I would go through all these . . . to get to Christ.'[50] Had not the author accompanied his cousin James Guthrie when he went to the scaffold in June 1661? How effective must these words of Guthrie's have been to those who had been brought to serious concern about spiritual matters: 'ordinarily the Lord prepareth His own way in the soul by a work of humiliation, and discovereth a man's sin and misery to him, and exerciseth him so therewith, that he longs for the Physician, Christ Jesus'.

This was also the age of pamphlets and cheap literature, scattered throughout the land, and the enthusiasts had not neglected this medium. 'The Marrou people . . . print and scatter papers and sermons very cheap throu the country, and are popular', Wodrow reports in November 1726.[51] Two years later, Erskine of Grange informed Wodrow of his intention to encourage the printing of selections from the writings of Joseph and Richard Alleine, in a 6d or 8d pamphlet. These cheaper forms of reading were distributed by the chapmen, or 'flying stationers', who were often the only merchants in rural districts. Bad roads, the absence of wheeled transport in many areas, the non-existence of any cheap post and the distances of small country hamlets from a market made these itinerant salesmen a necessity. Success depended on good manners and genial conversation and, if he could 'entertain the good-wife with all

48 M'C. Mss. i *p* 24 (Janet Jackson).
49 *Ibid.* i *p* 310.   50 *Ibid.* i *p* 313.
51 *Anal.* iii *p* 360.

the latest news and "clish-ma-claver" of the countryside at the same time that he disposed of his wares, then John Cheap was a welcome and important personage at every fireside.'[52] Such chapmen as Dougal Graham (*fl* 1724–79) and Peter Duthie (*fl* 1721–1812) were known the country over.

There were pamphlets for every kind of taste, such as *Jockie and Maggie's Courtship*, or, for those who wanted more serious reading, *The Life and Prophecies of Alex. Peden* or Ebenezer Erskine's sermon *The Plant of Renown*. Some of them were full of appeals to superstition, with accounts of witchcraft and astounding prophecies. In 1737 there was published in Glasgow *The Wonderful Scotch Prophecy, or the Whole Visions, Discoveries, and Warnings which were revealed to John Porter of Crossibeg to this very day &c*. The blind old man had been seeing apocalyptic visions for about eight years, and his little book had a wide circulation in the west of Scotland. None other than 'Jupiter' Carlyle gives testimony to the effect of a similar, and even better-known pamphlet, namely Peden's *Prophecies*. In March 1744, he was at New Port Glasgow with a friend, waiting at an inn for dinner, when they were alarmed by the loud weeping of about half a dozen women servants in the kitchen. When he went to investigate, Carlyle 'learnt from the calmest among them that a pedlar had left a copy of Peden's *Prophecies* that morning . . . they found that he had predicted woes of every kind to the people of Scotland; and in particular that Clyde would run with blood in the year 1744'. Carlyle, however, was able to quieten them by pointing out that they had in fact misread the pamphlet.[53]

The early eighteenth century was also the age of journalism. The *Edinburgh Evening Courant*, edited by Thomas Ruddiman, began in 1718, and in 1720 the *Caledonian Mercury*, edited by James McEuen, started. Each paper appeared three times a week.[54] In January 1739 there came a forty-eight-page octavo volume priced sixpence monthly; it was the *Scots Magazine and*

52 Fraser, John: *Humorous Chap-Books of Scotland. p* 181.
53 Carlyle, A.: *Autobiography. p* 89.
54 Cowan, R. M. W.: *The Newspaper in Scotland. p* 7.

General Intelligencer, modelled on the *Gentleman's Magazine*, started in 1731 in London. It aimed to give more adequate space to Scottish affairs 'that the Caledonian muse might not be restrained by want of a publick echo to her song'.[55] It became exceedingly popular; in the early issues one could read about foreign affairs and the problem of Spain, or of how the notorious horse-stealer John Palmer, under the name of 'Richard Turpin . . . look'd impudently around him, and after speaking a while to the topsman, flung himself off and expired in about five minutes'.[56] In 1742 there was the disturbing news from Edinburgh that 'the unjustifiable practice of stealing corpses out of their graves is become too common here'.[57] As a result of this traffic in bodies for the purpose of dissection, the mob broke many of the surgeons' windows and burned down the house of a beadle suspected of complicity.

Beginning in the second issue in February 1739, by far the largest amount of column-space was given to 'the preaching of a very young man named Whitefield'. For months every kind of abuse was heaped upon him. Appeals were made to 'our Christian magistrates' to note that probably Jesuits in disguise would mix with these enthusiasts. This man, and others like him, must be stopped. For six months the campaign of vituperation went on.

In June 1739 a lengthy letter was inserted 'to the more celebrated Apostle WH–T–D', proposing an alliance between him and the Quacks of Kennington Common. Were their aims and methods not the same? Says the quack: 'Do you pocket the fee when 'tis offered? I do the same; are the mob your customers? they are mine likewise . . . No body, I thank God, can upbraid me with devouring widows' houses, leading captive silly women, ruining the peace, preaching up Christ and playing the devil . . . squeezing out the last mite out of the pockets of the poor . . . to make room for that fiend Enthusiasm; blind, undistinguishing Enthusiasm! What have we to do with

55 Couper, W. J.: *The Edinburgh Periodical Press. pp* 71–83.
56 *Scots Mag.* April 1739. *p* 185.
57 *Ibid.* March 1742. *p* 140.

innocence? – Gain, I take it, is your godliness, as it is my publick spirit; for gain, I practice, and you preach . . . let us fairly divide the mob between us; the fleece is large enough for us both . . . when your zeal becomes madness, send your lunaticks as fast as you can make them to me.'[58]

These and many similar charges were spread throughout Scotland by the pages of the *Scots Magazine*, and many must have learned to loathe and fear the young English preacher, without any accurate information about his work or character. His aims were suspect from the first, and the charge of using for personal gain the collections he obtained for supporting the Orphan House he had founded in Georgia was to linger for a long time.

In May 1741 he was described as 'an incomparable master of the groan';[59] in June, loud ribaldry was directed against 'Tom Tickle-Text . . . more ready at words than ideas . . . He plays on the surface of things and raiseth a froth . . . let him pump, let him thump, let him flounce and trouble the waters, till he raise a tide of devotion, and set the people afloat, and the old women a see-sawing like steeples when the bells are rung'.[60] In the very next issue, July 1741, was the announcement that Whitefield had arrived in Edinburgh and was preaching every day.

Not all the people in Scotland were, however, prepared to accept the judgment of the correspondents of the *Scots Magazine* as the last word. Some, who were familiar with his writings, were awaiting his ministry with expectation. Thus, Mary Scot, a woman of twenty-four with a most unusual style of spelling and calligraphy reported: 'In reading Mr Whitfilds 2 leters to Bishop Tillitson I was much afected with yr last, so I had strong inclination to hear him.'[61] Another young woman wrote: 'When I read Mr Whitefields Journals before he came to Scotland, I was glad that God had raised up so remarkable

58 *Ibid.* June 1739. *p* 250.
59 *Ibid.* May 1741. *p* 218.
60 *Ibid.* June 1741. *p* 269.
61 M'C. Mss. ii *p* 244.

an Instrument of good to many . . . and I thought that if I might hear him, I might get good also.'[62]

There was a close and long-established association between America and Scotland by means of the printed page, personal letters and the transatlantic contacts of Scottish emigrants; revival news from New England was often connected with the labours of Whitefield, who first went there in the summer of 1739.

Thus W— D—, 'a young Man, who went from Glasgow about four Years ago, and is now living . . . about twenty miles from Boston' wrote 'to his Friend in the Gorbels of Glasgow': 'There has been a glorious spring time indeed in Boston . . . hundreds of converts'; he also tells of Whitefield's meetings as 'thronged every night' (24 May 1741). In a letter (3 June) he describes Boston as 'like Heaven upon Earth . . . there is a Sermon almost every Night with Candle Light to crowded Auditories'.

The Reverend John Moorhouse of Boston (19 June 1741) wrote to this 'same person in the Gorbels' that 'The blessed Whitefield came here . . . The Town in general appears a Sanctuary for God . . . What cannot God do? . . . My Friend, be earnest with God that you may have the same reviving Time with you . . . this would soon bring you to an Agreement among yourselves.'

Even before the young evangelist went there, news of the Great Awakening of 1734 at Northampton in New England, under the ministry of Jonathan Edwards, was being received with joy in Scotland. In 1735 Edwards wrote *A Faithful Narrative of the Surprising Work of God in the Conversion of many hundreds of souls in Northampton*, and this was circulated in Scotland. Henry Davidson, minister at Galashiels, wrote to Edwards some years after this, informing him: 'My acquaintance with you commenced in that remarkable period of the century, the 35th, and since that time it has been maintained by the perusal of a great many of your letters to your worthy correspondents in Scotland; and by reading all of your printed

62 *Ibid.* ii *pp* 334–5. (Margaret Richardson).

pieces that are come over here.'[63] The laity as well as the ministers had learned of the revival in New England. Margaret Richardson, whom we have already shown to be conversant with Whitefield's Journals, also said: 'About five or six years ago, when I heard Mr Edwards' *Narrative of the Surprizing work of God at Northampton* read, I was very glad, to hear that there was such a work of conversion in those far distant places.'[64] M'Culloch at Cambuslang was greatly moved by these reports from New England and made it his practice to take some of them into the pulpit during worship, and to read to his congregation the latest news from overseas.[65] In the autumn of 1741, one of his congregation reflected: 'hearing a minister [M'Culloch] on a fast day, after sermon, read some papers relating to the success of the Gospel abroad; I was greatly affected at the thought that so many were getting good, and I was getting none'.[66]

Some few weeks later the Cambuslang minister took another step to arouse still greater interest. Whitefield had been at Glasgow in September 1741 for a few days. On 18 November 1741, the following advertisement was printed on the back of a pamphlet containing letters from Gilbert Tennent in America: 'Proposals that a paper be printed Weekly (Providence favouring and a sufficient Number of Subscriptions coming timeously in) and the several Subscribers or some by their Order shall once a Week, call for this Paper at William Duncan's Shop in the Salt-Mercat of Glasgow, James McCoul's Shop in the Trongate or (Blank) Shop above the Cross; and pay a Halfpenny at the Receipt of it and continue to do so for a Year, from the First of December 1741.'[67] The appeal must have been successful, for in December 1741 there was issued the first number of the first religious periodical ever to be published in Scotland, and its editor was William M'Culloch. '*The Weekly*

63 Davidson, H.: *Letters &c. p* 126.
64 M'C. Mss. ii *p* 333.
65 *Old Stat. Acc.* v *p* 242.
66 M'C. Mss. i *p* 103.
67 *Vide* Art. Couper, W. J.: 'The Glasgow Periodical Press' in *Recs. Glasgow Bibliographical Society.* viii *pp* 106–7.

History: or An Account of the most Remarkable Particulars relating to the Present Progress of the Gospel. By the Encouragement of the Rev Mr Whitefield. Glasgow. Reprinted by W. Duncan &c.' was thus begun. Each issue was of eight pages, and it was a compilation of reports, letters, poems and selections from devotional writers. At first, it was mainly a reprinting of matter from a London journal, the *Weekly History*, begun on 11 April 1741, but the revival which began at Cambuslang in February 1742 spread rapidly throughout the land, and soon provided more than enough material of purely Scottish interest. The paper ran for exactly fifty-two issues before M'Culloch discontinued it.[68]

It was to an informed people that the Cambuslang revival came; they had been reading about stirring events elsewhere, and were prayerfully wishing that it might happen with them. And it did!

68 After the *Weekly History* ceased publication the Rev James Robe began a somewhat similar venture, the *Christian Monthly History*, in November 1743. Something larger, its price was '6d for copies on fine paper, and 4d only on coarse'. It brought revival news and continued for two years. (*Edin. Per. Press*. W. J. Couper, *pp* 86–9.)

6

'*The Cams'lang Wark*'

There can be little doubt that the anarchy in the Cambuslang kirk session, leading to the drastic breach followed by the suspension of most of the elders in 1740, must have greatly disturbed the introspective M'Culloch. About this same time there were some unusual phenomena in the world of nature, which seemed to reflect and echo the violence and disorder within the church. It was cumulative evidence of the divine displeasure and discipline.

The first number of the *Scots Magazine*, January 1739, reported a storm of almost unexampled violence, following the sun's eclipse of 13 January; extensive damage had been done to shipping and property throughout Europe. Glasgow did not escape. In the civic records it is stated: 'By the late violent storm and hurricane which happened in the night betwixt the thirteen and fourteen days of January 1739, severall of the turretts of the speir of the Church (*ie* the High Kirk or Cathedral) and battlements surrounding the same were throun doun, part whereof fell doun upon the roof of the church and broke throw and damnified the roof . . . other parts . . . covered with lead and sclate was uncovered . . . several other parts of the church shattered and disordered and the top of the speir made to decline and bow doun, which will cost a considerable expence for repairing thereof and putting the said cathedral in any tollerable condition.' Also 'the spear and piramid of the tollbooth steeple . . . was throun doun by the storm'.[1]

Janet Hamilton has left us a graphic record of the adventures

1 *Glasgow Burgh Records*. 23 May, 27 June, 1739.

94

of her grandfather on this 'windy Saturday'; of thatch stripped from the roofs, falling rafters and tumbling gables, and of a journey of five or six miles which took him several hours. Often he was compelled to lie down at the bottom of grassy slopes to shelter from the fury of the gale. It was 'ever after spoken of by my grandfather as the most eventful and terrible day, or rather night, that he had experienced during his lengthened life'.[2]

So singular an event could not fail to impress M'Culloch, who, like most of his contemporaries, saw transcendental purpose in every unusual happening in the world of nature. One resident in Cambuslang, Andrew Faulds, a young man of twenty-one, recorded what happened: 'In all my Life, I never found any thing I read or heard come home with any Power to my Conscience or heart, till on a Fast day in the Parish, a little after the great Hurricane on the 13th of January (1740) . . . when hearing a Minister (26, *ie* M'Culloch) preach on that Text, Fire, hail, snow, vapour, stormy wind, obey his word, that Sentence he had in his Sermon, Will neither the Voice of God in the Tempests in the air, nor in the threatnings of devouring fire and everlasting Burnings awaken you? came home to me with a powerful Impression and made me see it as a Message sent from God to me.'

In a footnote he adds: 'N.B. On the very day when that great Tempest or Hurricane happened, that had been the Text, Who shall dwell with devouring fire who shall abide with everlasting burnings.' Reading from his Bible in February 1742, Faulds goes on: 'that word that had been before sent to Me, came home to me again with fresh Power, Will not the voice of God in the Tempest of air . . . awaken you?', and a new concern about spiritual affairs was created in him.[3]

After the catastrophic anger of the hurricane there came weary, famine-stricken months of dreadful hardship. During 1740 there was widespread distress throughout England, with hungry mobs attacking wagons taking grain to the ports. Cold

2 Hamilton, J.: *Poems &c. pp* 191–4.
3 M'C. Mss. ii *pp* 320–1.

and hunger reigned supreme.[4] Similar conditions obtained in
Scotland about the same time and for similar reaons. On 5
August 1739, Lord Elchies wrote from Shank to his factor at
Tanmore in the north; 'If you are burnt up with heat, wee are
drown'd with rains, in so much that I believe harvest will
hardly be begun in this countrey this month.'[5] On 17 January
1740, he wrote again: 'I doubt not prices will rise, tho' not
higher, I hope, than they are just now, on occasion of this long
continued frost, which is the most intense I ever saw in Scotland, and has rais'd the meal from 9d to 10d the peck.'[6] By
11 November of that same year, oatmeal was sold in the
Edinburgh market at 15d per peck.[7] In the *Scots Magazine*
which quotes this price, there is an account of rioting at Leith,
Edinburgh, Musselburgh, Prestonpans, etc, when troops fired
on large mobs.[8] Legislation was enacted forbidding the hoard-
ing of corn or any increase in the price of victuals. All corn had
to be threshed out before 1 May or be forfeited to the king. In
December 1740 the *Scots Magazine*, disturbed at the increase of
distress, with provisions scarcer and the number of beggars
vastly increased, put forward a scheme for licensing beggars,
to provide them with badges and collecting-boxes under the
control of inspectors. Within a few days the magistrates of
Edinburgh adopted this scheme, and more than 260 badges
were given out, in addition to the weekly allowances provided
for over 500 beggars by the churches.[9]

It has been estimated that at least 2,000 persons perished of
hunger and cold during the great famine of 1739–40, when the
frost was too severe for peat mosses to be dug, and the inland
waters were so frozen that wood and coals could not be carried.
Labouring men earning 4d a day had to pay up to 2s a peck
(about 9 lbs weight) for their staple diet of oatmeal; potatoes

4 *Vide* Wearmouth, R. F.: *Methodism & the Common People of the Eighteenth
  Century.* pp 20–2, 51–5.
5 *Letters of Patrick Grant, Lord Elchies* (ed H. D. MacWilliam). p 10.
6 *Ibid.* p 123.
7 *Scots Mag.* October 1740. p 487.
8 *Ibid.* pp 482–4.
9 *Ibid.* January 1741.

were not in general use and wheaten flour was a luxury. In the parish of Cambusnethan, when the long-delayed spring began to burst the buds and unfold the leaves, 'bands of haggard and emaciated women and pale, skeleton-like children, creeping slowly among the trees, stripping the branches of the beech of their tender leaves, returning to pick them day by day' could be seen. Little children searched among the miller's husks, hoping for some stray grains of corn, gnawing the stems of vegetables from the dunghill.[10]

James Robe, the minister of Kilsyth, wrote: 'Under the late Dearth the People suffered greatly, the poor were numerous, and many, especially about the Town of *Kilsyth*, were at the Point of starving.'[11] Upon 1 June 1740 the session in that parish appointed a day of fasting and prayer later that month 'upon account of the Dearth and Drought'.[12] It may be well to note that the elders collected through the parish in that very month for 'William Scot . . . lying in Prison in a Starving Condition'.[13] The chief thing that impressed Robe was: 'I could not see any one turning to the Lord who smote them, or crying to him because of their Sins, while they howled upon their Beds for Bread.'[14] On 4 June 1740 the Presbytery of Glasgow, 'considering the Extraordinary Drought, which at this time threatens both men and beast with famine, Thought proper to appoint, and hereby appoint Thursday the Twelfth instant as a Day of Solemn Humiliation, Fasting and Prayer, to be observed in all the Churches of this Presbytery'.[15]

Challenged by the many problems that surrounded him, and inspired by the news of revival that streamed in from New England, M'Culloch set himself to educate and enthuse his congregation to seek after similar results in their own community. On Sabbath evenings after the sermon, he 'frequently read to his hearers, missives, attestations and journals which he

10 Hamilton, J.: *Poems &c. pp* 194–6.
11 *Kilsyth Narrative. p* 68.
12 Kilsyth K.S.R.
13 *Ibid.*
14 *Kilsyth Narrative. p* 68.
15 Glasgow Pres. Recs.

had received from his correspondents, giving an account of conversions which had taken place in different parts of the world, especially in New England under Mr Whitefield's ministry'.[16] A new note was also heard in his preaching: 'in his ordinary Course of Sermons, for near a Twelvemonth before this Work began (*ie* from about February 1741), he had been preaching on these subjects which tend most directly to explain the Nature, and prove the Necessity of Regeneration, according to the different Lights in which that important Matter is represented in Holy Scripture', said the first reporter of the revival.[17]

It has been suggested that both M'Culloch and Robe 'were influenced by Doddridge's *Letters on Regeneration*, which were at that time in the enjoyment of a considerable popularity'.[18] This, however, could hardly have been the case, for Doddridge's *Practical Discourses on Regeneration &c.* were not published until 1742.[19]

It is not necessary to postulate any influence from outside Scotland to explain this preoccupation with preaching about regeneration. In 1726 the Society for Promoting Christian Knowledge reprinted a little book, *The Life of God in the Soul of Man*, by Henry Scougal. This was one of the most influential books in the early eighteenth century; 'one of the few produc-

16 *Old Stat. Acc.* v *p* 267.
17 *A Narrative of the Extraordinary Work at Cambuslang in a Letter to a Friend* dated 8 May 1742, with Preface by M'Culloch. *p* 4.
18 Couper, W. J.: *Scottish Revivals. p* 52.
19 In his Preface, written 7 November 1741, the Northampton divine speaks of treating the subject 'more largely than I had ever done before; knowing in the general how important it is, and observing that several controversies had about that Time been raised concerning it' (Preface, vi). He acknowledges the help of some of his friends who had taken notes 'after me in Characters' (*Ibid.* viii). Amongst those who took down Doddridge's discourses in shorthand was Thomas Gillespie, who became minister of Carnock in 1742 and was closely associated with the 1742 revival. *Vide John Fergusson 1727–50* – James Fergusson (London 1948), for further details about Doddridge's influence on Scotland through his academy. John, the eldest son of Lord Kilkerran; David, son of Colonel James Gardiner; David Dickson, son of a Peeblesshire laird, were his pupils. Also Irene Parker: *Dissenting Academies in England. pp* 77–95, 147–53.

tions by Scottish divines which has attained to the rank of a religious classic'.[20] From the first edition, published in 1677 in London, until 1733, six impressions appeared.[21] Naturally enough, this book by the son of Bishop Scougal, the friend of Leighton and Burnet, was highly prized by the Episcopalians. Susanna Wesley recommended it to her two sons Charles and John as 'an excellent good book . . . an acquaintance of mine many years ago'.[22] It influenced both of them greatly.

Charles, founder of the Holy Club at Oxford, gave this book to a perplexed young undergraduate there, George Whitefield. We have the latter's own account of his visit to Charles Wesley; he had been diligently going the round of such pious duties as fasting, watching and praying, and receiving the sacrament, 'yet I never knew what true religion was till God sent me *that excellent treatise* by the hands of my never-to-be-forgotten friend'. He went on:

'At my first reading it I wondered what the author meant by saying "that some falsely placed religion in going to church, doing hurt to no one, being constant in the duties of the closet, and now and then reaching out their hands to give alms to their poor neighbours". "Alas!" thought I, "if this be not true religion, what is?" God soon showed me; for in reading a few lines further that "true religion was union of the soul with God, and Christ formed within us", a ray of divine light was instantaneously darted in upon my soul, and from that moment, but not till then, did I know that I must be a new creature.'[23]

Many years later, in 1769, recalling Charles Wesley and the loan of Scougal's book, Whitefield confessed that 'whenever I go to Oxford, I cannot help running to the spot where Jesus Christ first revealed Himself to me, and gave me the new birth'.

Whitefield at first had feelings of great apprehension about the book, like a pauper facing an imminent revelation of bankruptcy, and he questioned: 'Shall I burn this book? shall I

20 Scougal, H.: *The Life of God &c.* Preface. *pp* 15–16.
21 John Newton acknowledges the influence of Scougal's *Life &c.*, on him in 1752. (*Works.* i *p* 56.)
22 Clarke, A.: *Memoirs of the Wesley Family.* i *p* 103.
23 *George Whitefield's Journals* (Banner of Truth editn). *p* 47.

throw it down? or shall I search it?' Following the latter course, 'O what a ray of divine life did then break in upon my soul!'[24] Thus did a quiet Scottish teacher in Aberdeen, who died at the age of twenty-eight, mould the life and inspire the preaching of the greatest pulpit orator of the eighteenth century. It was this message of the new birth that Whitefield proclaimed everywhere; it was his clarion-call to Scotland.

The book was also appreciated by Scottish Presbyterians; Principal William Wishart, writing from the College of Edinburgh, 26 April 1739, gave his warm approval to a proposal for a cheap edition of the book, to be published by Thomas and Walter Ruddiman, 'price 6d or 5s a dozen for giving away'.[25] May it not be that one of these cheap copies came into the hands of M'Culloch and Robe and inspired their preaching?

The theme of regeneration was not new for M'Culloch. One of his parishioners, Janet Struthers, aged thirty-two, who set down her experiences in 1743, recalled that 'about 9 years ago, Mr M'Culloch coming thro the Parish visiting, took me aside by my self, and among other things told me, Except you be born again, you can never see the kingdom of heaven; that word for a long time haunted me often & came frequently into my mind, but I knew not what to make of it'.[26] Even before the revival of 1742, the conscientious faithfulness of M'Culloch was not entirely unfruitful. One young woman writes: 'Some years before the Awakening came, I was in service in a Ministers (M'Culloch's) family, who took a great deal of pains upon Me to instruct Me.' As a result she became impressed by the need to perform outward religious duties. 'About five years ago, at a Communion Occasion, when I saw some Young Folk coming to my Master about their soul concerns ... I wondered what it was that affected them ... Next Year, 1739, when the Communion came about, something of a concern about My Soul revived in Me ... Only I thought it would be well enough with Me, if I carried as I saw other Douce folk carry:

24 Quoted in D. Butler. *Scougal &c. pp* 104–5.
25 Scougal: *Life of God &c.* Preface by Cooper. *p* 17.
26 M'C. Mss. ii *p* 558.

and so I kept up a form of duty, but rested there.'[27] It was at this same sacrament in 1739 that the minister of Bothwell, Mr Hamilton, preached on Revelation 22.17: 'The Spirit and the Bride say Come'. This puzzled one of the young people from Cambuslang . . . 'like Nicodemus, I never knew that there was such a thing as a New Birth. My thought all this while was, that I could grow good of Myself.'[28] On 1 June 1740, M'Culloch preached at Cathcart on the text 'Wherefore He is able to save to the uttermost', and in the audience was a young woman from Cardross who was 'distinctly made to close with Christ Jesus in all His Offices as an All-Sufficient Saviour'.[29] Faithfulness, even of a pedestrian fashion, was laying the foundation for still greater things.

Next summer there came a visitor to Scotland, whose vivid and passionate preaching aroused tremendous interest. A press notice announced from Edinburgh that 'the famous Mr George Whitefield arrived here from England about the end of July. He preaches every day when in town to very numerous audiences.' Then follows a new note, after all the harsh criticisms that had been printed in earlier issues of the *Scots Magazine*: 'This gentleman recommends the essentials of Religion, and decries the distinguishing punctilios of parties.'[30]

This first visit to Scotland – he was to make fourteen before his death in 1770 – lasted for thirteen weeks; his correspondence and diary reveal how abundant and exacting were his labours, with preaching services every day, long private discussions with troubled people, and the arduous toil of writing many letters, often after 'the clock has struck twelve'.

On 15 August 1741, Whitefield wrote to a friend in London: 'It would make your heart leap for joy, to be now in Edinburgh. I question if there be not upwards af 300 in this city seeking after Jesus. Every morning I have a constant levee of wounded souls . . . At seven in the morning, we have a lecture in the

27 *Ibid.* i *pp* 17–20 (Janet Jackson).
28 *Ibid.* i *p* 103 (Elizabeth Jackson).
29 *Ibid.* i *p* 134 (Sarah Gilchrist).
30 *Scots Mag.* July 1741. *p* 331.

fields, attended not only by the common people, but persons of great rank. I have reason to think several of the latter sort are coming to Jesus ... Congregations consist of many thousands. Never did I see so many Bibles, nor people look into them, when I am expounding, with such attention ... I preach twice daily, and expound at private houses at night, and am employed in speaking to souls under distress great part of the day.'[31]

Towards the end of August, Whitefield made a preaching tour of the Scottish provinces;[32] coming to Glasgow, he preached ten times in five days, chiefly in the High Church (*ie* the Cathedral) yard from Friday to Tuesday (11–15 September). The congregations were very large and many people were deeply moved. 'With great regret we parted',[33] was his comment. Some little time later, M'Culloch wrote to Whitefield about this visit: 'It is a matter of great Joy and Thankfulness to God, who sent you here, and gave you so much Countenance, and so remarkably crown'd your Labours when here at Glasgow with Success ... I am well informed by some Ministers and other judicious and experienced Christians, that there are to the Number of 50 Persons already got notice of in and about Glasgow, that all that can be judg'd ... are savingly converted by the Blessing and Power of God, accompanying your ten Sermons in that Place, besides several others under Convictions.'[34] He then describes the great difference made in the behaviour of many young people and comments on the new zeal they were displaying for the conversion of others. This 'great visible Change' had aroused widespread interest; also the newly-converted 'have all a great love to one another and to all good Christians'.[35]

When M'Culloch was collecting his reports from men and women who had been influenced at Cambuslang, he found still more definite evidence of the impressions made by this first visit of Whitefield to Glasgow. At least fourteen people declared

31 *George Whitefield Works.* i pp 315–16.
32 Details of the places are given in Gillies' *Life of Whitefield.* pp 78, 96–7.
33 *George Whitefield Works.* i p 319.
34 *Glasgow Weekly History* No 13.
35 *Ibid.*

that they were present at the services in the 'High-Church Yeard'.

One 'heared nine sermons of him in Glasgow and fouer in Paisley';[36] another 'was impatient to hear him . . . my great concern was to experience what it was to be born again'.[37] A young woman from Greenock also heard this 'Stranger-Minister . . . preaching concerning conversion . . . I thought he was just speaking to me, and was going to name me out . . . I was afraid I would cry out, and rather than do that, I choosd to withdraw from among the people and did so and heard him no more.'[38] The preacher's words 'came with a dint' on the heart of one young man . . . 'I felt my heart turn hot and melt and overboil in tears.'[39]

There were those who would have liked to hear him, but could not attend. Agnes More of Carmunnock tells a pathetic story. Servant at a minister's house, she became the mother of an illegitimate baby. 'Often wishing to be turn'd', she heard of Whitefield's coming to Glasgow. 'I long'd much to hear him preach, having heard that he spake much of Conversion . . . but having a Child on my breast, and being in low and straitning Circumstances, I could never get the Opportunity to hear him.'[40] But she did so in the next year, to her great happiness.

Whitefield's visit confirmed M'Culloch in the programme he was already carrying out . . . 'preaching much on regeneration'; his people testified to the effect upon them of this reiterated theme. One 'thought that My own Minister preached much better than He used to Do'.[41] A young man, John Aiken, a weaver in the parish, declared that 'the first time that ever I heard the word with power, was on a Sabbath, about Martinmas 1741'. M'Culloch's sermon was on John 3.5 on the new birth. 'That was the first time I heard the call of the gospel come home to Me in particular. And that day I thought, Either The

36 M'C. Mss. ii p 243 (Mary Scot).
37 Ibid. ii pp 334–6 (Margaret Richardson).
38 Ibid. ii pp 28–9 (Mary Shaw).
39 Ibid. ii pp 664–7 (John Parker).
40 Ibid. ii p 110.
41 Ibid. i p 21 (Janet Jackson).

Minister or I was changed.'[42] One could wish that Dr Robert M'Culloch, when he edited and published some of his father's sermons posthumously, had included certain ones which were made memorable for many listeners, especially the one preached in December 1741 from 2 Corinthians 6.1, 2 – 'We then as workers together with him beseech you also that ye receive not the grace of God in vain'. Many referred to it later, one of whom thought 'he was preaching to Me . . . pointing at Me as directly and distinctly as if he had named me out before the Congregation, so that I was like to cry out in the Kirk'.[43]

An air of expectancy was increasing throughout the parish of Cambuslang as the winter of 1741 wore on. One was 'much and oft taken up in praying for a Revival of Religion, that I seemd in a great measure to forget my self and my own concerns'.[44] John Aiken, when on a journey going to the East country, dreamed that he 'saw a great multitude of people about Cambuslang kirk'. When he told this to his companion next morning the latter informed him: 'Yes, there will be a general Meeting there very soon, and this happned, I think, in the first week of Jan. 1742, which was about six weeks before the Awakning broke out.'[45] This coming together of the various societies for prayer in the district would increase the sense of standing at the very threshold of some great and good work of God.

On 31 January 1742, M'Culloch preached to his own people on 'the abundance of divine consolation' with 2 Corinthians 1.3, 4 as his text. In his closing paragraph, he declared: 'When I look around me, blessed be God, I see marks of more apparent concern about Salvation, than in times past, among some of you. Beware of a noisy or ostentatious religion; and, at the same time, take heed that you run not to the opposite extreme, by endeavouring to stifle the convictions you may feel. "Follow on to know the Lord . . . and he shall come unto us as the rain, as the latter and former rain unto the earth" '.[46] The floods of

42 *Ibid.* i *p* 461 (John Aiken).   43 *Ibid.* i *p* 21 (Janet Jackson).
44 *Ibid.* ii *p* 343 (Margaret Richardson).
45 *Ibid.* i *p* 463.   46 M'Culloch: *Sermons &c. p* 241.

blessing were not far off now. One woman who had listened to M'Culloch preaching on regeneration through the whole winter became very troubled but decided that this feeling was foolish. 'People about Me will think I'm grown light in the head, and I may cast My Self into some sickness or distemper, and what will come of Me then, having no body to take care of Me.' On the first Sunday in February 1742 she heard him once again on the same theme, 'about the Necessity of Regeneration'. 'At the Close of the Sermon, the Minister Charged us to go home to a retired place, and fall doun upon our bended knees before God, and with all possible earnestness, as for life, to beg of him his Holy Spirit to renew and change our hearts and Natures, and take no Comfort in any thing worldly, till We got it.'[47]

Some of the most prominent laymen in the parish decided that this 'more than ordinary concern about religion' called for unusual and additional methods. About the end of January 1742, Ingram More, a shoemaker, together with Robert Bowman, a weaver, both converts of Whitefield's preaching, went from door to door with a petition which was to request M'Culloch to give a weekly lecture. Ninety heads of families, over half of the total households in the parish, subscribed the document. Thursday was settled on as being the most suitable day, and a start was made on 4 February.[48] The first two lectures produced nothing unusual, although one young woman, speaking of the second meeting on 11 February, informed M'Culloch: 'I had such a thirst after the Word ... that I sate up a good part of the night before, spinning at my Wheel, to make up the time at my work that I was to spend next day at the Weekly Lecture, that so my Master and Mistress might have no ground to complain that I neglected my Work with them ... tho' this was not what they required of me.'[49]

On the following Sabbath, 14 February, the kirk was full, 'and many standing for want of seats'.[50] M'Culloch preached

---

47 M'C. Mss. i *pp* 95–6 (Mary Mitchell).
48 *Old Stat. Acc.* v *p* 268; *Narrative of the Extraordinary Work &c. p* 5.
49 M'C. Mss. ii *p* 266 (Catherine Jackson).   50 *Ibid.* i *p* 26.

yet once more on 'Except a man be born again' (John 3.3, 5),
'on which he had been insisting for a long time before'.[51]
Catherine Jackson became extremely distressed and, with her
two sisters, was taken to the manse by Mr Duncan, 'a Preacher',
and 'another Person, now an Elder, *viz* Ingram More'.[52] It was
this incident, in all probability, that proved to be the spark
which ignited the ensuing blaze. A full account of what
happened that night was written down next morning by
M'Culloch, 'drawn up from his own Memory, and that of the
other two persons just now spoken of . . . and the truth of it can
also be attested by many others who were then present'.
Because it is so typical of what was to follow, we shall set it
down fairly fully. M'Culloch, who wrote a very detailed record,
seems to have been greatly impressed by this event.

In the manse, she cried out three times, 'What shall I do?'
and he called on her to believe on the Lord Jesus Christ and be
saved. Bitterly weeping, she declared that her sins were so
many that He would not receive her. The story goes on: 'But
he will, said the Minister; If you be willing to come to him and
accept of him; I can assure you in his name, he is willing to
accept of you; Whatever you have been, whatever you have
done, come to him, and he will not reject you. When there is a
Willingness on both sides – he is willing, and you, I think, are
willing – what should hinder the concluding of the blessed
Bargain, the match between Christ and your soul.'[53] To each
of her many semi-hysterical outbursts, M'Culloch replied with
some word of promise from the Scripture. 'Come, said the
Minister, Shall we pray for a Pull of God's almighty arm to
draw you to Christ. O yes, yes, said She, and got up on her
feet. Some of the company said, She would not be able to stand
(for that was the Posture design'd) in time of Prayer: There is
no fear of that, said one standing by, I will take care of that . . .
and so took hold of her arm.' During this prayer, 'She told the
Person who was supporting her, Christ says to me, He will

51 *Ibid.* ii *p* 266.
52 *Ibid.* ii *p* 267.
53 *Ibid.* ii *pp* 268–9.

never leave me nor forsake me, repeating it over and over; and immediately after, she said . . . He is telling me, He hath cast all my Sins behind his back.'[54]

There were many people present in the room, including several young women who were her personal friends, weeping and crying out. Pointing to them, M'Culloch said to her: 'You see that there are several Daughters of Jerusalem there . . . Have you anything to say to commend Christ to them? She immediately turn'd to them, and said in the most moving and feeling manner, My Beloved is . . . the chief among ten thousand, yea he is altogether lovely. O Sirs, will ye come to Christ . . . If ye cannot cry to him, O long after him . . . At this time there was a great Stir . . . The joys of some were plainly transporting and almost too strong for them to contain . . . and there was a sound of weeping among others, that might be heard at a considerable distance.' Then M'Culloch called on the company to compose themselves, and they all sang together the first eight verses of Psalm 103 before separating. We are told that these events in the minister's closet lasted 'above three hours' – and the days ahead were to see many more hours spent on similar attempts at spiritual counselling. M'Culloch wrote out the story in full next morning and this was 'read over by him to a General Meeting of the Socities [sic] for Prayer in the Parish that met at his House that day; they were greatly affected in hearing it'.[55]

In the evening of that same Monday, Janet Jackson, sister to Catherine, whose story we have just retold, 'went to my Experienced Christian Acquaintance's house [ie Jean Galbraith] where there were present about eight or nine young people, that had before that fall'n under trouble of mind'. Also present were Duncan, John Bar and Ingram More 'that had been awakned at Glasgow the Harvest before'.[56] That same night, at family worship in the house of Bartle Somers, when he gave out the 130th Psalm, 'O who shall stand if Thou, O

54 *Ibid.* ii *pp* 270–1.
55 *Ibid.* ii *pp* 272–4.
56 *Ibid.* i *pp* 28–9.

Lord, Shouldst Mark Iniquity', 'they [the words] struck Me with much terror, and Made me weep', said one of his young weavers.[57] On the following evening, Tuesday, 16 February, there was another meeting of 'several serious Christians' at the Manse for prayer,[58] and at the schoolhouse a similar meeting was conducted by Jonathan Bar.[59] One young woman who left this latter meeting, 'going away to a Relations house . . . could not forbear bursting out into tears and breaking out before all in the house to speak in commendation of Christ'. When many of the neighbours came flocking in, she continued to speak at length and with great freedom to them all. 'I was before this time ashamed to open my mouth and speak anything almost before others: But now I thought if a whole Congregation had been present, I could not have been able to hold my peace.'[60] Still a third meeting was held that week on Wednesday evening at the manse, when M'Culloch preached on 'He shall feed his flock like a shepherd'. But it was the next day, Thursday, 18 February, that became memorable – the day of days, commemorated in the parish and beyond for many years afterwards. (M'Culloch, and probably many of his parishioners, could not have failed to recall that it was on 18 February 1731, also a Thursday, that the parish of Cambuslang had met to elect and subscribe a call to him as their intended minister.)

The sermon was preached from Jeremiah 23.6: 'And this is the Name whereby he shall be called, THE LORD OUR RIGHTEOUS-NESS.' There is no record of it, but we know of some of its effects. One 'thought that sermon was, as it were, a new Gospel to me';[61] a young man 'wept almost all the time',[62] and a young woman 'was so affected . . . that the tears ran down My Cheeks, all the time I was hearing'.[63] Mary Mitchell also

57 *Ibid.* i *p* 77 (John McDonald).
58 *A Short Narrative etc. p* 5.
59 M'C. Mss. i *p* 77.
60 *Ibid.* i *pp* 107–8 (Elizabeth Jackson).
61 *Ibid.* i *p* 30.
62 *Ibid.* i *p* 77.
63 *Ibid.* i *p* 9 (Mary Lap).

wept and added: 'My heart beat so violently, that I tho't it would have leapt out at My side', but 'I did not cry out in the Kirk, nor did any there cry out that day'.[64] In the closing prayer after he had lectured, M'Culloch exclaimed: 'Where are the fruits of my poor labours among this people?'[65] He had not long to wait now! After the lecture ended, a number of men and women, who were in considerable distress, went to the dining room in the manse for prayer and conversation with the minister. Several 'had some difficulty to get into the hall, there was such a croud of people there'.[66] The total number was about fifty, and M'Culloch exhorting, psalm-singing and talking with individuals, went on throughout the night, but there were 'only about 15 who that night got any outgate or relief from their soul distress'.[67]

When the news of the happenings at Cambuslang on this night became known, hostile critics began immediately to rush into print and condemn the work. Within three weeks, one of them asserted in a pamphlet that at this lecture, some of the people 'expressed their Agony not only in Words, but by clapping their Hands, beating their Breasts, terrible Shakings, frequent Faintings and Convulsions; the Minister often calling out to them, Not to stifle or smother their Convictions, but encourage them'.[68] These are not the words of an eye-witness, and we have already seen that M'Culloch closed the lecture with a cry almost of disappointment and failure. John Erskine, writing in October 1742, alludes to this pamphlet as 'malicious ... This for some Time prejudiced People at a Distance, till Persons of Credit, who had gone there, declared it was a Bundle of Lies'.[69] Another objector wrote in similar terms in the *Scots Magazine*;[70] M'Culloch aptly replied that 'they were not brought, but all of them came without help of their own

64 *Ibid.* i *p* 97.
65 *Old Stat. Acc.* v *p* 268; *A True Account &c. p* 3.
66 M'C. Mss. i *p* 98.
67 *Ibid.* ii *p* 101.
68 *Letter from Gentleman in the West Country &c. pp* 4–5.
69 Erskine, J.: *Signs of the Times Considered. p* 21.
70 *Scots Mag.* 1742. *p* 233.

accord: there were none of them screaming nor crying, and they could not come in a faint'.[71]

After this eventful night, crowds of people began to flock to Cambuslang from all quarters, and sermons had to be provided for them almost daily. M'Culloch, aided by two probationer ministers living in the district, James Young and Alexander Duncan, and several neighbouring ministers, laboured day and night, teaching and exhorting the ever-growing crowds. In spite of his fifty-one years, he seemed 'to renew his strength'.[72]

Not only did the local ministers join whole-heartedly in the onerous task of promoting the work of revival in Cambuslang; ministers of the highest repute travelled from distant parts of the country to see for themselves what was taking place. Many of these sent written attestations to M'Culloch, which he published in order to disarm suspicion and dispel false rumours.

John Willison of Dundee (1680–1750) was one of the most prominent and respected ministers in Scotland. When Whitefield first came to the country in 1741, he gave him a warm invitation to visit Dundee, and the youthful evangelist promised to do so at the first opportunity. In this selfsame letter, Whitefield administered a gentle rebuke to his venerable correspondent: 'I wish you would not trouble yourself or me in writing about the corruptions of the Church of England. I believe there is no church perfect under heaven.'[73] The promise was redeemed in September 1741, and Whitefield wrote back to Willison: 'Blessed be God for any good done at Dundee! . . . I do not despair of seeing Scotland like New-England.'[74] Willison, in his reply, thanks God for the many tears he had seen during Whitefield's preaching in Dundee and for the many young people who had joined societies for prayer. There was some persecution, but there was also much faith: 'But O if Christ would Smile no matter tho' the Devil Roar.'[75] In the Preface to his book, *The Balm of Gilead*, written in January 1742,

71 M'C. Mss. i *p* 101.

72 *A True Account &c. p* 6. *Letter from a Gentleman in the Gorbals of Glasgow to his Friend at Greenock.*

73 *George Whitefield Works.* i *p* 310.

74 *Ibid.* ii *p* 319.   75 *Glasgow Weekly History* No 11. *pp* 6–7.

Willison speaks of revival as having already begun, and urges ministers in particular to try and arouse their churches.[76] After referring to the 1596 Assembly, the events of 1625 and 1630, and the Awakening in New England, he writes, 'Let us all cry for a general revival, and for poor Scotland, that it may not be past by when other places are watered'.[77]

News of the revival at Cambuslang must have filled Willison with joy, and soon he was making his way south 'to enquire and get satisfaction about it'.[78] On 15 April 1742 he was one of the ministers who sent to M'Culloch attestations about the revival. 'Having resided several Days in Mr *M'Culloch's* House,' wrote Willison, 'I had occasion to converse with many who had been awakened ... some who had been very wicked and scandalous, but now wonderfully chang'd ... very rude and boisterous before, they now had the mildness, and meekness of the Lamb about them ... Tho' I conversed with a great Number both Men and Women, Old and Young, I could observe nothing *Visionary* or *Enthusiastick* about them ... Upon the whole, I look on the Work at *C——g*, to be a most singular and marvellous Out-pouring of the *Holy Spirit.*'[79]

Among the first to receive news about Cambuslang was Whitefield himself. On 4 March 1742 he noted: 'In Scotland, the awakening is greater and greater', and on this same day he wrote to Mr A—— at Heriot's Hospital, Edinburgh: 'I hope, at my return to Scotland, to see greater things than ever.'[80] On 22 March he replied to a letter from M'Culloch: 'I rejoice to hear of the great work begun in Scotland, and doubt not of its continuance.'[81]

On 1 April Mr A. T. sent an urgent plea to Whitefield that he should seek to return to Scotland. He quotes from a letter from M'Culloch to him, dated 18 March, which says: 'I have the greatest Regard to that dear Servant of Christ Jesus,

76 Willison, J.: *The Balm of Gilead.*
77 *Ibid. p* 130.
78 Gillies. *Hist. Coll.* ii *p* 344.
79 *A Short Narrative of Cambuslang &c. pp* 11–13.
80 *George Whitefield Works.* i *pp* 375–7.
81 *Glasgow Weekly History* No 17 *p* 1.

Mr Whitefield . . . I go on to preach every Day . . . I daily see new Instances of Conviction and Conversion . . . about an hundred and thirty Souls here have been wounded with a deep Sense of their perishing Condition . . . of which about eighty have been comforted. I suppose there was between thirty and forty distress'd Souls in my House this Night, of which three received Comfort. One of them a great Debauchee, Another a Moral young Woman; Another a Boy about eight Years of Age. The first Week this Work of God was chiefly among the People of this Parish, but these ten Days past, it has been particularly among Strangers that resort here.'[82]

The writer informs Whitefield that, because there had been a lull in the work, M'Culloch decided to tell the people that there would be preaching only on Sundays and Thursdays, but that very evening, 'such an extraordinary Awakening came among the People, that above thirty were convicted'. As a result, daily preaching was continued. He then ends his letter: 'O, Mr Whitefield. Why are you so long a coming to poor Scotland again? How many say, When is he coming? For the Lord's sake do not lay aside Thoughts of coming, what ever Work you may have in England.'[83]

Later in that same month, on 28 April, M'Culloch himself wrote to Whitefield, pointing out that he had been employed daily in the Lord's work and had not the leisure to write as often as he wished. 'Yet I cannot forget you one Day . . . I believe that in less than three Months past, about 300 Souls have been awakened . . . more than 200 of these, I think, are hopefully converted . . . Some have computed the Hearers, these two last Lord's-days, to have been Nine or Ten-thousand . . . We continue still to have a Sermon here every day. I long much to see you here. Let me know by the first opportunity when you think to be with us.'[84] There could be no greater attraction for Whitefield than to hear such news; like the war-horse sniffing up the smells and knowing the sounds of battle, he longed to hurl himself into the fray.

82 *Ibid.* No 22 *p* 4.   83 *Ibid.* No 22 *p* 5.   84 *Ibid.* No 27 *p* 4.

7

The Two Communions at Cambuslang

It will be unmistakably clear that the revival at Cambuslang had begun and was going on from strength to strength before Whitefield arrived to move the crowds by his amazing eloquence. The work was no foreign importation, but had issued directly from the faithful preaching and labours of a somewhat colourless parish minister, assisted, as the labours became more abundant, by his brethren. To say this is not to underestimate the value of the contribution made by Whitefield. His first coming to the west of Scotland in the summer of 1741 provided a much-valued inspiration, and his second visit in the following summer proved an irresistible magnet for the multitudes.

During May 1742, Whitefield had embarked on a new enterprise of preaching to the great crowds thronging Moorfields in London, and patronising the many booths, which contained every kind of mountebank, player, puppet-show and the like. His own estimate of the numbers there was between twenty and thirty thousand. His success angered 'Beelzebub's agents', and he was honoured, as he says, 'with having a few stones, dirt, rotten eggs, and pieces of dead cats thrown at me'. A merry-andrew, balanced precariously on the shoulders of another man, tried several times to lash him with a heavy whip, but without success. A recruiting sergeant, complete with drum, marched through the listening crowds which, at Whitefield's invitation, opened up to give him passage. One young rake tried hard to stab the preacher with his sword, but a bystander struck up the weapon with a cane. Another climbed a tree near to the pulpit, and 'shamefully exposed his naked-ness before all the people' and thus provided the evangelist with an illustration for his theme. Amid all the tumult and bestiality, men and women knelt seeking for pardon and peace.[1]

Immediately after this field-preaching in London, 'fighting with wild beasts' in very truth, Whitefield embarked on the *Mary and Ann* bound for Scotland, expecting 'great things' there. He arrived on 3 June. Five days later he wrote to M'Culloch, rejoicing at the continued progress of the work at Cambuslang: . . . 'I believe you will both see and hear of far greater things than these. I trust that not one corner of poor Scotland will be left unwatered by the dew of God's heavenly blessing. The cloud is now only rising as big as a man's hand; yet a little while, and we shall hear a sound of an abundance of gospel rain . . . God willing, I hope to be with you the begin-ning of next week.'[2] Exactly one week later he was met at Glasgow and welcomed 'in the name of twenty thousand . . . By three o'clock this morning [16 June], people were coming to hear the word of God. At seven, I preached to many, many thousands.'[3]

On Tuesday, 6 July 1742,[4] he came to Cambuslang at mid-day, and preached at two, six and nine o'clock at night. 'Such a commotion surely never was heard of, especially at eleven at night. It far out-did all that I ever saw in America.' For about an hour and a half there were scenes of uncontrollable distress, like a field of battle. Many were being carried into the manse like wounded soldiers. 'Mr. M['Culloch] preached after I had ended, till past one in the morning, and then could scarce persuade them to depart. All night in the fields, might be heard the voice of prayer and praise.'[5] Writing to his steward in Georgia, Whitefield described the awakening as unspeakable, akin to an experience they had once shared at Fogg's Manor in Pennsylvania: 'I never was enabled to preach so before.' In a

1 *George Whitefield Works.* i pp 384–8.   2 *Ibid.* i pp 398, 401–2.
3 Tyerman, L.: *Life of Whitefield.* ii p 5.
4 Not 19 June as in Tyerman (*Life,* ii p 5). We might also note Tyerman's habit of rewriting Whitefield's *Letters* or touching them up.
5 *George Whitefield Works.* i p 405.

letter that same day to his wife, he tells her that this far out-
does all that he had ever witnessed in America: 'I am persuaded
the work will spread more and more.'[6] Invited by M'Culloch
to assist at the annual communion services, Whitefield wrote to
Willison at Dundee: 'On Friday, God willing, I go to Cambuslang, where I expect to see great days of the Son of man.'[7]

He arrived at Cambuslang on Friday, 9 July, and preached
the following day to more than twenty thousand people. Of the
next day, the communion Sabbath, he declares that 'scarce
ever was such a sight seen in Scotland'.[8] The sacrament was
celebrated in the fields, a custom which aroused nostalgic
memories of the days of persecution. Whitefield notes elsewhere
that 'a brae, or hill, near the manse at Cambuslang, seemed to
be formed by Providence, for containing a large congregation.
People sat unwearied till two in the morning to hear sermons,
disregarding the weather. You could scarce walk a yard, but
you must tread upon some.'[9] Apparently services were frequently held out-of-doors about this time because the kirk was
too small and out of repair. The place chosen was 'a green brae
on the east side of a deep ravine near the church, scooped out
by nature in the form of an amphitheatre . . . sprinkled over
with broom, furze and sloe-bushes'.[10]

Two wooden preaching-tents were set up along with the
communion-tables; throughout the long summer day, a group
of ministers, which included Alexander Webster of Edinburgh,
served the tables and preached to the multitudes. Writing on
14 July, M'Culloch reckons that the total of communicants,
judging by the tokens gathered in, 'was about 1700'. Some
people had estimated that the congregation exceeded 30,000,
but 'Mr Wh——d, who is used to such Things . . . made them
about 20,000'. In this same letter, the minister of Cambuslang
believes that 'above 500 Souls . . . have been savingly brought
home to God . . . Nor do I include those who have been awakned
by Means of Mr Whitefield's Sermons in this Place (he had

6 *Ibid.* i *p* 405.   7 *Ibid.* i *p* 407.   8 *Ibid.* i *p* 409.
9 Gillies, D.: *Life of Whitefield. p* 124.
10 *New Stat. Acc.* vi *p* 426.

preached seventeen sermons in Cambuslang) because I cannot pretend to compute them.'[11]

In the evening, when the sacrament was over, Whitefield preached again at the request of the ministers[12] for about an hour and a half to the whole congregation. His text was from Isaiah 54.5: 'Thy Maker is thy Husband; the Lord of Hosts is his name.' This was the sermon most frequently referred to by the converts, as the M'Culloch manuscript volumes show. The theme of a marriage-contract would be understood by everyone and provided him with a magnificent opportunity to plead for the consent of his hearers.

One of Whitefield's biographers, Gledstone, complains of this particular sermon that 'we look in vain for a single passage of interest or power in it. The thought is meagre, and the language tame; there is a total absence of the dramatic element which abounds in all his treatment of narrative and parable.'[13] Surely this is to overlook completely the preacher's habit of illustration. The printed sermons of Whitefield, as of M'Culloch and others, were really outlines, frameworks into which were fitted anecdote and illustration to drive home the argument.

We may find glimpses of his approach in the testimony of his hearers. 'He said he was sent to take a wife for his Master's Son, asking if there was any there that wanted to take Christ for their Husband, and bidding them come and he would marry them to Christ, after which he laid out the Terms and I found my heart made Sweetly to agree', says one young man of twenty-one.[14] A married man of thirty also found help in this sermon: 'where he described the articles and terms of a marriage agreement between Christ and Beleivers [sic]'.[15] Daniel McLarty, single and twenty-one, 'almost cried out for joy at the sweet offers of Christ as a husband to my soul, and I was ready to strike hands on the Bargain'.[16] Meeting another young

11 *Glasgow Weekly History*. No 30 *pp* 1–2.
12 *George Whitefield Works*. 1 *p* 409.
13 Gledstone, J. P.: *The Life & Travels of George Whitefield*. *p* 286.
14 M'C. Mss. ii *p* 325. (Andrew Faulds).
15 *Ibid*. i *p* 7. (Wm. Baillie).
16 *Ibid*. ii *p* 163.

man whom he knew, he threw his arms around him and said that Whitefield had married his soul to Christ. Both men and women were attracted by this appeal. When Margaret Borland heard the plea and invitation, 'I thought, Willing! who would not be willing?'[17] Sixteen-year-old Margaret Carson recollected vividly the alternative; not to be married to Christ was 'to have the Devil for your Husband and you sleep all night in the Devil's arms'.[18] It seems obvious that Whitefield had fastened on the story of Abraham's steward Eliezer, journeying east to seek a wife for his master's son, Isaac, and the ready assent of Rebekah to agree to the terms and go with him.[19] And the same analogy is strengthened by Paul's conception, in his letter to the Ephesians, of the Church as the Bride of Christ.

Throughout that Sunday night, 'in different companies, you might have heard persons praying to, and praising God. The children of God came from all quarters.'[20] The weather does not seem to have been altogether favourable, as may be seen from one delightful reference in the account of Daniel McLarty. He lay down on the brae, filled with the love of Christ, and wishing that he might die on the spot, if it should be the Lord's will, 'yet, rain coming on, I thought it was not my duty to ly still there, but went to a House for Quarters'.[21] On the Monday morning, Whitefield preached to a crowd almost as large as that of the Sabbath and wrote to John Cennick: 'such an universal stir I never saw before. The motion fled as swift as lightning from one end of the auditory to another. You might have seen thousands bathed in tears. Some at the same time wringing their hands, others almost swooning and others crying out'.[22]

17 *Ibid.* ii *p* 541.
18 *Ibid.* ii *p* 500.
19 The same emphasis is found in Hosea. McDonald, 'The Apostle of the North', preached on a similar theme to a congregation of ten thousand at an evening service in the same week that his young wife died in 1814. 'Few eyes were tearless in that vast assembly.' (Kennedy: *The Apostle of the North, pp* 78–80.)
20 *George Whitefield Works.* i *p* 410.
21 M'C. Mss. ii *p* 163.
22 *Letters.* i *pp* 409–10.

Many of those who sat down at the Lord's Table had overcome great difficulties to do so. One young journeyman weaver from Glasgow, after listening to the preaching at Cambuslang on the Saturday, went 'away with Haste to Glasgow and got a Line to get a Token and came back with it to Camb. that evening and got one, and spent all that night in prayer'.[23] The small metal tokens that admitted would-be communicants to the Lord's Table were not given out easily. When Janet Struthers came to M'Culloch to ask for a token, 'he bade me look to it, that it was not to be seen of men and to get a name for Religion or for any other selfish end'.[24] Even coming to the table could be very difficult. Anne Wylie tells of her own apprehension about coming forward. 'When the 2nd Table was to be served The people being slow to come forward to it, A Minister (26 *ie* M'Culloch) saying, to excite them, "Is this your kindness to your Friend", I felt My heart Melted down and made willing to come. But not having access, because of the Great Crowd, My fears returned. At length, I said within My self, with the Lepers, If I stay here, I perish, and if I go forward I'll but perish, and so I came to The Table.'[25] She had spoken earlier in her account of having obtained a communion token, although under discipline for uncleanness. All four editors of the M'Culloch manuscripts note this, and take exception to the absence of any information about public repentance.

So impressive was this first sacramental occasion that, there and then, Dr Webster of Edinburgh moved that another similar communion should be observed very soon at Cambuslang. Whitefield readily seconded this, although such an event was altogether contrary to custom; 'a thing not practised before in Scotland', says Whitefield.[26] 'It hath not been known in Scotland that the Lord's Supper hath been given twice in a summer in any congregation before this revival', wrote James Robe.[27] M'Culloch favoured the idea, and justified the unusual

23 M'C. Mss. ii *p* 383. Duncan Alge.
24 *Ibid.* ii *p* 564.
25 *Ibid.* i *p* 68.
26 *George Whitefield Works.* i *p* 413.
27 *Christian Monthly History.* November 1743. *p* 28.

proposal by the extraordinary nature of the events of that year. 'Care was therefore taken to acquaint the several Meetings for Prayer with the Motion, who relish'd it well . . . The Session met next Lord's-Day.'[28] After considering the Scriptural injunction to celebrate the ordinance often, the great benefits that had accrued from the recent sacramental occasion, and the fact that many who had intended to participate had been hindered for various reasons, the session resolved that the sacrament should be dispensed again in the parish of Cambuslang on 15 August. Special meetings for united prayer were held at the manse and, when this place proved to be too small, in the church. Among the matters mentioned in prayer were 'the Seceders and others, who unhappily oppose the work here'.

On this second sacramental occasion, the crowds were enormous, greater than ever. 'None ever saw the like since the Revolution in Scotland, or even any where else, at any Sacrament Occasion; Some have called them fifty Thousand; some forty Thousand; the lowest estimate I hear of . . . makes them to have been upwards of thirty Thousand.'[29] In a letter to Georgia, Whitefield confirms this statement. It is easier to grasp the significance of this when one recalls that the total population of Glasgow in 1740 was estimated by the magistrates to be only 17,034.[30] The size of the crowds may be gathered from the details of the collections, as noted in the Session records, in Scots money. A normal Sabbath day offering ranged between £3 and £12; the first communion Sabbath brought in £117 12s and the second £194 2s. The money collected from February–December 1741 was £146 13 9d; for the same period in 1742 it was £1,445 17 9d.

From near and far, the people flocked to Cambuslang; there were two hundred from Edinburgh and the same number from Kilmarnock. They must have walked, for there was only one stagecoach weekly between Glasgow and Edinburgh at this time. A hundred came from Irvine and the same number from

28 *Glasgow Weekly History.* No 39 *pp* 1–2.
29 *Ibid.*
30 Pagan, J.: *History of Glasgow. p* 101.

Stewarton; strangers were also present from England and Ireland. M'Culloch lists the names of the ministers who assisted. In addition to Whitefield, there was 'Mr Webster from Edinburgh, Mr M'Laurin and Mr Gillies from Glasgow, Mr Robe from Kilsyth, Mr Currie from Kinglassie, Mr M'Kneight from Irvin, Mr Bonnar from Torphichen, Mr Hamilton from Douglas, and three of the Neighbouring Ministers, *viz* Mr Henderson from Blantyre, Mr Maxwell from Rutherglen, and Mr Adam from Cathcart'.[31] There were also present 'Several Persons of considerable Rank and Distinction who were Elders' and who assisted in serving the tables, including 'the Honourable Mr Charles Erskine, Advocate, Bruce of Kennet, Esqu; Gillen of Wallhouse, Esqu; Mr Warner of Ardeer, and Mr Wardrope Surgeon in Edinburgh'.

The number of communicants was about three thousand, and this is no haphazard guess, for a man sat near to the table with a pen in his hand and carefully marked each table – and again there were many who could not get tokens. M'Culloch estimated these at about a thousand more. Margaret Borland of Bothwell would have given much for a token, and was uneasy until someone beside her 'bade me sit down and settle myself; God would accept of the will for the Deed'.[32] Jean Hay of Lesmahagow could get no token and 'beg'd the Lord that He might make up that loss another way'.[33] Elizabeth Dykes of Carmyle, having no token, sat on the brae and 'thought if I had wings, I would have flown over the heads of the People to have got to the Table'.[34] Worship began at 8.30 on the Sunday morning and the last table was being served at sunset, 'the Precentor having so much Daylight as to let him see to read four lines of a Psalm'.[35] About 10 pm Whitefield exhorted in the churchyard, but without any particular text. When he had been serving the tables it had been noticed that he appeared to be almost carried away in an ecstasy.

31 *Glasgow Weekly History.* No 39 *p* 3.
32 McC. Mss. ii *p* 542.
33 *Ibid.* i *p* 267.
34 *Ibid.* i *p* 212.
35 *Glasgow Weekly History.* No 39 *pp* 5–8.

Services were held again on Monday, large crowds still attending, and more than twenty-four ministers and preachers were present. One of them is specially mentioned by Whitefield – 'good old Mr Bonner'.[36] John Bonar (1671–1747) was noted for piety. He was one of the 'Twelve Apostles' who presented the petition to the General Assembly of 1721 defending the *Marrow of Modern Divinity*. He was minister at Torpichen for over fifty years, and was the ancestor of one of the most distinguished evangelical families of the nineteenth century, Horatius, John and Andrew all being direct descendants. In 1740 he had written a short letter 'On the Duty and Advantages of Religious Societies' for a small group in Edinburgh, warmly encouraging union among Christians. It is not surprising to find him in close contact with M'Culloch soon after the awakening began at Cambuslang. On 16 March 1742, Bonar wrote to him, declaring that he had known 'for some weeks the refreshing news ... We heartily pray for a continuance of it with you, and that we and many others may be partakers of it in a large measure ... Pray let me hear if it be true that there are so many converts among you ... that I may be more enabled to rejoice with you, and to pray for you.'[37] Writing again in the same month, he expresses the hope that the converts would so live that no ill-wishers could speak evil of the work and adds, 'I would gladly have visited you, and preached with you, but am neither able to ride nor walk; it is a burden to me to go to church on the Lord's-day'.[38]

The stirring news of the first communion season at Cambuslang must have given the venerable minister a new lease of life, for M'Culloch writes that 'old Mr Bonner, tho' so frail that he took three Days to ride 18 miles from Torphichen to Cambuslang, yet his Heart was so set upon coming here, that he could by no Means stay away, and when he was help'd up to the Tent, preach'd three Times with great Life; and return'd with much Satisfaction and Joy'.[39] Standing on the stairhead at the

36 Gillies, J.: *Life of Whitefield. p* 124.
37 *Edinburgh Christian Instructor.* August 1838. *p* 362.
38 *Ibid.*   39 *Glasgow Weekly History.* No 39 *p* 3.

manse when he was about to leave Cambuslang, he said his goodbye in the very Nunc Dimittis of another aged priest, Simeon.[40]

This second communion at Cambuslang represented the high-water mark of the revival. Of these unforgettable days, Whitefield wrote: 'Such a passover has not been heard of.' He had spent his days among revivals, yet he testified that this was the greatest he had ever witnessed – 'Our Saviour loves to let us see yet greater things'.[41] M'Culloch closed his account of the day: 'May our exalted Redeemer still go on from Conquering to Conquer, 'till the whole Earth be filled with his Glory.'[42]

The youthful John Erskine, later to become the famous minister of the Old Greyfriars Church, Edinburgh, and leader of the evangelical party, was so impressed by what he saw and heard at Cambuslang that in the autumn of that same year he published a pamphlet of thirty-six pages, entitled *Signs of the Times Considered, or the high PROBABILITY that the present APPEARANCES in New England, and the West of Scotland, are a PRELUDE of the Glorious Things promised to the CHURCH in the latter Ages*.[43] In the Preface, dated 28 October 1742, he avows it to be his aim to show that the 'work now carrying on at Cambuslang' is but a prelude of greater things to come. Whilst denying any knowledge of the exact times and seasons for the fulfilment of the Scriptural prophecies, he argues that certain signs contained therein are being seen on every hand. He concludes one of his major sections by a fervent prayer, prophetic of his own future concern to forward the cause of overseas missions. 'It is to be hoped that this Work will not only go through our Land in the Length of it and the Breadth of it,

40 *Kilsyth Narrative pp.* 297–8; *Glasgow Weekly History.* No 39 *p* 6.
41 *George Whitefield Works.* i *pp* 428–9.
42 *Glasgow Weekly History.* No 39 *pp* 6–7.
43 Erskine, J.: *Signs of the Time considered p* 18. Another effect of Cambuslang upon Erskine was probably the arousing of his concern to promote more frequent communion services. In 1749 he published a pamphlet, *A Humble Attempt to promote frequent Communicating*, suggesting four times a year (*vide Life* by Moncrieff – Wellwood *pp* 147–57). But he also suggested fewer sermons at each occasion and that all the churches in a presbytery should have the communion on the same day – a highly unpopular suggestion.

but spread from Kingdom to Kingdom, till all the Kingdoms of the Earth shall become the Kingdom of God and of His Christ.'

It is now time to consider the progress of the revival throughout Scotland and beyond the seas, watching the ever-widening circles which spread out from the awakening at Cambuslang.

8

Kilsyth – and Beyond

Reports of the awakening at Cambuslang spread rapidly through the country, and, for a variety of motives, crowds flocked from all quarters to that parish. On 9 March 1742, within three weeks of that memorable outbreak, Colonel James Gardiner, an outstanding Christian soldier, wrote to the Rev John M'Laurin, minister of the Ramshorn or North West Parish Church, Glasgow, requesting him 'to let me know what truth there is in this wonderful account we have had . . . in the conversion of so many in the parish of Cambuslang . . . I am very willing to believe the truth of it . . . But I should be glad to have it confirmed by so good a hand as yours.'[1] On 17 March Alex Gillon of Wallhouse wrote to M'Culloch, asking for definite news 'which cannot be had with equal certainty from any other'. His letter closed with the hope that 'our gracious God . . . may not confine his mercy to your corner only; but graciously visit this, and every corner of the land with a like plentiful effusion of his spirit'.[2]

John Hamilton, minister of the Barony, Glasgow, wrote to the Rev T. Prince of Boston, New England, on 13 September 1742, about the unusual nature of the scenes accompanying the revival at Cambuslang – bodily agonies, faintings and outcries. 'This made the Report of it spread like a Fire . . . in less than two Months after the Commencement of it, there were few Parishes within twelve Miles of Cambuslang, but had some more or fewer awakned there . . . and many at a much greater

1 *Edin. Christian Instructor.* 1839. *p* 336.
2 *Ibid.* 1838. *p* 219.

Distance . . . The same Work is spreading . . . particularly at Calder, Kilsyth and Cumbernauld, all to the North and North-east of Glasgow . . . Since the middle of February . . . there are upwards of two Thousand Persons awakened.'[3]

Many places are known to have been affected, in greater or lesser degree, by the revival at Cambuslang; Irvine, Stewarton and Kilmarnock in Ayrshire; Bothwell, Blantyre and East Kilbride, each adjacent to Cambuslang; Glasgow and the nearby parishes of Cadder, Baldernock, Kirkintilloch and Campsie. With the extension of the revival, however, certain other places acquired more than ordinary significance. If Cambuslang was the focus of the movement, it is equally true that these places became the loci of analogous developments.

On 9 August 1743, M'Laurin also wrote to New England: 'the Corners where the Revival has appeared most remarkably are (1) Cambuslang . . . (2) Kilsyth . . . (3) St Ninians and Gargunnock . . . (4) Muthil . . . (5) Torryburn and Carnock . . . also a Corner about 100 Miles North from Aberdeen'.[4] We shall seek to examine these developments as they centred in Kilsyth, Muthil and Nigg, before glancing overseas.

Kilsyth is situated about nine miles from Glasgow, and was on 21 June 1603 the birthplace of 'that burning and shining light, worthy and warm Mr Livingstone, who used to preach as within the sight of Christ',[5] and who was so intimately associated with the revival at the Kirk o' Shotts in 1630. It was at Kilsyth too that Montrose, on 15 August 1645, inflicted the heaviest defeat ever sustained by the Covenanters. That summer afternoon the claymore, the dirk, the clubbed musket and the Lochaber axe wrought fearful destruction; the sturdy Highlanders, clad only in their shirts, and therefore fleet of foot, left 6,000 dead on the field of battle. The parish historian, Anton, pertinently comments concerning the revival of 1742: 'The parish of Kilsyth, being of all the parishes in Scotland the most heavily drenched with Covenanting blood, there is a

3 Prince, T.: *Christian History.* 1743. *pp* 77–8.
4 *Ibid.* 1744. *pp* 353–4.
5 Anton, P.: *Kilsyth – A Parish History. pp* 106, 122.

certain spiritual propriety that it should also have been the scene of the richest outpouring of the heavenly Grace.'[6]

James Robe became the parish minister there in April 1713, and continued in that charge until his death at the age of sixty-five, in May 1753. We are very fortunate in the source-material available for studying the revival that broke out within his parish when he was a mature and experienced minister, fifty-four years of age. Scholarly, industrious and methodical, he was impressed by the necessity for publishing the fullest possible account of events in his parish and throughout the land. His compilation, *A Faithful NARRATIVE of the Extraordinary Work of the SPIRIT OF GOD at Kilsyth and other Congregations in the Neighbourhood,* published at Glasgow in July 1742, is an amazing quarry of facts about these days. In the Preface, he stated that his intention was to awaken praise in the godly, to allay prejudice and fears in others, and that posterity should also reap some benefit. He was concerned primarily with fact and a strict regard for truth and exactness. 'A polished Stile is not to be expected from one, who must redeem time from Eating and Sleeping to carry it on. To write intelligibly is all I aim at.'[7]

In addition to this ample, printed, contemporary evidence, there are the session records covering the whole of his incumbency. Beneath his name on the opening page is the appropriate motto:

> . . . *Et ordinem*
> *Rectum evaganti. Fraena licentiae*
> *Injecit emovitque culpas.*
> Horace Liber 4, Ode 15

Here is set down for us the fluctuating religious history of his parish of 'above eleven hundred examinable Persons'. At first they appeared to benefit from his ministry. We have already noted the session proposal to set up societies for prayer in

6 *Vide* comment by Livingstone's contemporary Robert McWardin 1677. (Stevens, *A History of the Scots Kirk in Rotterdam p* 53.)
7 *Preface. pp* xxii, xxiii.

1721. On 14 June 1722, agreement was reached whereby 'the Isle Loft should be built and seats therein',[8] to meet the demand for increased accommodation.

But there were more melancholy factors present also. In the summer of 1723 an overture was brought by the minister to the session 'against consulting the Devil's servants, or Instruments, anent stollen goods, fortunes, health or recovery from sickness' and it was agreed that a congregational rebuke should follow such misdemeanours.[9] This arose out of the disclosure that Margaret Grahame, relative to one of the session, Robert Grahame, had consulted 'the Dumbie . . . at the wood', giving to this speechless man twelve pennies to gain information about 'who stole her cloaths'.

The session frequently met three times a week, for there was much to do. Again and again James Ronald, the local butcher, had to appear and be rebuked for profanity, selling drink on the Sabbath, 'lying Drunk like a Dead man upon the street' – obviously a man of incorrigible character.[10] There were violent men like 'James Livingstone in Brea' who, after pleading guilty to cursing and blasphemy, was rebuked and 'fell into a great Rage and Passion . . . stamped with his feet, and shook and wagged his staff in the face of the Session'.[11] Likewise, Alexander Forrester, an elder, and later baillie-depute of the town, in an argument about land ownership, called John Hamilton 'a Damn'd Eternal Lyar a Villain and a Rascall . . . in the presence of the magistrate of the place, in the face of the sun, in the publick street'.[12] There was also the ever-recurring problem of fornication, when the 'medwife Janet Bankier', with a panel of three women, examined cases of suspected pregnancy under the surveillance of the session. Often their negative reports were contradicted by the arrival of babies some months afterwards.[13] Pestilence brought at least sixty burials within

8 Kilsyth K.S.R.
9 *Ibid.* 30 June 1723.
10 *Ibid.* 28 February 1734, 18 January, 20 September, 10 October, 1736 *et al.*
11 *Ibid.* 19 May 1734.
12 *Ibid.* 12 December 1735.
13 *Ibid.* 3 September, 5 November, 1738. (Case of Eliz. Rennie.)

three weeks in January 1733, including 'the most religious and judicious Christians';[14] during this period Robe visited his people every day from morning till night. In June of that year a dreadful storm of hail and rain wrought extensive havoc, 'as no Man living had ever seen'.[15] The societies for prayer dwindled away, and the unhappy divisions connected with the Secession of 1733 aroused a spirit of contention on every hand. We have already seen the effects of the famine of 1740.

In this same year, 1740, Robe began to preach a course of sermons upon the doctrine of regeneration, just as M'Culloch was to do a little later. Robe gives a complete outline of his scheme,[16] and wistfully remarks that his hearers listened attentively and approved, but no visible change was to be seen in their behaviour. Then, early in 1742, came the amazing news from Cambuslang; Robe found fresh cause for hope and tried to interest his congregation but, in spite of all his efforts, 'few of the People under my Charge went to Cambuslang'.[17] One encouraging result emerged; the societies for prayer, long abandoned, began afresh.

On Thursday, 15 April, John Willison of Dundee wrote from Glasgow to M'Culloch, with whom he had been staying for a few days, expressing his satisfaction with what he had observed at Cambuslang. He ended by regretting that he could not stay to give any further help 'but my Business and Circumstances oblige me to return homewards'.[18] That same evening he arrived at Kilsyth, and Robe prevailed upon him to preach the following morning when 'a great Multitude of People met tho' the warning was very short'.[19] Many were to date their first real concern about spiritual things from that sermon.

Robe frequently went across to Cambuslang to help in the work, and riding home from that place on the morning of Friday, 14 May, he was constrained to travel by a little-known

14 *Kilsyth Narrative.* p 66.
15 *Ibid.* p 67.
16 *Ibid.* p 68.
17 *Ibid.* p 70.
18 *Ibid.* p 11.
19 *Ibid.* p 70.

but nearer path. Calling at a friend's home, he found several servants in distress, twelve in all, and talked and prayed with them. His friend said that it was providential; he 'must needs go through Samaria'. The following Sunday, 16 May, he preached with unusual power; many, including 'some strong and stout men', cried out in distress. These troubled people were sent along to Robe's barn, which proved to be too small to hold them, and so they came back to the church. Psalms were appointed to be sung, and two or three elders were instructed to pray with the distressed, but were forbidden to exhort or speak in the congregation. Robe decided to interview the troubled, as he reports, 'in my Closet one by one', and sent for Mr John Oughterson, minister at the neighbouring parish of Cumbernauld, to come and help. Altogether the ministers spoke to about thirty people, twenty of them belonging to Kilsyth.

The following Wednesday, 19 May, there was the first preaching on a week-night, the Rev John M'Laurin having come at Robe's special request to undertake this. By July, Robe estimated that about 200 of his parishioners had been awakened. From Kilsyth, the revival spread to Kirkintilloch, Gargunnock and especially to St Ninians; and the track between Kilsyth and Cambuslang was well worn by the comings and goings throughout the summer months.

The revival at Kilsyth came later than that at Cambuslang, and Robe was well aware of the objections noised abroad by opponents of the whole movement. The loud cries and bodily distresses to him 'appeared unpleasant, yea even shocking',[20] and he planned to have anyone who so behaved removed from his audiences to a place made ready for them. Elders were detailed to carry them off, but experience taught him that more disturbance was made by removing them than by letting them stay. Also their example of acute distress was a pointed reminder to others as yet undisturbed.

At first Robe intended to have preaching only on Wednesdays, so that daily work might not be hindered, but eventually

20 *Ibid. p* 85.

they had to 'embrace every opportunity of stranger ministers coming to the place to give Sermon to the People'. He worked on the principle suggested by one of his friends: '*While the Wind blows fair croud on all the Sail you can.*'[21] His own people 'needed rather a Bridle than a Spur in hearing', and so the mid-week services were held usually in the evening when toil was over. On Tuesday, 15 June, Whitefield wrote that he had preached twice at Kilsyth 'to ten thousand; but such a commotion, I believe, you never saw. O what agonies and cries were there!'[22] It ought to be noticed that, as at Cambuslang, so at Kilsyth, the revival had been in progress before Whitefield came. Before he even arrived in Scotland, the penitents at Kilsyth numbered nearly a hundred.[23]

The session set apart Wednesday, 30 June, for 'solemn Publick Thanksgiving . . . for the Extraordinary out-pouring of the Spirit of God, upon this and other Congregations in the Neighbourhood'.[24] The fields were indeed white unto harvest and Robe heard, as he said, the Lord of the Harvest commanding him to put in his sickle and reap. He appointed each week-day except Wednesday and Saturday for the awakened to come to see him; 'I looked upon my Pulpit-work, tho' great, as but a small part of my Task'[25] and, although he begrudged giving up his Saturdays, the anxious were not sent away if they came then. Ministerial friends assisted in the work, and 'of all others, the Rev Mr Thomas Gillespie, Minister of the Gospel at Carnock, was most remarkably God's send to me'. Both were kept busy from morning to night. Some well-wishers cautioned the over-worked minister to slacken his hand and take care of his health but, believing that God had promised needful strength for the doing of His work, Robe 'resolved not to spare myself. It became soon the pleasantest Work ever I was engaged in . . . Tho' I was wearied when I went to bed . . . I was fresh by the Morning.' After four months of incessant labour, he grate-

21 *Ibid. p* 93.
22 Tyerman, L.: *Life of Whitefield.* ii *p* 5.
23 *Ibid.* ii *p* 3.
24 Kilsyth K.S.R. 27 June 1742.
25 *Kilsyth Narrative. p* 95.

fully rejoiced that his bodily ills were in no wise increased.[26]

Embodied within Robe's *Narrative* are the individual accounts of many who were awakened and converted at Kilsyth. These follow much the same pattern as those preserved by M'Culloch.

The sacrament of the Lord's Supper was observed at Kilsyth on 11 July, the same day as the first communion at Cambuslang; there is no record of anything unusual at this time. Robe attended the memorable second communion at Cambuslang on 15 August; M'Culloch suggested to him privately that something similar might be a good thing at Kilsyth. Robe demurred: he had 'never thought of it', and he 'had a rooted Aversion at any thing that looked like affecting Popularity'.[27] To celebrate the sacrament twice within three months would leave him open to misunderstanding, and so he was unwilling to acquiesce in M'Culloch's proposal. One of Robe's elders, whom he greatly respected, brought forward the same proposal in a private conversation with him, and the matter was then discussed at the session meeting and passed on to 'several Societies for Prayer, to seek Light and Direction'. On 2 September 'the Session, at the General desire of the Parish unanimously agreed, that the Sacrament of the Lord's Supper be given a second time in this place, the first Sabbath of October, and for several weighty Reasons – particularly the Extraordinary out-pouring of the Holy Spirit upon Numbers here'.[28]

Although autumn, with its shortening days, had arrived, many of the services were held in the open fields; several ministers came to help, including M'Laurin of Glasgow, Gillespie of Carnock and M'Culloch of Cambuslang. On Sunday, 3 October, great crowds gathered including 'many Strangers from a great Distance'.[29] Public worship began at 8.30 in the morning and continued without a break for twelve hours. There were twenty-two services and about 1,500 communicants. Robe's account of this second sacramental season

26 *Ibid. p* 98.   27 *Ibid. p* 141.
28 Kilsyth K.S.R.
29 *Kilsyth Narrative. p* 144.

is completely unadorned; reading it, one would hardly antici-
pate the enthusiastic testimony of Whitefield on 6 October:
'The work in the west still goes on and increases. Last sabbath-
day, and Monday, very great things, greater than ever, were
seen at Kilsyth. There is a great awakening also at Muthel
...'[30] Five days later: 'The work is still increasing in Scotland,
especially in Kilsyth. Surely we shall see great things ere long.
Dear friend, my soul is on fire.'[31] A countryman, living about
fourteen miles from Kilsyth, wrote to Robe about this memorable week-end: 'O Lord, never let my Soul forget, what I did
see at *Kilsyth* and *Cambuslang* . . . on *Saturday's* night before the
Sacrament, I did not go to seek Lodging with the rest of our
Town's People that were there: . . . I went to the Braehead
Eastward, and looked around: The Candles were burning in
every Place; that blessed Echo of Prayers, and sweet singing of
Songs, made me almost faint for Joy.'[32]

Beyond Kilsyth, the revival made its way. On 14 June 1742,
Willison wrote from Dundee to Robe, rejoicing that the work
had spread so many miles on this side of Glasgow to Kilsyth.
Wistfully, he speaks of the need of his own locality. 'Ah! our
ground is very dry, but blessed be God, the Shower seems to
point Northward.' He pays tribute to the good work done by
M'Culloch's paper, the *Weekly History*, read by many people
throughout the land.[33]

In southern Perthshire, another awakening found its centre
at Muthil, four miles north-west of Auchterarder. William
Halley was called to this charge on 4 August 1704 by the
Presbytery, *jure devoluto*; he had to be ordained in the churchyard because the parishioners, devoted to episcopacy, resisted
with swords and staves and stoned the presbytery. After seven
months, he managed to gain the use of the church.[34] It is said
that he was chosen to be minister as much for his physical
strength as for his spiritual graces.[35] This was not a very

30 *George Whitefield Works.* i *pp* 446–7.
31 *Ibid.* i *p* 449.
32 *Kilsyth Narrative. p* 193.
33 *Ibid. pp* 199.   34 *Fasti.* iv *p* 285.
35 Cunningham, J.: *History of the Church of Scotland.* ii *p* 312.

promising start, but he eventually secured the affections of his people; he had been minister for thirty-eight years, and was sixty-five years of age when the Cambuslang revival began. In several letters to Robe and others, Halley gives an account of the awakening in his own parish; he was 'averse from publishing any Thing about it, fearing it might savour too much of Ostentation and Vain-glory', but he did so rather than 'run into another Extreme, viz. smothering the Redeemer's Glory'.[36]

Writing on 28 September 1742, he testified that 'for about a Year hence, there has been an unusual Stirring . . . through this Congregation'.[37] The first Sabbath of January 1742 – just about the same time that matters were coming to a head at Cambuslang – was a stormy day. Expecting a small congregation, Halley abandoned his prepared discourse and changed his text. He found so much freedom in his preaching that day that he continued with his substituted theme. Deep concern was created and contact was made with the awakening at Kilsyth. On 5 July 1742, Robe wrote to M'Laurin: 'I had with me on Saturday an honest man from Muthil . . . who informs me that there have been, since March, fifty awakened in that parish'.[38] Expectation mounted until the third Sabbath of July, the Sunday following the first communions at Cambuslang and Kilsyth, when the Lord's Supper was dispensed at Muthil. Says the minister: 'God was in the Place . . . Many were brought to the Conqueror's Feet.'[39]

From this time onward, 'unusual power hath attended the Word preached every Sabbath-day since'. The evening services were especially successful and, immediately after these were over, 'such crouds of People come to the *Manse*, as fill the House and the Closs before the Doors', overwhelming the minister's voice by their cries. For hours afterwards, Halley was occupied in dealing with them. Formerly there were only

36 Letter from 'the Rev Mr Haly to the Gentlemen at Edinburgh, as transmitted hither in the last Ship from SCOTLAND.' Prince, T.: *Christian History*. 1744. *pp* 183–4.
37 *Kilsyth Narrative. p* 146.
38 Gillies, J.: *Historical Collections.* ii *p* 364.
39 Prince, T.: *Christian History*. 1744. *pp* 183–4.

two praying societies in the parish; within a year there were eighteen, many flocking in to them.[40] About twenty-seven members of Halley's parish travelled down to the second communion at Kilsyth in 1743, walking the distance of almost thirty miles. On the way back, they were overtaken by Mr Porteous, minister at Monivaird near Muthil, Mrs Erskine and Mr David Erskine (son of Ebenezer), who were able to help them with spiritual counsel. By this time the Sabbath evening fellowship could not be contained in the manse, for almost the whole congregation stayed behind. Says their minister, 'Many of them not regarding the Difficulty of travailing [sic] through a long dark Moor, under Night'.[41]

News of these astonishing events at Cambuslang, Kilsyth and Muthil travelled still further north, and there were some who came to see for themselves. Amongst these was Dougald Buchanan (1716–68), the greatest of all the Gaelic religious poets.[42] Distressed about his spiritual condition, in 1741 he came to believe that his 'sins were pardonable'. He went along to the sacrament of the Lord's Supper at Muthil in July 1742, where Mr Halley 'was wonderfully helped to speak home to the hearts of the hearers, speaking on flight into the City of Refuge'. 'Hearing a great noise about the work of God at Cambuslang',[43] Buchanan journeyed there and 'was greatly comforted to hear the people speaking of their experience to one another. On the Sabbath there was a great multitude gathered together. Such a sight I never saw before'. A little later he went to Kilsyth, hoping 'that the Lord would knock off my fetters . . . and came away rejoicing'.[44] Dougald Buchanan later became one of the schoolmaster-evangelists employed by the S.S.P.C.K., and was settled in 1755 at Rannoch, where he laboured with eminent success until his death in 1768. John

40 *Kilsyth Narrative.* p 148.
41 *Ibid.* p 150.
42 *Vide* MacInnes, Dr John: *The Evangelical Movement &c.* pp 280–3.
43 *The Diary of Dougald Buchanan* with a Memoir (Edinburgh 1836). pp 96–7, 100. See also Sinclair, A.: *Reminiscences of the Life & Labours of Dougald Buchanan with his Spiritual Songs.*
44 *Diary of Dougald Buchanan.* pp 102, 117–9.

Porteous[45] (1704–75), 'a preacher of great eloquence . . . and a man of deep piety', for over forty years the well-loved minister of Kilmuir Easter, visited Kilsyth in 1742. Doubtless the journey was made by many others who have left no written record.

News of the awakening in the Lowlands would serve to add fuel to a flame already burning in the north. John Balfour, appointed to the parish of Nigg in 1729, became the acknowledged leader of the revival movement in Ross-shire and beyond. About 1739, a 'most considerable concern appeared among his people, 'though there were no unusual bodily symptoms to be seen'.[46] After five years he informed Robe that 'not one in forty, who have been awakened, have fallen off . . . or given open scandal'.

Numerous societies for prayer were established, every member undergoing examination by the minister and some of the elders before being admitted. Almost every household practised family worship. 'The civil magistrate has had no crimes here . . . for many years'; and the kirk session had very little to do by way of discipline.[47] This revival at Nigg owed nothing to Cambuslang in its origins; it antedated it by about three years, but it did draw added strength from contact with the southern movement. M'Laurin wrote to Cooper of Boston, New England, on 9 August 1743, about some ministers from 'a Corner about 100 Miles North from Aberdeen' who attended the General Assembly in May 1743, after first visiting Muthil, Kilsyth and Cambuslang. They were surprised with what they saw of bodily agitations – something new to their experience – but were full of admiration for 'a praying Society of young Ones in the parish of Muthill' meeting two miles from the manse.[48] In 1744, Balfour wrote to Robe, commending the earnest way the converts were trying to learn to read the Scriptures and giving themselves to prayer. 'Surgunt indocti, et

45 *Fasti.* vii *p* 28. Kennedy, J.: *Days of the Fathers in Ross-shire.* pp 39–45. MacInnes, J.: *The Evangelical Movement &c. p* 156.
46 Gillies, J.: *Hist. Coll.* ii *p* 381; Robe, J.: *Monthly History.* 1744. ii *p* 41.
47 Robe, J.: *Monthly History.* 1744. ii *p* 45.
48 Prince, T.: *Christian History.* 1744. *p* 355.

Coelum rapiunt. The men of letters dispute Heaven, these live it . . . I beg the help of your prayers still.'[49]

Into the nearby parish of Rosskeen 'there came a surprising revival and stir among the people' about the end of October 1742.[50] Daniel Bethune, or Beton, was inducted in 1717, following an Episcopalian, and had to surmount great opposition. When he celebrated his first communion in 1721, only six or seven people attended. One of his converts, an elder, was formerly leader of the shinty players; he stopped his former companions from playing shinty on Sundays and brought them to church under threat of physical violence.[51] Good reports were soon to hand of awakenings in several other places in the Presbytery of Tain and round about; 'Rosemarky, Logie, Alness, Kilearn, Cromerty, Kirkmichael and Avon'.[52]

North of the Dornoch Firth, Golspie became another northern revival centre. In this stronghold of episcopacy (a modern historian assures us that in this district the post-1688 'pioneers of Presbytery had a stern and difficult task'),[53] John Sutherland was appointed minister of Golspie in 1731. One day he overheard the catechist and some others praying that their minister might be given the Holy Spirit. He asked to be allowed to attend the meeting and join in the prayer; this was granted and he found a new spiritual power and 'so the taught became the teacher'.[54] With mingled hopes and fears, Sutherland informed his people of the 'wonderful success of the gospel in the British Colonies of America . . . I likewise communicated to them the displays of divine mercy as known at Kilsyth, Cambuslang and other places'. Returning from the General Assembly of May 1743, he tried, unsuccessfully, to stir up his people by first-hand

49 Robe, J.: *Monthly History.* 1744. vi *p* 39.
50 *Ibid.* vi *p* 45.
51 MacInnes, J.: *ut supra.* *p* 44.
52 Robe, J.: *Monthly History.* vi *p* 47. Alex Ross of Cromarty became a merchant in London. In a letter to M'Culloch (20 July 1758) he begins: 'It is some years since I had the pleasure of being in your house . . . is there any motion now among the dry bones? . . . Is honest Ingram still in the land of the living?'
53 MacInnes, J.: *ut supra.* *p* 39.
54 Robe, J.: *Monthly History.* 1745.

reports about Cambuslang, Kilsyth and Muthil, which he had visited.

Bewailing to Balfour his lack of success, whilst assisting at the sacrament at Nigg in August 1743, he was told that societies for prayer lay behind any good achieved at Nigg. He then set up three distinct societies in Golspie, which met each Saturday evening. After a year of earnest intercession, 'upwards of seventy persons' had been awakened and consulted the minister. Dr John MacInnes, in his recent admirable study of evangelical developments in the Highlands during this period, points out that Ross-shire was the 'scene of the dourest and most bitter episode in the Post-Revolution struggle of Episcopacy and Presbytery'. He makes clear that the revivals associated with Nigg, Golspie and the surrounding districts were of pre-eminent importance in capturing the whole of the Northern Highlands for evangelical religion, establishing Ross-shire as the home of the 'Fathers', the Holy Land of Highland Evangelicalism.[55]

M'Culloch and Robe were indefatigable correspondents, writing to many parts of Scotland, throughout the British Isles and overseas. On 19 June 1742, a minister in Dublin acknowledged M'Culloch's letter to him containing news of Cambuslang. On 26 October of the same year, a dissenting minister in Wales sent news about the state of religion in that country to the minister of Cambuslang.[56] A very voluminous correspondence was kept up with ministers in New England. Alexander Webster's pamphlet *Divine Influence &c* was sent to the Moravian leader, Jacob Hutton, in London, who forwarded it to Augustus Spangenberg in Yorkshire. Spangenberg, in turn, wrote to M'Culloch in Latin, and this letter, along with an English translation, was published. Spangenberg gave cautious approval, adding that 'we always rejoice with Trembling' and advising humility upon those who had been used in the work of revival.[57]

55 MacInnes, J.: *ut supra. p* 28.
56 *Glasgow Weekly History.* No 30 *p* 3, No 48 *pp* 1–8.
57 *Ibid.* No 47 *pp* 5–7.

There was a close connection, both economic and religious, between the eastern seaboard of Scotland and Holland; it was intimate and of long standing, for the Scots were the first foreigners to settle in the enterprising city of Rotterdam – the Cunninghams having emigrated from their native Dumfries to settle at Veere. They took a keen interest in the welfare of the Scottish Church there and, in 1643, a 'church for the Scottish nation' was established at Rotterdam, through the friendly help of the Presbytery of Edinburgh.[58] In the troubled days of seventeenth-century Scotland, Holland became a haven for persecuted ministers and laymen. William Carstares, later Principal of the University of Edinburgh, was the confidant of William of Orange; John Livingstone, of Kirk o' Shotts revival fame, died at Rotterdam in 1672.[59] Robert Fleming, torn from his flock at Cambuslang, became minister of the Scots Church at Rotterdam in 1677. Prominent laymen also sought asylum in Holland, and amongst them was Colonel John Erskine of Carnock, grandfather of John, the leader of the evangelicals in the latter part of the eighteenth century.[60] Writing to Robert Wodrow on 4 February 1728, Colonel Erskine sent some information which he had requested about church government in Holland. He noted that 'What looks likest Erastianism in ye church of Holland is the power ye Magistracy of a town has to reject the election of a Minr made by the Consistory . . . before he's called, the burgomasters must be acquainted . . . If they regret the choice, the Consistory must proceed to a new one.'

Less than ten years later, such a problem vexed the Scots Kirk at Rotterdam. During a space of fifteen months, three elections were made from short leets that included Henry Lindsay of Bothkennar, Thomas Mair of Orwell, Robert Riccaltoun of Hobkirk, John Balfour of Nigg (all outstanding evangelical ministers in Scotland), and all were rejected by the burgomasters. Finally, in April 1737, they agreed to the choice

58 Steven, W.: *History . . . Rotterdam. pp* 1, 3; *The Journal of Thomas Cunningham of Campvere 1640–54.* Preface xi.
59 Steven, W.: *History &c. pp* 53, 105.
60 *Journal of the Hon. John Erskine, &c. of Carnock.* 1683–7. (Edited W. McLeod.) *pp* 108–14, 160–201.

of Hugh Kennedy of Cavers. Steven, the historian of this Scots
Kirk, asserts that 'the dominant party in the Assembly' of the
Church of Scotland, not content with manipulation at home,
'privately exerted their influence to thwart the measures taken
by the Consistory to obtain a minister of evangelical sentiments'.[61]

Hugh Kennedy was born of Scottish parents in Northern
Ireland in 1698 and was 'one of the best pulpit-men' in Scotland. In 1742 he was invited to leave Holland and succeed
Ralph Erskine at Dunfermline, but he declined, and ended his
days in 1764 at Rotterdam. It is not surprising to learn that
news of the revivals at Cambuslang and Kilsyth reached
Holland quickly. Hugh Kennedy informed a friend in Edinburgh that he had 'got by accident a *Narrative of the Work at
Cambuslang* with the Attestation; which is printed in Dutch'.[62]
He confessed to having been deeply moved; 'it is as Life from
the Dead', and he wrote a Preface in Dutch for a new edition,
in which he pointed out that he was acquainted with the
ministers who had attested the narrative, and they were
'Worthy of all Credit'. Other friends in Scotland 'of unquestion-
able Capacity and Integrity' had also visited Cambuslang and
had written approvingly to him of what they found there.

'The Lord seems to have some great Event upon the Wheel
just now', wrote Kennedy, in prophetic mood, 'and I would
fain hope, the Glory of the latter Days is not far off. The present
Convulsions and Reelings among the Nations, as well as the
Stirring among the dry Bones in Scotland, America and other
Places, confirm me more and more in this Opinion.'[63] He ended
by earnestly requesting that all who read the *Narrative* would
pray for the success of the work in Scotland which 'is begun
and going on, and also for a notable Reviving to the Lord's
Work in these united Provinces ... that Ministers may be made
divinely Wise to win Souls to Christ'. This Preface was issued
at Rotterdam and dated 26 July 1742. The *Narrative* itself was
translated into Dutch by three members of Kennedy's session,

61 Steven, W.: *History &c. pp* 161–71.   62 *Glasgow Weekly History.* No 43 *p* 1.
63 *Ibid.* No 43 *pp* 3, 7.

and went through six editions.[64] On 22 December 1744, Robert Wightman, Dean of Guild in Edinburgh, wrote to M'Culloch, and in his letter mentioned that 'This week I had a copy of a letter sent me, which came from Rotterdam, dated the 15th of October, giving an account of a great revival of religion in the town of Tergoes in the island of Zeland . . . He says Mr Robe's *Narrative* has been of use towards it.'[65]

Within eight years of his commendatory preface, Kennedy was forwarding encouraging news to his 'Correspondents in Scotland and at London'. This was 'read publicly to a numerous Company of Christians purposely met together at one of their appointed Seasons, for learning what concerns the Success of real . . . Christianity, in any Part of our own Island, or up and down the World'.[66] Thus, 'God sheds forth his Spirit abundantly . . . from Friesland to Zealand, as hath been in Scotland and England'.

Writing from Rotterdam on 2 October 1750, Kennedy tells of an awakening at Nieuwkerk, which began under the ministry of Gerardus Kuypers in 1748. This young man had been an assistant in Amsterdam in 1744, where people cried out during his preaching. At Nieuwkerk, he began a system of weekly catechising and set apart some time 'for a sort of Fellowship Meetings', held in private houses. Kennedy comments that these were similar to private meetings of Christians held in Scotland for prayer and religious exercises.[67] At them, Kuypers questioned the members about the 'truths delivered in public'. Hundreds frequented these meetings after their daily labour was over, and on Monday, 17 November 1748, as Kuypers was catechising in church, there was a general outcry and many fell down upon the ground. The following day, from early morning until late at night, the minister and some trusted private

64 Steven, W.: *History &c. p* 199.
65 *Edinburgh Christian Instructor.* 1839. *p* 340.
66 *A Short Account of the Rise & Continuing Progress of a Remarkable Work of Grace in the United Netherlands.* In several LETTERS from the Reverend Mr Hugh Kennedy, Minister of the Gospel in the Scots Congregation in Rotterdam (Publisher's Preface).
67 *Ibid. pp* 11–12.

Christians went from house to house, giving counsel. The work increased and spread beyond all description; Kuypers could only compare it to the Day of Pentecost.[68]

Kennedy concluded his *Short Account &c.* by pointing out that spiritual awakening was 'in substance the very same Work which was some years ago carried on so remarkably in your happy Corner of the Lord's Vineyard'. On 5 January 1751, Kennedy rejoiced that the work was still spreading to Aalten, Rheed and Groningen. He was not able to finish his story because the bearer of the letter 'tells me his Ship must leave this Harbour in a little time', but he does pause to underline the fact that 'the Narratives of the great Work of God in Scotland . . . are blessed to Multitudes in these Provinces and through Germany'. It bore an exact resemblance to the work in Scotland, and the friends of the work in Holland 'tell the World so: Therefore the Opposers do their utmost to bring the Work in Scotland into discredit'.[69]

Kennedy became lyrical in his tributes to the amazing change that had come over the people affected by the revival; ignorance was being dispelled and the Scriptures studied; people 'infamous for Brutality, differing little from Hottentots', were now moral and sober; churches, recently empty, were well-attended. He was happy to say that violent bodily distresses had ceased, and then ended: 'In a word, the Subjects of this work are made another sort of People than ever they were before . . . They who don't think that the Spirit of God is truly the Cause of this happy change, ought to tell us fairly, soberly and rationally what other Cause is proportionate to such blessed Effects.'[70]

It would be too much to assert that the revival in Holland was inspired directly from Scotland, and that it would not have occurred had there been no awakening in this latter country.

68 Gillies, J.: *Hist. Coll.* Appendix, *p* 23. Letter of Kuypers to Gillies.
69 Kennedy, H.: *A Short Account &c. p* 26.
70 *Ibid. pp* 30-2. Jonathan Edwards wrote to John Erskine on 28 June 1751 about this revival in Holland and noted 'one important circumstance' not much mentioned in the Scottish Accounts *viz* that 'the STADHOLDER was pleased with the work'. (Dwight, S. E.: *Memoirs of Jonathan Edwards.* clxxii.)

But it is plain that, through Kennedy, in his influential position at Rotterdam, the work at Cambuslang and Kilsyth was made widely known in the Netherlands, and the literature that came from M'Culloch and Robe could not have failed to inspire many who were also waiting for some such outpouring in Holland. Both friends and foes of the work in Holland recognised it as being akin to that of Cambuslang in 1742; there was considerable interest taken in it by many in the west of Scotland, and those who were banded in the Concert for Prayer made mention of this revival in Holland in their intercessions.

The influence from Cambuslang spread into the four corners of Scotland, initiating, inspiring, confirming revival movements, and also made an impact upon Holland. Previously we noted how vital was the effect of the awakening in New England upon the whole movement that originated in, and associated itself with, Cambuslang. In return, Cambuslang, and all that it stood for, contributed generously to the quickening of spiritual life in New England. On 12 May 1743, Jonathan Edwards wrote to M'Culloch, telling him that 'We were informed last year by the printed and well-attested narrative, of the glorious work of God in your parish . . . especially by Mr Robe's *Narrative*, and I perceive by some papers of the *Weekly History* sent me by Mr M'Laurin of Glasgow, that the work has continued to make glorious progress . . . it is the fore-runner of something greater . . . I believe God will revive his work again before long, and that it will not wholly cease till it has subdued the whole earth.' On August 13 1743 the minister at Cambuslang replied that he had been impressed by the prophecy in Isaiah 59.19 *viz* 'So shall they fear the name of the Lord from the west &c.' and saw in this reference to occidental priority that 'the glorious revival of religion . . . should begin in the more westerly parts, and proceed to these most easterly'.[71] Notable amongst these inspirations was the concept of the Concert for Prayer, and the religious journalism of Thomas Prince of Boston, so obviously inspired by, and imitative of, M'Culloch's weekly paper.

71 Dwight, S. E.: *Memoirs &c.* cxiv, cxv.

9
Danger Points

When we examine the results which emerged from the revival days at Cambuslang, we notice that some of the by-products of the unusual events of 1742 were not altogether healthy, and these, but for the vigilance and authority of the ministerial leaders might have deteriorated into disorder and disgrace. Fortunately, a very adequate curb was put upon such aberrations, and little harm was actually done.

Critics of revivalism have frequently pointed out the close connection between spirituality and sensuality; the excited state of mind that issues from heightened religious emotions and the inevitable lack of control are presumed to throw wide open the door for sexual licence. There is, however, not the slightest evidence to support such a conclusion with regard to the movement under consideration. The facts suggest rather the opposite result. One of the favourite religious authors of the day was James Durham, who wrote a commentary on the Song of Solomon. The language of the ancient Hebrew love idyll had been given a hidden, allegorical meaning, and its *ipsissima verba* were constantly upon the lips of preachers and people as they sought to express their devotion to Christ.

Thus, one young married woman of eighteen years of age said: 'When I would sometimes have gone to bed, I thought I would have had Christ between my arms; He was a Bundle of Myrrh to me and sweet to My soul'. But this young lady was in the habit of using such language; she 'gave up whole soul and Body to Him ... my Heart was in a flame of Love to Him.'[1]

1 M'C. Mss. i *pp* 327, 335 (Catherine Cameron).

Such emotive language would find a dubious welcome today, but was the religious fashion among those who crowded to Cambuslang, and we may safely be sceptical of any extreme Freudian interpretation.

There were some attendant circumstances which might have aroused suspicion, especially the fairly common practice of both men and women spending the whole night out in the fields. References are frequent. One young girl of seventeen 'lay all night in the Church-yard by my self'. On another occasion, she, with two other young women, stayed out in the fields praying and singing psalms from ten o'clock until six o'clock in the morning. Young people of sixteen years of age kept late hours, some staying all night at the manse, others until one o'clock in the morning.[2] Here at last was abundant opportunity for ir-regularity! Yet no breath of any such scandal touched the re-vival movement to bring sorrow to its friends, or jubilation to any would-be detractors.

Only once is even the indecorous mentioned in the case-histories. One young married woman of twenty-three, overjoyed by a sense of relief after her sore distress, 'could not forbear getting up . . . and taking the minister in my arms and crying out, O my Dear Minister' and then shaking hands warmly with all the company. M'Culloch himself deleted this phrase before sending out the story for editing.[3] With this type of hostile criticism in mind, the records of the Presbytery of Hamilton for the ten years 1741–50 have been examined with care. During this period there were eighty-three cases of presbyterial discipline for sexual offences – twenty-five coming from Hamilton, six-teen from Avendale, thirteen from East Monkland, but only one case from Cambuslang – and he was the servant of M'Culloch's persistent adversary, Hamilton of Westburn!

One charge laid specifically, and with slightly more warrant, against the converts was that of 'idleness and neglect of civil affairs'. M'Culloch himself speaks of 'numbers of idle boys in *Glasgow*, apprentices and others, who . . . came often out to

2 *Ibid.* ii *pp* 474, 479 (Jean Wark).
3 *Ibid.* i *p* 100 (Mary Mitchell).

Cambuslang, . . . and they brought much reproach on the work here, by so often leaving their masters work, and strolling idly through the fields'.[4] Sir John Clerk, of Penicuik, wrote to his brother-in-law Moncrieff, one of the four Seceding Brethren of 1733, finding fault with Whitefield for inducing men to neglect their business, since they 'goe a gading after conventicles as they doe at present', estimating the loss to the nation of one day's work in the week at 'eight millions of sixpences'.[5] There were certainly some who felt that secular responsibilities, if not irrelevant, were certainly not 'the better part'. One who lost her employment made no secret of her delight, 'thinking I would have greater liberty to come to the preachings at Cambuslang'.[6] Webster deletes this passage, with the marginal comment 'as giving some Continence to the Charge against the Subjects of this work as if they were bad servants'.

Many must have been taxed by the long distances they walked to the services and the late hours at which they left Cambuslang. A boy of fifteen 'was enabled to walk home with a Comerad to My Fathers House about five Miles of way from that place, about Sun rising next morning'.[7] Another, this time a young woman, spent all night in the fields with a companion, talking and praying. Alas, the next entry says so much: 'Next day I intended to have spent all next night in prayer; But when night came I fell asleep'.[8] These people were but human after all! An aged widow of sixty-five wrote: 'For six weeks I was obliged to leave off every thing with which I us'd to win my bread, and I could not apply My self to any Worldly bussiness at all'.[9] Repeatedly the story is told of lack of sleep, loss of appetite, fasting (once for sixty hours), weakness and exhaustion. The leaders, however, were well aware that a price had to be paid for such maltreat-

4 *Kilsyth Narrative pp* 300–1.
5 Clerk of Penicuik. *Memoirs 1676–1755* (S.H.S.) *p* 248. In this same letter he says: 'I wish you would only imitate him in the main thing, to wit, in a peaceable, charitable disposition'.
6 M'C. Mss. i *p* 53 (Anne Wylie).
7 *Ibid.* i *p* 173 (Alexander Rogers).
8 *Ibid.* i *p* 182 (Jean Robe).
9 *Ibid.* i *p* 114 (Sarah Strang).

ment of the body – and that this would have to be paid in other than physical coin. One girl of eighteen went for two months with little sleep and ate very little too, 'for meat would not go down with me then . . . But hearing some people telling me, Satan would take advantage of My bodily weakness, occasioned by my Fasting, I essayed to take some.'[10]

Yet the tasks of the country-side were not seriously hindered by the revival. Dr Webster, in his book *Divine Influence the True Spring of the Extraordinary Work at Cambuslang &c*, written in 1742, set himself to answer this accusation among several others. He pointed out that persons stricken by conscience could hardly be expected to enter wholeheartedly into the business of daily life; 'we don't find Paul making Tents when lying on the Ground through the o'erwhelming Influence of the heavenly Vision'.[11] Webster affirmed that, when the violence of the convictions was over, the converts, 'went in their respective Callings with uncommon Cheerfulness and Alacrity'. Revivals are assets – not liabilities!

Meetings for prayer and fellowship had been so organized as not to interfere greatly with duty to employer and family, 'of which their present plentiful Crop is sufficient Evidence'.[12] As a Parthian shot, Webster noted that many of the critics could 'spend away whole nights' in drunkenness and sensual excesses.

On 22 June 1831, the Rev John Robertson, then minister of Cambuslang, wrote a lengthy letter to the press, in which he charged his predecessor, Dr Meek, with bias in the account he had written of the Cambuslang revival for Sir John Sinclair's *Statistical Account*. A certain John White was an aged man who remembered the revival (his wife recalled the beginning of M'Culloch's ministry); he had lived next door to Dr Meek, who had asked him many questions about parochial interests. The old man affirmed that 'Dr Meek never put to him a single question respecting the work at Cambuslang'.[13] Dr Robertson goes

10 *Ibid.* i *pp* 570–1 (Jean Dickinson).
11 Webster, A.: *Divine Influence &c. p* 25.
12 *Ibid. pp* 25–6.
13 *Edin. Christ. Instr. 1831.* Letter 'On the Work at Cambuslang'. *pp* 552–4.

on: 'When I came to the parish in 1785 . . . I found one uniform tradition prevail among the old people, who then distinctly remembered the work, *viz* that the *labour* of the parish was never in a more *forward state than in 1742;* and that the poor's roll was far from being enlarged by the events which took place in the course of that season.' This fact was to some extent explained by making up at a future day what was deducted from a day's labour earlier and, 'in harvest, the reapers would in the evening have come to church with their sickles on their shoulders'.

In his 1751 Attestation, M'Culloch revealed that the time of the Thursday evening lecture was altered at harvest and 'the reapers came running from the fields, where they had been toiling all day'.[14] We read of others sitting through the night at their tasks, stealing time from their sleep, in order to attend the meetings. Robe said of Kilsyth that the work done by the labourers in the fields and workshops was better done than before the revival.[15]

Another more dangerous tendency which aroused violent opposition and led to charges of delusion was the temptation, revealed by some of the converts, to lay stress upon visions, inward light, and the varying eccentricities which went with such claims. Such irrational behaviour was indeed a scandal in an 'Age of Reason', and there has invariably been with most people a deep-rooted 'dislike of the unlike'.

In the sphere of religion, eighteenth-century thought considered the greatest danger to be enthusiasm, a term equivalent to our modern fanaticism, perhaps even stronger. There was sufficient evidence to provide good grounds for caution about unbridled subjectivism, especially the crop of new and extravagant cults which were thrown up in England in the days of the Commonwealth. George Fox, with his doctrine of the Inner Light and his high ethical standards, had gathered around him the earnest Quakers; so many people were tired of words and wanted deeds. The stress put on inwardness led, however, to anarchy in some cases and found its ultimate expression when James Nayler

14 *Kilsyth Narrative. p* 315.
15 Anton, P.: *History of Kilsyth. p* 138.

rode into Bristol in 1656, and was hailed as the Messiah by a few excited women. Brought to trial for blasphemy, he was pilloried, whipped through the streets, branded with a 'B' on his forehead and had his tongue bored through. This was an indication of popular repugnance to such claims, and for most people it seemed but a short and easy step from Quakerism to Naylerism.

When the revival began at Cambuslang, the participants were suspected of this heresy. One visitor was astonished to hear people crying out in time of prayer and 'got up again off my knees in great fear'. The report she had heard 'that a Quaker Spirit was got in among them'[16] seemed true, but she soon altered her opinion when she saw them making so much use of their Bibles. Another, trembling and overcome with despondency, was sitting in the house when 'a Mighty and heart-overcoming power and a sweet light shining into my Mind, brighter than the sun'[17] brought peace. She stayed in this semi-conscious state for an hour, and then 'began to think that that was the way the Quakers were, and what I had met with was not from God, but That the Spirit they spake of was come upon me'. That was enough to thrust her once more into the Slough of Despond. Some time later, hearing M'Culloch preach, she surmised that someone must have told the minister about her, for he said: 'They that had got a light within them and joy, and trusted therein, more than in Christ's righteousness, were free to shake hands with the Quakers.'[18]

Often we hear of experiences of a trance-like nature. Alexander Bilsland was so preoccupied coming home from the Monday thanksgiving service that 'when I came to the Close where I live, I mistook it and went into another'.[19] Such absent-mindedness is not really very dangerous. That same day he was transported and 'thought My Soul would have taken its flight on high... and My body was almost taken off from the place where I was.'[20] This state lasted for at least two hours, and neither he nor his wife had any 'mind or need of bodily refreshments'. Towards

16 M'C. Mss. ii *p* 137 ('Sarah Gilchrist in Cardross').
17 *Ibid.* i *pp* 44–5.   18 *Ibid.* i *p* 55.
19 *Ibid.* i *p* 135.   20 *Ibid.* i *p* 136.

evening he became utterly exhausted, and recounted a vision of
dead men's bones, similar to that told by the prophet Ezekiel.
These turned into 'living Men, walking about me . . . strong
Country men with Staves in their hands, runing to Churches . . .
After which I thought there was a sweet and thick white and
soft refreshing shower, falling about me . . . Manna'. Needless to
say, all the editors who read the case-histories deleted this story.
Margaret Clark in the manse at Cambuslang 'verily thought I
saw with my bodily eyes, Christ as hanging on the Cross, and a
great Light about him in the air'.[21] It was a similar testimony to
this, given by a younger woman, that furnished the Seceders
with one of their strongest criticisms of the revival.

Mystical tendencies, with the conviction that nothing more
was needed but immediate illumination by the Holy Spirit,
were to be found among the converts. One who walked the
many miles from Shotts to Cambuslang, and found great blessing, went home rejoicing. 'I began to think with My self, This
blessed Bible that I carry with me, where everything I now see
there is so plain and sweet, will tell me all the things I need to
know: and therefore I need not care tho' I never come back to
Cambuslang again, or go to publick Ordinances elsewhere . . .
the Lord soon made me sensible of my folly.'[22] This belief that
extraordinary spiritual experiences make normal means of ac-
quiring knowledge unnecessary, a perverted interpretation of
the Johannine dictum, 'Ye have no need that any teach you',
is a constant attraction to subjects of unusual religious phenomena. Long ago Tertullian dismissed philosophical enquiry in
pungent epigram: 'What has Athens to do with Jerusalem?' His
argument was: We know: why then try to learn? We have
arrived; why talk of travelling? Throughout the centuries,
speakers in unknown tongues, dabblers in glossalalia, have been
convinced that knowledge divinely given is far better than
knowledge painfully and assiduously gained by hard endeavour.[23]

21 *Ibid.* ii *p* 450.
22 *Ibid.* ii *p* 193 (Agnes Buchanan).
23 Calamy, Dr E.: *Caveat against the New Prophets. p* 47. 'Go to argue with
them and they will stop your mouth with the plain *Revelation from Heaven*;
and they expect their Affirmation should be credited without proof.'

Some of the converts at Cambuslang were tempted to believe that a prophetic gift had been given to them. Alexander Bilsland, on the morning that news reached Glasgow of the victory over the French at Dettingen, June 1743, and before anything was known to the public, read from Psalm 18. His thoughts dwelt upon Pharaoh's drowned host. 'I immediately said to My wife, Surely the Lord had been doing some great things . . . to our Armies abroad. And within about an hour after, My wife happ'ning to open the window . . . she heard the Musick-Bells ringing . . . Within a little, a Man came and told me that . . . the Bells were ringing for that victory of Dettingen; and he did not believe it: I told him I had got notice of it another way and did believe it.'[24] Such a story would have greatly impressed many, but the editors Webster and Gillespie rejected it completely. Had the leaders in the revival not set their faces firmly against these visionary proclivities, the damage would have been irreparable. Religious opinion in Scotland was inexorably bound up with the Bible and the Psalter, the Shorter Catechism and the definitive written formulae of belief. Devotees of the mystic way, hearers of the inaudible, and those who saw great lights were regarded with suspicion. Everything had to be tested by and brought to the plain words of Holy Writ.

During the early years of the eighteenth century, another movement of similar genre to the Quakers had created considerable discussion in Scotland. The Flemish Pietist, Antoinette Bourignon (1616–80), seeking for a fuller spiritual life amid the arid wastes of superstition, formalism and dogmatism, had gained many adherents on the Continent. Her teaching crossed to Scotland and was particularly successful in the years between 1695 and 1715, when 'religion was singularly dry, harsh and pedantic'.[25] Her teaching spread around 'like a devouring fire' about 1700 and received the enthusiastic support of Dr George Garden, the close friend of Henry Scougal. In 1701, the General Assembly of the Church of Scotland took Garden to task and

24 M'C. Mss. i *pp* 130–1.
25 MacEwan, A. R.: *Antoinette Bourignon.* *p* 209.

deposed him, declaring A.B.'s (the customary designation for Antoinette Bourignon) doctrines to be 'impious, pernicious and damnable'. This did not check the movement and, in 1711, the questions addressed to ordinands for the ministry of the Church of Scotland included: 'Do you disown all Popish, Arian, Socinian, Arminian, Bourignian and other doctrines . . . ?',[26] and this continued until 1889.

As late as April 1738, Francis Hutcheson was 'surprised to find some people of very good sense, laymen more than clergy, not a little pleased with some of the notions of the foreign mystics'. Hutcheson wrote that his curiosity was roused and he intended to pursue the matter further. 'I am going to read Madame Bourignon when I have leisure.'[27]

Opponents of the revivals also sought to link them with yet another imported movement which followed closely behind that inspired by Antoinette Bourignon – the Camizards, or French Prophets. These comprised chiefly the extreme groups of the French Huguenots, who emerged in 1688, and were notorious for their convulsions, prophecies and speaking in tongues. In 1706, three or four members came to London and their number increased to about three hundred within the year, John Lacy becoming the chief English prophet. In November 1710, Wodrow notes: 'We have had the Prophets of Stirling and Glasgow . . . I have heard it remarked, that none of any sense have been gained by them, but either these that wer Bourignians or Jacobites.'[28] Five years later he says: 'The Prophets, as they call them . . . make some noise with their warnings and agitations . . . . . . at this time in Stirling and other places, as Aberdeen.'[29] Until the revival began at Cambuslang, little had been heard in Scotland of the extravagant emotionalism and physical disturbances associated with the Camizards. Then indeed, there was plenty for critics to protest

26 *Ibid. p* 16.   27 McCosh, J.: *Scottish Philosophy. p* 463.
28 *Anal.* i *p* 309.
29 *Narrative, of the Faithful Account of the* FRENCH PROPHETS *Etc.* ANTI-ENTHUSIASTICUS. *pp* i, xv. (90 *pp.*) Printed and sold by Robert Foulis at Glasgow 1742.

about, and for earnest-minded, sober people to reflect upon. Robe takes great pains to dissociate supporters of the revival movement from the charge of being crypto-Camizards.[30]

Routine in church services was frequently interrupted; everything was unpredictable. One Sabbath after noon in April, Jean Robe was on the brae at Cambuslang. She had, with difficulty, restrained herself from crying out earlier in the day, but now became 'over-charg'd with joy, that I could no longer contain; but got up on my feet and cry'd aloud, That Christ had glorify'd himself . . . in My redemption . . . and I took the Minr. and all the people witnesses to it; and holding out my Bible, I said . . . that Bible is witness sufficient'.[31] Gillespie adds: 'Tho this Passage is Good tis liable to be Abus'd', and Webster concurs: 'I aggree', and so it is marked for deletion. One young woman was 'forced to cry out, before the whole Congregation in the Colledge Church, O Praise the Lord, for I could not contain My self'.[32] Another, whilst sitting in Carmunnock Church reported 'seeing several persons who us'd to mock at the Work at Camb; and the crying out there . . . begg'd of the Lord, that if it were his holy will, I might be kept from crying out in the Congregation, and becoming an Object of derision to them or others'.[33] But this was all to no purpose, for she cried out during the sermon. Some of these outbursts, especially among the throngs at Cambuslang, can be attributed to mass influence and suggestibility, but there are instances of individuals, away from the centres of agitation, most anxious not to exhibit themselves, and yet doing what they wished to avoid.

One of the dangers inherent in this situation was that many were prone to make the unusual the criterion of their own earnestness and sincerity, with all the torment this must have involved for sensitive, introspective souls. Thomas Barclay averred: 'I never cry'd out in publick . . . but hearing so many cry out, I have suspected My exercise was not so deep as it should.'[34] Another, this time a woman, confessed that her 'Con-

30 *Kilsyth Narrative.* pp 53–5.   31 M'C. Mss. i pp 185–6.
32 *Ibid.* i p 599.   33 *Ibid.* ii p 121 (Agnes More).
34 *Ibid.* i p 353 (Thomas Barclay).

victions and sense of sin . . . were not so sudden and violent as with some others . . . and would have wish'd to have been put to a Necessity of crying as others did.'[35] Obviously the agitations became associated, among the converts, with a spiritual élite, although the unbelievers derided. M'Culloch, looking back from 1751, summed up the situation by stating that 'As to outcries, in the time of public worship, it is best to avoid extremes.'[36] On the one hand, hearers should not give vent to their feelings if they can possibly avoid doing so, for 'they mar the attention of others, and their own, to the word of God's grace'. Ministers should beware of trying to excite their listeners to such behaviour. On the other hand, those who could listen with composure should not judge harshly those who were unable to contain themselves. He pointed out that some who endeavoured to refrain from crying out in 1742 'fell a bleeding at mouth or nose . . . for a considerable time'.

These demonstrations did, however, serve some useful purpose in arousing interest and curiosity throughout the countryside, and also in impressing some with the need for serious reflection about their own condition.[37] Janet Lennox worshipped with the Seceders in Glasgow and came out to Cambuslang on a Thursday in March 1742, impelled by curiosity. She heard sermons 'both from the Tent, and at night in the Kirk, but was not touch'd with what I heard. I was however somewhat affected to hear and see severals crying out in distress in time of Sermon and after in the Manse . . . all the way almost as I went home that night to Glasgow, that word haunted my thoughts, We have seen strange things today.'[38]

Dr Meek spoke of the sermons during the revival as being addressed 'especially to the passions of fear and hope', and im-

35 *Ibid.* i *p* 539 (Janet Reston).
36 *Kilsyth Narr. p* 306.
37 'Had not our Lord come with Such mighty Signs & Wonders, not half as many had heard of Him . . . Through Report of Things happening out of the usual course (in Cambuslang) MANY flock from all Corners; they come, they see, they hear, they feel, they Rejoice.' Webster: *Divine Influence* &c. *pp* 45–6.
38 M'C. Mss. ii *p* 524.

plied that much of the distress arose from 'dread of everlasting punishment'.[39] Too much has been made of this criticism that people were frightened through lurid descriptions of hell. Not that there was no appeal to such ideas; far from it. The preachers at Cambuslang believed in a literal hell, with all its torments and, thus believing, they were too much in earnest not to warn their hearers of imminent danger. They were understood by many. A twenty-one-year-old man at Cambuslang one evening 'thought I saw hell as it were at a distance from Me, as a pit where the Wicked were frying, and the Devils going among them'.[40] This is disallowed by the editors. A boy of fifteen, before he fainted away, 'thought I saw the flames of hell coming up to Me'.[41] One young woman, with her breath almost taken away by the smell of brimstone, 'took it to be the smell of the lake of fire and brimstone in the bottomless pit'.[42]

In spite of these instances, there is abundant evidence that fear was not, for many, the strongest motive for their state of distress. Often they stated categorically that they 'had no dread of hell'; probably frequent repetition had dulled the edge of this stimulus. What melted down many was not the thought of reward or punishments, but the love of Christ. 'The awful terrors of the Law . . . had very little effect on me; but what then affected me most was the sweet and gracious offers of Christ', said one of the converts.[43] On the first Thursday in April 1742, one listener heard M'Culloch say: 'Those that loved God served him out of free choice . . . and would do so tho' there were no rewards or punishments hereafter.'[44]

For some, threatenings had the opposite effect from that desired. 'In hearing of threatenings, I always find my heart turn harder, but in hearing of the love of Christ and his Death, my heart is melted down', said one young woman;[45] and, this time

39 *Old Stat. Acc.* v *p* 273.
40 M'C. Mss. i *p* 309 (John Wier [*sic*]).
41 *Ibid.* i *p* 172.
42 *Ibid.* ii *p* 148 (Margaret Shaw).
43 *Ibid.* i *p* 139.
44 *Ibid.* ii *p* 575 (Mrs Baillie).
45 *Ibid.* ii *p* 153.

from a young man: 'When I read my Bible and meet with the Threatenings there, I am not at all moved by them: but when I meet with the Promises, I find my heart melted with love and joy'.[46]

There were many peculiar physical and mental consequences associated with some who were subjects of the work at Cambuslang, and these are easily recognisable as various manifestations of hysteria. One youth of nineteen 'lost all power of walking Myself... was not able to speak or scarce draw my breath... I stayed all night in Camb'.[47] A young woman 'fell into such a sweat, that one might have wrung my gown... as if it had been drawn thro' the water'.[48] Margaret Clark, forty-two years of age, declared: 'I have born several children', but her pains under spiritual convictions were equally severe, ' . . . if I had not got my Cloaths loosd when I found my Side rising, I had been in hazard of my life . . . all sore and pain'd as if bruised by beating'.[49]

Some of these physical results associated with the revival must have created social problems within the home. One wonders what were the repercussions of such an experience as that told by Janet Barry, the wife of a carter in Rutherglen. After family prayers, she 'was made to roar out twice in hideous and terrible manner . . . not like a human voice'. Her frightened husband ran out to bring the neighbours who had to hold her, for she 'was all like to shake to pieces with trembling'. She goes on to speak of a terrible thirst that 'made me drink water much and oft' and of a deep loathing for her own body and she 'could not endure that My Husband should come near me'. Often she detected a smell 'like the Stinking Smell of hair when it is burning, which I took to be the Smell of the bottomless Pit'.[50] As we might expect, there were the feeble and unbalanced of mind, who found much in the excitement to fire their fancies. Some sat in the house, hearing voices although no one could be

46 *Ibid.* ii *p* 164.
47 *Ibid.* i *p* 189 (Robert Shearer).
48 *Ibid.* ii *p* 18 (Margaret Boyle).
49 *Ibid.* ii *p* 453.
50 *Ibid.* ii *pp* 91, 94.

seen, or hearing bells ringing and drums beating. The devil was never far away. One morning, before the break of day, Jean Hay 'saw something like a Brown Cow with a White Face,... it look'd in at Me,' and she had no doubt that it was the devil.[51] Another, under terror, saw Satan 'whom I tho't I saw at the side of the bed as a rough tautie dog'.[52] A neighbour who was called in told her that the night was ordained for sleep. What must he have thought of the revival which produced such fantasies?

Amid so much that was curious, it is little wonder that one of the ministers in Lanarkshire, Mr Lining, told one of the converts, 'If this be the way of the working of the Spirit of the Lord, it is Strange'.[53] The peculiar aberrations that were associated with the Cambuslang work did leave a legacy of unbalanced extravagance to bedevil the future, although these can be more readily understood in the light of modern psychological insights.

Surely it is not without relevance that most of the leaders, and many of the strange participants, in the Buchanite delusion of 1784, should have come from some of the revival centres of 1742. This was when a company of men and women forsook homes and occupations to follow Elspeth Buchan, this female Moses – this 'woman clothed with the Sun' – into another Promised Land. The processions started from Irvine, and consisted mainly of members of the congregation of the Rev Hugh White, who was a native of St Ninians in Stirlingshire. Several who joined this fantastic experiment in communism came from Muthil, including the last surviving member of the sect, Andrew Innes.[54] Irvine, St Ninians and Muthil – places strongly influenced by the revival of 1742! John Barclay, the founder of the Berean Church, was born in Muthil in 1734 and spent his early impressionable years in the unusual atmosphere of the revival in that place.[55] Andrew Moir, who became Seceding

51 *Ibid.* i *p* 256.
52 *Ibid.* i *p* 522 (Isobel Matthie).   53 *Ibid.* i *p* 276.
54 Cameron, John: *History of the Buchanite Delusion*; Train, Joseph: *Buchanites from First to Last.*
55 *Vide* Berean Church. J. Campbell in *S.C.H.S. Records.* vi *p* 135 *ff*; Also *D.N.B.* iii *pp* 164–6.

minister at Selkirk in 1758, was 'expelled and extruded from the University of Edinburgh as being the author of a tract charging his fellow-students with impious principles and immoral practices'. He was also a native of Muthil.[56]

Turning to yet another of the charges laid against the revival, we are told that it bolstered false hopes of salvation and tended to foster spiritual pride; the converts were 'vain and self-conceited'. In 1739 a well-known divine, Dr Trapp, had preached four sermons under the title, *The Nature, Folly, Sin and Danger of being Righteous Overmuch*, and three editions were issued in the course of a year.[57] Why could not these people at Cambuslang believe and behave as other folk did? asked their exasperated neighbours. There is, however, very little indication of any spirit of boasting; instead, we find hesitation to make definite claims to be converted, self-abnegation and the 'fear of a false hope'. M'Culloch and his colleagues, by their own words and spirit, set the standard and strove to maintain it. In his 1751 Attestation, he desired 'that the entire glory of the revival should be given to God whose work it was'. Several eminent ministers had helped, both by preaching and conversation with those in trouble, but 'ministers are but instruments . . . no *praise* was due to the *Ram's-horns*, though *Jericho's* walls fell down at their *blast*'.[58] James Jack closed his account by asserting: 'I can lay claim to assurance of God's love, and peace of conscience and joy in the Holy Ghost; but am a little in the dark as to increase of Grace: tho' it may be, if it were explained to Me, I might also lay Claim to that.'[59] All the four editors protested at this. Webster and Willison agreed that 'there is something visionary in this man's experiences' and suggested they be not published. Ogilvie concurred, and Gillespie added that, if this should hap-

56 Small, R.: *History of the U.P. Congregations.* ii *p* 441.
57 Speaking of Whitefield's Journal, Trapp writes: 'that rhapsody of madness, spiritual pride and little less than blasphemy . . . to pray, preach and sing psalms in the streets and fields, is worse, if possible, than intruding into pulpits by downright violence, a shame and reproach, not only to our Church and country, but to human nature itself'. *pp* 57–8.
58 *Kilsyth Narrative.* *p* 310.
59 M'C. Mss. i *p* 514.

pen, 'it would do hurt'. There was 'not the Humility and Self-
Denial one would Wish and Expect where extraordinary At-
tainments are pretended'.

Occasionally there are hints of censoriousness, ever the besetting
sin of the righteous. Jean Hay heard Mr Steel of Dalserf preach
at the Bothwell sacrament 'in such a legal strain that by the time
he had done, my heart was as dead as a stone'.[60] At another time
'sitting in the Kirk thinking on heaven . . . as soon as Mr Steel
came up to the pulpit, whenever I saw his face . . . these thoughts
instantly vanished . . . I fell into great distress and was straight-
way carried out of the Kirk.' Hearing Steel in the afternoon,
she 'fell into the old confusion again, but resolved to hear him
out and heard his sermon 'with much pain of heart'. His text
'well reported on for good works' was 'pressed, if I mistake not,
in such legal strain; that there was little or nothing of Christ in
the Sermon.'[61] The four editors were unanimous about deleting
this; they were unwilling to have their brethren in the ministry
so censured; but the point of view represented must have engen-
dered strife. In the main, however, the converts were far too
busy fault-minding in themselves to go fault-finding in others;[62]
usually they told their stories with reluctance and reserve. One
was 'most of all affraid of Pride';[63] another had a great fear
'that I may be soft to My self and fall back into my former
ways'.[64] The mind of several was expressed by such a phrase as:
'I have no assurance for the ordinary of Heaven and Salvation;
but . . . I am not without hopes of it; Only I am afraid of a false
hope.'[65] One young man marked the change in his attitude
thus: 'Formerly I went away from a Sermon . . . How well he

60 *Ibid.* i *p* 265.
61 *Ibid.* i *pp* 274–5.
62 Welch, Jno.: *Fifty and Two Directions &c.* (c 1740 reprinted) *p* 40. 'Be
sure that your own Hearts and Ways be the matter o your daily study,
when Hypocrites have their work abroad, let yours be much at Home,
while they make it their business to censure this Man and that Man, let
it be your main task to be looking in to the inner Man of your own Heart,
and to be keeping all right betwixt God and you.'
63 M'C. Mss. i *p* 545 (Janet Reston).
64 *Ibid.* i *p* 352 (Mary Colquhoun).
65 *Ibid.* i *p* 92 (Janet Reid).

preach'd! but now, I oft go away with that, How ill have I liv'd.'[66]
This uncertainty about the assurance of personal salvation is
often found along with very definite claims to some transforming
experience. So we read of one who 'cannot pretend to a stated
Assurance, that I am in a gracious State; But I would not for a
thousand worlds be in the State I was';[67] another affirms: 'My
heart is much changed from what it was once: but it is not so
right as I would have it.'[68] A young man writes: 'I cannot say
certainly whether I am converted or not: but I find a very remarkable change in My spirit: So that in some measure I may
say all old things are passed away . . . I do not find ane inclination to any of these sins I was addicted to before.'[69]

Always present is the fear of trusting to any human effort or
merit; salvation must be from God alone – the undeserved, almost unsolicited gift of sovereign grace. Emotion is not decried;
happiness might often be one of the things accompanying holiness. The danger lies in the possibility, even probability, of seeking gifts rather than the Giver. So Margaret Barton concludes:
'As for good frames and manifestations of the love of God, they
are very desirable, and what My soul cannot but earnestly pant
after and desire more and more of: yet it is neither the perfor-
mance of duties nor good frames, nothing either done by me or
wrought in me, I desire to rest on as the ground of my hope of
the pardon of Sin, peace with God, and eternal life . . . all My
hopes of them, I desire to build entirely on what Christ has done
and suffered and is still doing in Heaven for his people.'[70] There
were some who put too much reliance upon pleasurable emotions, such as Mary Scot, who confessed that 'losing my feelings,
I lost my Beliving (sic)',[71] but the greater number testified that
they had surrendered to Christ as King, irrespective of any
thrill; they were 'as willing and desirous to be ruled by his Laws
as to be saved by his love'.[72]

66 *Ibid.* ii *p* 326 (Andrew Faulds).
67 *Ibid.* i *p* 110 (Eliz. Jackson).
68 *Ibid.* i *p* 473 (Helen Shearer).
69 *Ibid.* i *pp* 519–20 (James Neil).
70 *Ibid.* ii *p* 522.   71 *Ibid.* ii *p* 241.
72 *Ibid.* ii *p* 598 (Agnes Young).

It was recognized, more or less clearly, that Christ was the hunger as well as the food; that he was the goal, and the way in which progress could be made towards the goal. John Parker heard George Whitefield, at Glasgow in September 1741, exhort the people 'to come and cast themselves at the feet of his mercy . . . where never one had perished yet', and found this good news.[73] That very night, in his prayers, Parker renounced all righteousness of his own, 'knowing that I had nothing that was good, and could do nothing but look to that All-fulness treasured up in . . . the Lord Jesus'. His closing words – and they were also the last in M'Culloch's second manuscript volume before his *Finis Coronat Opus* – are well said: 'Since that time, Septr. 1741, the habitual prevailing bent of my heart is after communion with God in Christ and conformity to him: and tho my heart oftimes wanders and runs off from God in duty, yet himself know it, That I am very uneasy when it is so, and that my heart is just like the mariners needle, which tho it may be jogg'd to the one side and the other; yet it is never quiet till it point to the North Pole; so neither does My poor heart ever settle or take rest, till it fix on God in Christ, and find rest in him.'[74] Perhaps that is as far as he would wish to go. M'Culloch reported that many attained to the full assurance of faith during the revival days.[75] Margaret Shaw of Rutherglen was quite explicit on this point. Travelling to Cambuslang, she 'essayed by the way to plead for the Faith of Assurance and the Seal of the Spirit and the answer came at length . . . I had a full assurance of My interest in Christ and of Eternal Salvation by him . . . And thus it continued with me . . . to this day [21 January 1743]. I have never been left under deadness nor doubts and fears, except for some little time for a day or two or so.'[76]

Such definiteness is, however, rare. In spite of Whitefield's reiterated exhortation that 'it was great presumption for any to rest in the faith of Adherence, and not seek after the faith of As-

73 *Ibid.* ii *p* 666.
74 *Ibid.* ii *p* 680.
75 *Kilsyth Narrative p* 297.
76 M'C. Mss. ii, *p* 154.

surance', few would claim so much. M'Culloch said in 1751 that, when he spoke of those who had persevered since 1742, he did not 'pretend to determine that all these are converted'. Assurance was sometimes given and that infallibly, 'yet this is not the attainment of every true believer neither, nor perhaps of the greatest part of believers'. Willison had said in his sermon at Cambuslang on the communion Sabbath: 'The believer had to climb to heaven between the two sharp rocks of presumption and despair'.

This note points to a difference between the revival in Scotland and the contemporary Methodist revival, led by John Wesley, in England. In the north, the Calvinistic emphasis upon salvation as a divine and sovereign work, wrought in men, rather than upon something which a man could readily secure by a faith he was able to exercise, led to caution. While M'Culloch and his colleagues taught that faith in Christ was the way to peace with God, they also warned their hearers against regarding *any* faith as evidence of regeneration. Wesley, on the other hand, pressed the duty of faith upon his hearers along with earnest persuasions that salvation was a gift, never deserved, but needing only to be taken. Receive salvation on these terms, said Wesley, and seek assurance which comes when the 'Spirit witnesseth with our spirit'. This latter viewpoint did not stress sufficiently the possibility of presumption and deception. The strong emphasis upon the certainty of the justification of all who receive the gospel offer, and upon the appropriating act of faith, gave birth to a carefree abandon of joy.

It is unlikely that any of the converts at Cambuslang would have sung 'My God, I know, I feel thee mine', or 'Now I have found the ground wherein, Sure my soul's anchor may remain', or 'And my heart it doth dance at the sound of his Name'.

To have sung such words as:

> That sinner am I,
> Who on Jesus rely,
> And come for the pardon God cannot deny

would have seemed to the ministers and people of Cambuslang to be at best presumption, at worst blasphemy. Thus the Methodists made music and turned England into 'a nest of singing birds'. But if the Scottish song was, by comparison, muted, the experience of grace was no less wonderful.

10

Results: Individual and Immediate

From the beginning, the revival at Cambuslang, with its associated movements, aroused both detractors and defenders to
vehement zeal, and one of the most bitter controversies known
in Scotland emerged. Pamphlets on both sides were issued in
abundance, following each other in hasty succession.[1] There
were three main groups of opinion concerning the revival, said
Dr Meek,[2] who succeeded M'Culloch as minister of Cambuslang.
Its supporters, 'the high party of the Church of Scotland',
ascribed it to the operations of the Holy Spirit. Its opponents,
the Seceders and other extremists, denounced it as of diabolical
origin, 'delusions of Satan, attending the present awful work
upon the bodies of men, going on at Cambuslang.'[3] The 'Moderate party', to which Meek belonged, discounted all supernatural implication and explained the unusual incidents by
natural causes. 'We are disposed', said he, 'to imitate the actions
of others.'

The strictest set of Presbyterians, those primitive Cameronians with their declared antipathy to episcopacy, obsessed with
the supreme necessity to live and die by the Covenants, bustled
into the fray with 'The *Declaration, Protestation* and *Testimony* of
the Suffering *Remnant* of the *Anti-Popish, Anti-Lutheran, Anti-
Prelatick, Anti-Whitefieldian, Anti-Erastian, Anti-Secterian,* true
Presbyterian Church of *Christ* in *Scotland, Published against Mr*

1 In the *New Stat. Acc.* vi *pp* 4–8 there are listed fifty-eight different books
  and pamphlets on the subject, all except seven having been written before
  1751, and the list is by no means complete.
2 *Old Stat. Acc.* v *pp* 271–4.
3 Act at Dunfermline 15 July 1742.

George Whitefield and his Encouragers, and against the Work of Cambuslang and other places'.[4]

Whitefield was 'a limb of anti-Christ . . . an abjured prelatick Hireling . . . a base English Imposture [*sic*] . . . a scandalous Idolater . . . a wild beast from the Antichristian Field of England to waste and devour the poor erring people of Scotland'; his friends and followers were 'drinking even the poisonous Puddles of Prelacy and Sectarianism . . . as far forsaken of God, and as far ensnared by Satan' as the children of Israel dancing round the golden calf. The whole affair, it went on, 'looks like the Time wherein the Devil is come down to Scotland'. A later Cameronian historian, Matthew Hutchison, wrote: 'It is a matter of regret that such declarations were given forth by Christian communities against a work which . . . is all but universally acknowledged to have been a genuine spiritual awakening.'[5]

In addition to the strong criticisms and misrepresentations that were filling the country, M'Culloch had also to face opposition inside the parish, principally from Hamilton of Westburn, the man who had opposed his coming in 1731. On 26 June 1744, Hamilton complained to the presbytery that M'Culloch was not 'preaching regularly in the Kirk', and requested that an *ad hoc* committee should meet at Cambuslang 'that Misunderstandings Might be Removed, the peoples privilidges ascertained and manifold Disorders Rectified'. The matter was sent back to him for 'More Special Condescensions,' but he does not appear to have made his charge any more explicit, and no more was heard of it officially. Early in 1749 a Committee of Presbytery reported on its examination of the Cambuslang records 'with respect to the poor's money'. There were some very slight errors due to converting Scots into English money, totalling 'only to two shillings five pence five twelts sterling in which they have overcharged themselves'. It was suggested that 'by gone interest be demanded att least every two years and not delayed for twelve years . . . as in the case of Westburn'. It concluded that the

4 *The Declaration of the True Presbyterians. p 3.*
5 Hutchison, Matthew: *The Reformed Presbyterian Church in Scotland. 1680–1876. p 179.*

management of the poor's money by the minister and session of Cambuslang 'appears to us careful and honest'.[6]

Hamilton of Westburn came back again to the attack, bringing against M'Culloch and his elders an action which came before the Court of Session in July 1752.[7] He protested about certain payments from the poor's money: 'in 1742 there was an article of two guineas for having a field to preach in, an article to a Constable to keep the peace and 17 shillings for repairing a dyke that the congregation had broken'. To this, answer was made that 'the Church could not hold the tenth part' of the crowds that resorted thither, and 'there was no other remedy than to preach in the fields'.'The poor' it was pointed out 'instead of losing, were great gainers by that expedient, in so much that their stock, from £500 Scots, that it was before 1742, is now increased to £3000 Scots.' Lord Elchies, from whose record of judicial cases we learn these facts, commented that 'Some of the Lords highly condemned the practice of preaching in the fields and proposed that we should put a mark of disapprobation upon it'; he himself objected that this was *ultra vires* and their only concern was with the poor's money. The Court of Session gave its verdict in favour of Hamilton.[8] It is worth while to realise that, while M'Culloch was spending himself in forwarding the revival in his parish, he had to face this interminable, petty persecution by litigation.

What, it may be asked, were the results of this revival? Dr Meek, by no means in sympathy with the aims, methods, and results of the awakening that had taken place in the parish under his predecessor, wrote: 'The Cambuslang work continued for about 6 months, that is from the 18th February till the second communion. Few or none were convicted or converted after this last period.'[9] It is certainly true that many of the most unusual features of those stirring days – physical convulsions, loud outcries and similar phenomena – disappeared, but the

6 Hamilton Pres. Recs. 31 January 1749.
7 *Decisions of the Court of Session*: Patrick Grant of Elchies, one of the Senators of the College of Justice. ii *p* 238.
8 *Ibid.* ii *p* 239.
9 *Old Stat. Acc.* v *p* 270.

leaders of the movement had never set great store by them, and would always have preferred to be without them. They were more of a liability than an asset. Also, the attendance at communion decreased year by year, although this still remained very large, greatly exceeding the numbers before 1742. M'Culloch supplies the figures. There 'used to be but about 400 or 500, before 42 ... at the second sacrament ... in 42 ... was reckoned 3000; in 43, about 2000; in 44, about 1500; in 45, about 1300'.[10]

It would, however, be quite misleading to assume that the results of the revival were as ephemeral, or negligible, as Meek suggests. In M'Culloch's case-histories, there are accounts of conversions as late as 1748. Whitefield, who kept in touch with his friends in Scotland, wrote on 23 July 1748: 'As for poor Scotland, what shall I say? ... Awakening times are always like the Spring. Many blossoms appear, and perhaps but little solid fruit is produced after all. O that the Lord of the harvest, if I am to see Scotland again, may send me to call some backsliders to return.'[11] This sounds far from encouraging. Later that same year he revisited Scotland, and on 28 September wrote from Glasgow: 'Great multitudes in Scotland flock to hear. Some of my spiritual children, I hear, are gone to heaven, and others come to me, telling what God did for their souls when I was here last.' On 1 October he added: 'Many come to me, telling what the Lord did by me the last time I was in Scotland, and also the time before'.[12]

Eight days later he wrote from Cambuslang itself: 'At present I am in the place where the great awakening was about six years ago. *The fruits of it yet remain.*'[13]

Perhaps the best evidence as to the extent of the movement, and its value – as far as statistics can take us – is to be found in the closing chapter of Robe's *Kilsyth Narrative* (1789 edition): 'Concerning the perseverance of those who appeared to be hope-

10 *Kilsyth Narrative. p* 297. In 1754 John Mill of Dunrossness assisted at the communion at Cambuslang and preached to about 8,000, who behaved decently. *Diary &c. p* 16.
11 *George Whitefield Works* ii *p* 154.
12 *Ibid.* ii *pp* 184, 189.
13 *Ibid.* ii *p* 191 (Italics mine).

fully changed, during this extraordinary season of grace.'[14] After observing that many had warned him in 1742 not to be too hasty in approving the work of revival, or in asserting that people had been converted, Robe states his present purpose of supplying evidence about the results of that awakening. 'Such a statement as was now offered had been long delayed, and that partly by design.' Time tests all things, and nine years had now gone by.

His mind had been made up by an entreaty sent from a minister in Holland. Many of the false reports circulating in Great Britain and Holland, *viz* 'that this work in Scotland was all Enthusiasm, that it is come to nothing, and that the subjects of it are fallen away and become worse than they were before,'[15] were being used as a stick with which to attack a similar movement in Guelderland, to which reference has already been made. Hence this *cri de coeur* from Holland for the facts about the perseverance of the converts; the minister of Kilsyth was asked 'to publish something to shew that the blessed work at Kilsyth, Cambuslang, &c. was not abortive; but the happy fruits thereof endure'.

Robe sets down an account concerning his own parish, with corroboration from his session, and there are similar declarations from other ministers about their respective parishes. Although the attestation by M'Culloch concerning Cambuslang is given at the end, as the last item in the book, it may be considered first.

M'Culloch underlined the fact that, in view of opposition and misrepresentation, he had felt it to be his duty to make 'particular enquiry' both about residents in Cambuslang and those from elsewhere, who had been awakened during the revival. Quoting the parable of the sower (Matthew 13), he owned frankly and with sorrow that a considerable number had backslidden since 1742. Discounting these, and even those who had lapsed but were anxiously seeking restoration, M'Culloch went on to speak of those 'who bring forth fruit'. 'I do not

14 *Kilsyth Narrative. p* 265 *ff.*
15 *Ibid. p* 268.

talk of them at random, nor speak of their number in a loose, general and confused way; but have now before me, at the writing of this, *April* 27, 1751, a list of about four hundred persons, awakened here at Cambuslang in 1742, who from that time, to the time of their death, or to this, that is, for these nine years past, have been all enabled to behave ... as becometh the gospel.'[16]

The kirk session, besides confirming this, added that 'seventy out of this four hundred lived in this parish', and that the figure of four hundred was really an understatement, for in the returns, 'there were no accounts sent up from the West country,' *ie* Kilmarnock, Stewarton, Irvine and other places in Ayrshire, 'where we know great numbers of the subjects of the late work lived, and do live.'[17]

Robert M'Culloch, speaking of the revival during his father's ministry, made it clear that he could not 'possibly have the least rememberance of any thing that occurred at that period' – he was not born until 21 July 1740 – 'yet having spent about twenty years of my life in that parish, I have had the best opportunity of strictly inquiring into facts'.[18] He agreed with Dr Webster, whom he cites, that faith clearly shows itself by works, and declared that he had seen with pleasure the happy fruits of the ministry of the gospel 'in the place of my nativity'.[19] Dr Robertson, a later minister of Cambuslang, paid tribute to the converts of 1742, some of whom were alive when he began his ministry, for they 'gave evidence, by the piety and consistency of their conduct of the reality of the saving change that had been wrought in their lives'.[20]

Before we examine in fuller detail further evidence of the spiritual and ethical results of the revival, we might look at some of the attestations given in response to Robe's inquiry of 1751. First of all, Kilsyth itself.

16 *Ibid. p* 308.
17 *Ibid. pp* 319–20.
18 M'Culloch, W.: *Sermons. Preface. p* 8.
19 *Ibid. p* 10.
20 Dr John Robertson, nephew of Principal Robertson, in the *New Stat. Acc.* vi *p* 427; *Fasti.* iii *p* 238.

Robe had already issued an attestation about the work at Kilsyth in the earlier phase; on 5 September 1742 the kirk session, fourteen in all, with five of the heritors, headed by Robert Graham of Thomrawer,[21] men 'who have Access to observe the daily Conversation of the People', paid tribute to the transformation among the people of the parish. Sins of body and disposition were no longer to be found. Added weight was given to this testimony by Alexander Forrester, baillie depute of Kilsyth, who evidenced the new spirit of friendship by the fact that 'there hath been no pleas before our Court for these several Months past: Whereas formerly a great many were brought before me every Week'.[22] In the first issue of his *Christian Monthly History*, November 1743, Robe wistfully compared the present with the previous year; no longer could he talk of harvesting for it was 'only like the gleaning of grapes when the vintage is done, and as the shaking of an olive tree, two or three being in the uppermost bough'. The years brought a winnowing and sifting and, in 1751, Robe acknowledged that some had lost their first love. The records reveal serious problems within the session itself.

John Forrester demitted office as an elder for 'several sins ... particularly Drunkenness and Swearing'.[23] On 20 May 1745 it was unanimously agreed to depose from the eldership James Rennie, appointed treasurer only two months before, for sexual offences with his servant. On 9 July 1748 Alexander Forrester was 'dropped' for not attending Session Diets, 'alleged Drunkenness, swearing and other irregularities'; two elders were appointed to interview him, and warn him 'not to meddle with any service at the Communion for this Time'. On 21 June 1748, one of the deacons, William Adam, demitted his office because the 'Session would not grant him liberty to run uncustomed goods' – trafficking in spirits being named.[24]

There were others who must have been a heart-ache to Robe,

21 Robert Graham was the first man to cultivate the potato commercially in Scotland. *Vide* Anton, P.: *History &c. p* 157.
22 *Kilsyth Narrative. p* 112.
23 Kilsyth K.S.R. 10 December 1744.
24 *Ibid.*

such as James Grindlay, 'son to Mary Brown Innkeeper in Town of Kilsyth'. Within the space of two months he made several appearances before the session for being the putative father of Mary Chambers' child, assaulting her by fist and foot, blaspheming before the session itself, and causing a riot at New Year's Fair night by knocking down several men.[25] 'He, refusing, said he would compear no more.' After all this, Robe still delayed reading to the congregation the verdict of the Lesser Excommunication passed upon the offender, because Grindlay had made promises to him to do better.

When Robe came to assess the situation in 1751, he found cause for satisfaction that there were 'also some who continue not only living but lively Christians'.[26] Some of the societies for prayer were defunct, but marriage, removals into other work, and amalgamations could partly explain this. He submitted to his kirk session a list of people who had been blameless in their lives, omitting all who had fallen into gross sins, even though they had since repented and reformed. The session queried this decision, pointing out that some of those omitted were in good standing now and regular communicants. 'But', said the cautious Robe, 'I chuse rather to lessen the number of the persons attested, to cut off occasion of cavilling and objection from those, who desire and wait for it.'[27]

The minute of the Session runs thus:

'Manse of Kilsyth, March 19, 1751. THE Session being met for prayer, according to a former appointment; the minister read unto them the names of above an hundred persons who were the most of them brought under NOTOUR* SPIRITUAL CONCERN, in the years 1742, and 1743; and of whom he had good ground to entertain good hopes.

The under-subscribing members of the session, elders and deacons, hereby testify and declare, That all those of them, who

25 *Ibid.* 1 December, 17 December, 1749, 7 January, 28 January 1750.
26 *Kilsyth Narrative. p* 274.
27 *Ibid. p* 276.
* Determinedly persistent (*Scottish*)

are now alive, have been, from year to year, admitted by the kirk-session to the Lord's table, since their first admission, either in these fore-mentioned years, or since; and, in as far as is known to the said members, they have had their conversation such as becometh the gospel; as also, that four or five of the said list, who are now removed by death, behaved until their said removal, as became good Christians . . .'

Five of the session appended their signatures on this day, and ten others, who had been absent, added their agreement on 24 March 1751.[28]

John Warden, minister at Perth, but formerly at Campsie, said of his former parishioners that not more than four of those whom he had known to be concerned had fallen from their profession of faith up to the time of his leaving. Of the many others, 'I could not but entertain the highest opinion, and the greatest hopes . . . In a word, their devotion is exemplary.'[29] John Erskine, by this time minister of Kirkintilloch, wrote two lengthy letters to Robe, paying tribute to his predecessor, James Burnside, who had been minister at Kirkintilloch during the revival days. 'No man had less of a turn to Enthusiasm . . . None ever charged him with endeavouring in his pulpit performances to work up people.' On the contrary, he 'used the utmost pains to discourage . . . noisy religion'; 'probably', added Erskine, 'his caution carried him too far'. It was no wonder if foolish virgins mixed with the wise, and tares resembled wheat, but 'is it not a matter of wonder . . . that so great a proportion of the awakened, should not only hold on their way, but wax stronger and stronger?'[30] On 22 February 1751, Erskine wrote again: 'My Sentiments of the religious concern in this place, are the same, as when I wrote you April 1748.' He praised the behaviour and spirit of his congregation in generous terms, and commented on their teachable disposition, even when he had thought it his duty to oppose some of their favourite opinions

28 Kilsyth K.S.R. 19 March 1751.
29 *Kilsyth Narrative.* p 279.
30 *Ibid. p* 281. (Letter of 25 April 1748.)

and practices. 'A thorough acquaintance with these people would effectually remove the prejudices of fair and honest minds.'

On 26 February 1751, William Halley, minister at Muthil, wrote that he was 'fully perswaded that the gracious fruits of that glorious work . . . abide'. Before dying, six of the converts had given 'a notable testimony to the truth and reality of religion'. If trees were to be judged by their fruits, then many had become the subjects of a saving work.[31] John Gillies, minister of the College-kirk in Glasgow, wrote to his people: 'I know there are some melancholy Instances of backsliding . . . But that the Revival which was at Cambuslang, and other Places in this Country in 1742, has come to nothing, has not been followed with any Good fruit in Peoples Lives . . . you and I both know this to be otherwise.' Then Gillies went on to give instances of awakening within his own congregation in 1751.[32]

Twenty-five members of the session in Glasgow wrote to Robe on 26 March 1751, 'anent the reputed subjects of the late revival of religion in *anno* 1742'. Judging from personal knowledge and credible information about the converts, they firmly declared that 'goodly numbers of them, both in town and country . . . give evidence of their perseverance'. From October 1743 onwards, the increase in communicants had remained steady at 'about twelve hundred'.

The increase was not only in quantity; the quality was far better. John M'Laurin, another minister in Glasgow, said that this 'must far surpass any thing of that kind known here these twenty-eight years, that I have been a minister in this place . . . or in the memory of any now living in it'.[33] From the earliest days of the outbreak of the revival in 1742, it had been understood that not all the converts would persevere. John M'Laurin wrote to Mr Cooper in New England: 'About the beginning of this Revival, in conferring and reasoning about it, it was sometimes argued that tho' only the half or third part . . . should evidence Sincerity by Perseverance; it ought to be esteemed an extra-

31 *Ibid. p* 2.   32 Gillies, J.: *Exhortations &c.* ii *p* 11. 16 February 1751.
33 *Kilsyth Narrative. p* 293.

ordinary Instance of the Success of the Gospel.'[34] After nine years there was much for which M'Culloch, Robe and their brethren could give thanks.

In his attestation of 1751, M'Culloch summarised his reasons for believing that many of his people were converted, giving both negative and positive arguments. The consequences indicated the cause![35] The converts were by no means free from common human frailties and faults; nor were their experiences of equal merit. In some, holiness shone so clearly in their lives as to provide a 'moral certainty, or very high degree of probability . . . concerning the goodness of their state'. Others offered evidence of somewhat less power, though a charitable judgment would include them among the converted. But every one on M'Culloch's list was vouched for by some minister, elder or private Christian of well-known character who had 'known them, and their manner of life, from 1742'.

M'Culloch singled out some obvious changes. Cursers and swearers spoke with new tongues; those who formerly spent much of their time in taverns, drinking and playing cards until morning, now found pleasure in their own homes. 'The formerly drunken or tipling sot, that used to ly a-bed till 8 or 9 in the morning, till he slept out last night's drunkenness, for these nine years, gets up at 3 or 4 in the morning, and continues at reading his Bible and other good books, secret prayer and meditation &c. till 7 or 8 o'clock in the morning, when he calls his household together for family devotions.' Wives who were formerly thorns in the flesh now lived in much love and peace with their husbands; should the husband storm against her, the wife hurried into another room and knelt, 'asking of God forgiveness and a better temper to the husband, and patience and meekness to herself'. The springs of generosity were flowing freely from what had been the stony hearts of selfish and worldly-minded people.

34 Prince, T.: *Christian History. 1743. p* 353.
35 *Vide* Baxter, Richard: *Works.* xx *p* 153. 'Section XIII Question: But how then shall I know that I have the Spirit of Christ? Answer: By the nature of its effects. . . . The Spirit of Christ is no fancy, dream or delusion nor worketh an imaginary change in the soul, but a real change.'

M'Culloch ended his attestation with characteristic caution, warning any included in the list of 'persevering subjects' against self-confidence and pride. 'What was *Judas* the better for being in the list, and in such repute among the other apostles? Men may approve thee, and God condemn thee.'[36]

Amongst these persevering subjects, there were many whose stories were collected by M'Culloch, and in them was much evidence of thorough-going reformation. They had found in the revival the power to transform the individual, and thereby to transmute society.

An examination of some of the individual results made manifest in these testimonies is revealing. Robert Hamilton was a twenty-nine-year-old weaver from the little village of Anderston near Glasgow. He was a drunkard, vexed with thoughts of suicide, and had been publicly censured for immorality. 'I listed my Self to be a Soldier, but was bought off again'. When he visited Cambuslang, he was sinking down into bankruptcy and ruin by neglecting his trade. Moral degradation and social failure disappeared, and a new sufficiency and responsibility replaced them.[37] There are others, from various social groups, set beside him – one of the Hamilton civic leaders whose remorse was over 'playing at Cards and drinking to excess';[38] an old soldier aged fifty-one, now a collier in Cambuslang, tells of a neglected childhood, and being 'addicted to all Evil, and indulg'd my self in the open practice of many vices'.[39] A girl of seventeen confesses that her 'former life was but very coarse ... scarce a sentence without profane swearing, and lying was habitual to me'.[40]

Thomas Foster of Ridley Wood, a man of forty years of age, tells of how he 'began to thrive very fast in the world'. Through 'a natural easiness of temper' he had been drawn into many harmful habits. When a boy of fourteen, two men had each offered him a penny if he would drink a cup full of ale and, after

36 *Kilsyth Narrative.* p 317.
37 M'C. Mss. ii *pp* 75–82.
38 *Ibid.* ii *p* 33 (Baillie Weir).
39 *Ibid.* i *p* 483 (David Logan).
40 *Ibid.* i *pp* 471–2 (Jean Wark).

that, he 'learned to drink better'. Excessive drinking brought rapid degeneration until he 'wrought each lawful day of the week and drank every night . . . day and night without sleeping any at all till Saturday night'.[41] Foster heard Whitefield and others at Cambuslang, reduced his drinking for a time, but soon lapsed into his former ways. He would have been written off as one whom the revival failed to help, but he reported: 'One day in July 1744, after I had been drinking hard two days and one night, and part of the third day all together without intermission . . . passed through the churchyard at Cambuslang and stopt a little and look't on a Grave-Stone lying above one I had been acquainted with'. Meditating on this, the certainty of his own eventual death, and the fact of his enslavement to drink despite his efforts to free himself, he decided: 'I'll go away in to the Minister there, and see if he will say anything to me that will rouse me and put me from it'.

Finding M'Culloch at dinner, he was invited into the dining-room and given something to drink from the minister's brew-house; when he got it into his hand, he said he 'had little need of drink, for . . . had been full of drink the day before . . . both of ale and brandy'. M'Culloch 'look'd me broad in the face' and called on all the company to witness this confession, which so distressed Foster that he ran from the room, troubled at having spoken in this fashion to a minister. He went to a public-house near the manse, fell to drinking again, and thereafter went from inn to inn, half a dozen or more, seeking to drink away his distress. Eventually, about midnight, he called at the house of an elder, where he found help.

There are, however, many other things of value to be noticed in these accounts besides such outward reformation. To many there came, along with conversion, the glory of the lighted mind, a fresh appreciation of beauty and of Nature as the vestment of God; there emerged a new sense of moral sufficiency and a warm, genuine brotherliness, which reached out not only to those within the fellowship but also to those as yet outside. Many historians have written about religion in Scotland as an

41 *Ibid.* ii *pp* 51–3 (Thomas Foster).

oppressive and gloomy thing; Buckle's caricature is well known, and the French scholar Taine to some extent agrees with him when he says: 'It seems as though a black cloud had weighed down the life of man, drowning all light, wiping out all beauty, extinguishing all joy.' A more recent American writer, Wallace Notestein, speaking of the eighteenth century, asserts that loveliness was banished and the beauty of holiness blotted out. 'From the seventeenth century to the last part of the eighteenth century, he [the Scot] was afraid to enjoy any thing, even the out-of-doors.'[42] Like all other sweeping generalisations, this says far too much. In this Age of Reason, this Classical Era, before the dawn of Romanticism, there are indications that the revival brought to some a new sense of the value of simple, everyday things in the world around them. One young woman of thirty-two, almost afraid to speak after finding peace in the manse at Cambuslang, told a friend: 'My heart was like a bird that had been long in prison in the cage, when it was first let loose . . . Next morning . . . everything I look'd at, fill'd me with wonder . . . the Birds on the trees, I thought, were singing their Creator's praise.'[43] Another, aged nineteen, when she 'walked in the fields everything looked to Me in another Manner than before.'[44]

Jean Hay, aged twenty-six, of 'Lismahago', said: 'One Night, looking up to the Stars twinkling in the Sky, I began to say within My self, If there be not a God in the Heavens, what could have put the stars there? and from the stars, I looked down to the spires of grass about Me, and wondered: and from these to My own body.'[45] A young woman of the same age from Cadder found a message for herself: 'One time in the Spring 1743 . . . looking about me and noticing the works of God; I thought now the grass is Springing, the birds are Singing, all things are reviving after the winter, all things are obeying and praising their Creator, but I, I am daylie and hourly dishonouring him,

42 Notestein, Wallace: *The Scot in History.* p 177.
43 M'C. Mss. i p 52 (Anne Wylie).
44 *Ibid.* i p 107 (Eliz. Jackson).
45 *Ibid.* i p 280 (Jean Hay).

I am withering and declining in Religion, if ever I had any.'[46]
All these witnesses could have sung, with understanding:

> Heaven above is softer blue,
> Earth around is sweeter green;
> Something lives in every hue,
> Christless eyes have never seen.[47]

In addition to this quickened appreciation of beauty, this stimulating of aesthetic taste, there came intellectual progress. Latent gifts were discovered; unrealised capacities developed. Prior to 1742, many people were able to read; others, however, did not even want to learn until they had been awakened at Cambuslang. A young Highlander reveals that he 'did not learn to read when I was a Child, nor till I put My self to School, when I was about 18 years of age; and even then I did not learn Much; but I am just now [at twenty-eight years of age] gone to school, to learn to read More distinctly'.[48] Other cases might be cited but one more will suffice. Janet Struthers, a married woman of thirty-two, confessed: 'I was careless about learning to read till last year [1742] when it pleased the Lord to take some dealings with my heart; and then I was much grieved that I had so long neglected to learn to read, and would have given never so much that I had learned to read the Bible: and by applying carefully to learn, I bless the Lord, tho I cannot pretend to read it perfectly, yet I can read much of it.'[49] So well had she availed herself of her newly-won privilege that she could find most of the passages of Scripture quoted by the minister, even when no reference was given.

Perception and progress were for some created by the revival

46 *Ibid.* i *p* 519 (Margaret Barton).
47 Jonathan Edwards, that 'Flinty minded Calvinist', as one critic has styled him, tells of a similar feeling: 'The appearance of everything was altered; there seemed to be as it were, a calm, sweet cast, or appearance of divine glory, in almost everything. God's excellency, his wisdom, his purity and love, seemed to appear in everything; in the sun, moon and stars; in the clouds, and blue sky; in the grass, flowers, trees, in the water and all nature' (*Works* i *p* 31).
48 M'C. Mss. i *p* 76 (John McDonald).
49 *Ibid.* ii *p* 557 (Janet Struthers).

– purpose too, for the ability to conform to higher ethical standards became apparent. A young shoemaker ended his account: 'as for my dealings with Men: I love plainness and simplicity: and tho' I could sometimes over-reach others, and they not know it; yet I abhor even the thought of doing so, because it is displeasing and dishonouring to God'.[50] Another man, who heard M'Culloch speak on the necessity for restitution, remembered that in his time as an apprentice he had 'kept up to my self some little thing of what I had got for my Master'. He became very uneasy and found no peace until he 'made offer to him of what I thought was the full value of what I had taken and more'.[51]

In the deeper and more vital fellowship created by the revival, contention was swept away and misunderstanding submerged.[52] We have already seen the unfortunate breach which split the Cambuslang session in 1740 and how one of the suspended elders, Archibald Fyfe, was reinstated. (Several of the converts were his employees.) John Bar, who was at the centre of the controversy, was frequently mentioned by the converts as a helper.

Many visitors to Cambuslang were impressed by the warmth of affection and the sense of community found amongst the people. 'Seeing two persons, *viz* Sergeant Forbes of Edinburgh and Ingram More of Cambuslang, who had never seen one another before, very lovingly embrace one another, at first sight,' filled Jean Hay with a sense of her own loneliness.[53] She felt like one outside, looking into the warmth of a home shared by others.

Archibald Smith of Kilbride determined to find out the truth about this revival at Cambuslang and, putting his Bible into his

50 *Ibid.* i *p* 357 (Thomas Barclay).
51 *Ibid.* ii *p* 674 (John Parker).
52 Webster wrote to Whitefield on 20 April 1742 about the stituation in Edinburgh: 'Religious Conversation has banish'd Slander and Calumny from several Tea-Tables' (*Glas. Wkly. Hist.* No 27, 2). Speaking of Kilsyth at this time, Robe said: 'Former Feuds and Animosities are in a great Measure laid aside and forgot! And this hath been the most peaceable summer amongst Neighbours that was ever known' (*Kilsyth Narr. p* 68).
53 M'C. Mss. i *p* 366.

pocket, set off one week-day. He became convinced that 'the Lord was among them, especially by seeing many of them . . . expressing so much brotherly love to one another, instructing and encouraging one another.'[54] Another man, sitting on the brae at Cambuslang in May 1742, listening to M'Culloch, saw his only brother, whom he hated, and 'then felt such a love to him, that if I could have got to him at that time, I would most heartily and lovingly have embraced him'.[55] This same man seems to have been difficult to live with, for he goes on to tell how, in the middle of the night, he felt impelled to ask forgiveness of his parents, but was reluctant to do so as it was one o' clock in the morning. Eventually he jumped out of bed, went to the adjoining room where they were, 'and coming to their bedside, all trembling and shaking, like the leaves of a tree shaken with the wind . . . beg'd forgiveness.'[56] Janet Struthers concluded her testimony: 'I bear no grudge or ill-will at any in the world. I pray for all, even for Enemies: and earnestly long for the advancement of the kingdom of Christ.'[57]

We shall have occasion in our concluding chapter to notice this eager outreach, with its implication for evangelism and for the growth of the concept of the Church's world mission. One cannot read the accounts of these 'Cambuslang converts', as they were sneeringly designated, without being conscious that something very wonderful had happened to some of them. Religion had ceased to be peripheral – something attached to the margins of life; now it was inward, focal and dynamic. In spite of many hesitations and qualifications, the converts were convinced of the reality of communion with a living Saviour, and from that they derived strength.

A young widow made it her 'constant business to travel betwixt the Redeemers fulness and My Own emptiness'.[58] A Glasgow tailor 'came oft to Cambuslang' and never came away 'without being strengthened to put on new resolutions'.[59] The

54 *Ibid.* i p 442.
55 *Ibid.* i p 499 (James Jack).
56 *Ibid.* i pp 502–3.   57 *Ibid.* i p 571.
58 *Ibid.* i p 535 (Isobel Matthie).
59 *Ibid.* i p 405 (Archibald Bell).

transformation was within. Margaret Borland from Bothwell wrote: 'Tho the world cannot observe any great alteration in my behaviour from what it us'd to be formerly ... yet I find a very great change in my self, even as great a difference between Light and darkness.'[60] Bessie Lyon, the daughter of a Blantyre cooper, declared: 'I have no good at all to say of my self ... I think I may venture to say this, to the praise of the Lord's free-grace, That I now for these two years past find it better with me when I am at my worst, than ever it was formerly when I was at my best.'[61]

We shall end with the account given by Mrs Marion Baillie, a woman of forty-four years of age, who visited Cambuslang in April 1742. 'From that time to this, Novr. 14, 1743, I have been kept trusting in him: tho I sometimes now and then ... fall under clouds and darkness ... so far as I remember I have not had any one Doubt or fear of my Interest in Christ. And the Lord has in mercy so sanctify'd and sweetned every Lot I fall into, that nothing now falls amiss to me, because it is the holy will of God ... I am now helped to bear with ease and cheerfulness, many tryals that were formerly most afflicting ... under which I was often ready to sink ... I have now no Cross in the world but a body of sin and death. So gracious has the Lord been to me ever since, that he never one day leaves me comfortless. Christ is now become all in all to me. I know not how to live without him ... I lov'd him for a while, mainly because he has done and suffered so much for me, but now I love him for himself, and because of his own Excellency and loveliness, which he hath discovered to me ... The thoughts of Eternity are sweet to me because then I'll get time enough to praise him and be put in a capacity to do it without any sinful imperfection ... I am now afraid of nothing but of offending and dishonouring him by sin.

'Death that was a terror to me to think of is now become a pleasure to me: he has been pleas'd (in condescending grace) to make it known to me, that he has taken me (poor deform'd hell-deserving me) for his Spouse ... and I now consider Death

60 *Ibid.* ii *p* 547 (Margaret Borland).
61 *Ibid.* ii *p* 256 (Bessie Lyon).

as a messenger to come and call me home to my Lord and Husband, to be where he is: and, tho' I do not know how matters may alter with me, yet for the present, and for a long time past, the thoughts of Death are as pleasant and delightful to me, as a message would be to a Loving wife to come away home to her Husband.'[62]

Here surely are genuine echoes of Francis of Assisi who more than 500 years earlier had sung the praises of:

> Thou, most kind and gentle death,
> Waiting to hush our latest breath,
> Thou leadest home the child of God.

Housewife and saint are at one here!

62 *Ibid.* ii *pp.* 578–9 (Marion Baillie).

11

The Evangelical Party

The last three pages of the conclusion of Robe's *Narrative* are taken up with the attestation of the kirk session of Cambuslang, dated 30 April 1751, in which they endorse the statement of their minister, and then add some observations of their own. The first of these is:

'The awakening in 1742, was so far from being a schismatical work, as it has been traduced by opposers, That numbers who had gone into a course of separation and division from their own ministers, and from the communion of the presbyterian church, established by law in *Scotland*, returned to their own pastors, and to communion with the national church, acknowledging God was in the midst of her of a truth. And many who were at the very point of deserting the communion of this church, and separating from their own pastors, were kept back from schismatick courses; and express a most tender regard to all true ministers of Christ, especially those who were their spiritual fathers in the Lord; and continue in full communion with this national church to this very day.' We may appreciate the change of emphasis when we recall Hugh Cummin and the deposition of the elders in 1740!

One of the most important consequences of the revival at Cambuslang was the stopping of a very considerable and growing drift towards the Seceders by some of the most earnest and sincere members of the Established Church. These people, retained within the fold of that church, became the evangelical salt which did so much to savour it when Erastian Moderatism was in control. They have a direct link with the Disruption leaders of 1843.

Perhaps the gravest criticism to be made against Dr Macfarlan, the nineteenth-century historian of the Cambuslang revival, is that he has made no reference in his book to the effect of the revival upon the Secession sympathisers. Probably anticipating such a criticism, he mentions in his Preface, after speaking of the painful controversy between the early Seceders and the friends of the revival in the Established Church, that 'it was thought injudicious to mix up matters of a controversial nature with the historical details of a work believed to be of God, but it was not meant to conceal or suppress these'.[1] Throughout the book, Dr Macfarlan keeps resolutely before him his declared purpose of seeking to 'awaken a thoughtless and sleeping generation', but however excellently the book may serve an hortatory purpose, it is distorting history to omit all mention of a theme running through the major proportion of the testimonies. Did Dr Macfarlan, writing in 1845, two years after the Disruption, feel that it would be indiscreet to uncover this earlier and similar situation?

It will be necessary to retrace our steps. The coming of George Whitefield to Scotland in July 1741, after two years of correspondence with the two Erskines and their friends of the Associate Presbytery, put before the Seceders an opportunity and a challenge in the sphere of evangelistic co-operation with many ministers and members of the Established Church who had mourned their departure. It is impossible to assess the costliness of the failure of the Seceders to discern and use this occasion.

At an earlier time, a certain catholicity had marked the outlook of the Secession leaders. When Ralph Erskine acceded to them in 1737, he made it clear that he still considered them to be part of the Established Church, witnessing against defections in doctrine and government. He went on: 'By joining with the said brethren, I intend and understand no withdrawing from ministerial communion with any of the godly ministers of this national church, who are groaning under, or wrestling against, the defections of the times . . . I am sensible what a bad tendency division natively has, and desire to abhor

1 Macfarlan, D.: *Revivals &c.* Preface. *p* v.

and shun all divisive principles and practices.'[2] It has been rightly commented: 'There is not one word either of schism or of bigotry in these sentences; how much is there of the spirit of the Christian reformer!' McKerrow, the historian of the Secession, owns that these sentiments 'were quite in unison with those entertained by all the members of the Presbytery'.[3]

Even as late as 10 August 1740, speaking to his congregation before the communion, Ralph Erskine posits the rhetorical question whether joining with the Seceders implies the obligation never to hear or join again with any in the Established Church of Scotland. His reply is categorical and crystal-clear: 'I answer, this would, indeed, be a very untender, unmerciful, and unreasonable term of communion . . . This would be to exclude ourselves and others from all occasional and providential communion with all the churches of Christ upon earth that are not just of our society. That would be . . . to cast off all that have Christ's image, unless they have just our image too. *We are far from thinking that all are Christ's friends that join with us, and that all are his enemies that do not. No, indeed!*'[4] Alas, within a year there was a change of mood and this stress on free communion vanished.

The invitation so warmly given to George Whitefield, an avowed Episcopalian priest, and Ralph Erskine's going with him into the pulpit of the Canongate church, Edinburgh, reveal how free from sectarianism the early Seceders were. The young Anglican evangelist had made his position quite clear before he came to Scotland. On 10 April 1741, Ralph Erskine wrote: 'Come, if possible, dear Whitefield, come. There is no face on earth I would desire more earnestly to see.' Anxious lest Whitefield's popularity should draw crowds to the pulpits of 'our persecutors', he gave his judgment: 'I know not with whom you could *safely* join yourself, if not with us.'[5]

Answering this letter on the day of its arrival, Whitefield is

2 *The Judicial Testimony.* p 155. Act concerning admission of the Rev Ralph Erskine and Mr Thomas Mair as members of Presbytery.
3 McKerrow, John: *History of the Secession Church.* p 112.
4 Fraser, D.: *Life & Diary of Ralph Erskine.* p 343.
5 Tyerman, L.: *Life of George Whitefield.* i p 504.

unequivocal: 'I come only as an occasional preacher, to preach the simple gospel to all that are willing to hear me, of whatever denomination ... My business seems to be to evangelize ... I write this, that there may not be the least misunderstanding between us.'[6] This was to be the theme of Whitefield's whole life. Writing on 13 July 1741 to a friend in London, he says: 'I have no freedom but in going about to all denominations. I cannot join with any one, so as to be fixed in any particular place. Every one hath his proper gift. *Field-preaching* is my plan.'[7] Few men at such an early age have seen their vocation so clearly, and fewer still have kept faith with the vision throughout life.

Whitefield spent his first night in Scotland with Ralph Erskine, who wrote to his brother the following day that Whitefield 'preached in my meeting-house this afternoon. The Lord is evidently with him.' But, rather ominously, 'he says he can refuse no call to preach Christ, whoever gives it.'[8] On Wednesday, 5 August, Whitefield met at Dunfermline the Associate Presbytery – 'a set of grave, venerable men'. They laboured hard to set him right about church government and, although they did not insist that he sign the Solemn League and Covenant at once, they did stipulate, he reported, that he was 'to preach only for them till I had further light'. The reason for this was that they 'were the Lord's people'. To this Whitefield replied that perhaps the Lord had other people too and, in any case, the devil's people needed him most of all.

He concluded: 'The consequence of all this was an open breach. I retired, I wept, I prayed ... Lord, what is man, what the best of men? but men at the best! I think I have now seen an end of all perfection.'[9] From this time the seceders disavowed all connection with him and preached openly against

---

6 *George Whitefield Works.* i *p* 262 (the letter is addressed to Ebenezer Erskine).
7 *Ibid.* i *p* 277.   8 Tyerman, L.: *Life of George Whitefield.* i *p* 507.
9 *George Whitefield Works.* i *pp* 307–8. An attempt has been made by Andrew Thomson in his *Historical Sketch of the Origin of the Secession Church* (1848), *p* 132 *ff.*, to vindicate the action of the Seceders against Whitefield, although he does describe it as an 'unhappy feud' with 'a little odium'. In my view it is an *ex parte* statement, written under the shadow of the

him. Even so noble and generous a soul as Ralph Erskine stooped to join in the violent attacks, and John Erskine noted of one of his namesake's sermons that it condemned the revival at Cambuslang, not openly but by innuendo. John Erskine commented: '*O Keep out of the Devil's Reach and keep out of his Ground*, the meaning of which is, no doubt, Don't go to Cambuslang unless you want to be possessed.'[10] Yet, when Whitefield heard of Ralph Erskine's death some years later, he mourned him as 'God's triumphant saint'.

Ralph Erskine suggested that Whitefield was 'trimming' and temporising in order to raise money for the orphanage he had founded in Georgia,[11] but it is apparent that the real problem was that Whitefield had no doctrine of the *ius divinum* of any particular form of church government: each had virtues and also defects. Writing to John Willison on 10 August 1741, Whitefield begged him to refrain from emphasising the corruptions of the Church of England: 'I believe there is no church perfect under heaven . . . The divisions in Scotland are affecting.' On the same day he wrote to Ogilvie in Aberdeen: 'I find it best simply to preach the pure gospel, and not to meddle at all with controversy . . . This is my comfort, JESUS is king. He will either heal, or bring good out of the present divisions . . . O that the power of religion may revive! Nothing but that can break down the partition wall of bigotry.'[12]

One defender of Whitefield pointed out, in a most reasonable fashion, that there had originally been no controversy between presbyterian and episcopal forms of government, and that the conflict had arisen from the religious struggle of 1638. After citing the example of Andrew and James Melville as hearers of bishops and deans of the Church of England in 1606, the writer continued: 'Chap. 26 of our Westminster Confession Parag. 2

1843 Disruption to justify secession in 1733 and 1843. The argument is that since Whitefield was invited to Scotland by the Erskines, he ought to have preached only for them. The great English evangelist had too great a concept of his ministry to be so confined.
10 Erskine, John: *Signs of the Times Considered.* p 23.
11 *George Whitefield Works.* i p 311.
12 *Ibid.* i p 310.

asserts, That Saints by Profession are bound to maintain an holy Fellowship and Communion in the Worship of God . . . which Communion, as God offereth Opportunity . . . is to be extended to all those who in every Place call on the Name of the Lord Jesus.'[13] Not until this was accomplished, affirmed the writer, quoting John 17.21–3, would the world be convinced of the mission of Jesus, by 'this very Unity of His Members in Him, and among themselves'. Oecumenicity is not as modern as some people imagine.

To this gentle plea for kindly tolerance, there came a counter-blast of scurrilous invective from the Rev John Bissett, a minister of the Established Church of Scotland in Aberdeen. In a bitter pamphlet of 112 pages, dated 26 October 1742, he labelled and libelled Whitefield as 'the strolling Priest' with 'the Art of a Quack', suspect of being 'a *Romish* emissary, a strolling Imposter, whose Cheats in due Time, I hope will be discovered'. So he ended his diatribe, but not before setting down that: 'It is evident Mr Whitefield hath in five Years Time collected himself rich. We commonly say, he is a sorry Cook who may not lick his own Fingers.'[14] It is no credit to James Fisher that he quoted from Bissett and added: 'I hope the Reader will be well pleased with this quotation.'[15]

The campaign of obloquy and insinuation against Whitefield was intensified as it became evident how successful was his ministry in Scotland, and it reached its climax and continued with relentless vigour when the revival began at Cambuslang. The Seceders had decided, *a priori*, that God could not bless this evangelist, minister of an uncovenanted church; this must, therefore, be a delusion, diabolically contrived.

James Fisher, one of the Four Brethren who were deposed in 1733, and the first Secession minister at Glasgow, beginning there in October 1741, had reason to be annoyed by the turn of events. Thomas Clarke, who 'kept a School in *Wester-Weems*'

13 *An Apology for the Presbyterians of Scotland who are Hearers of the Reverend Mr George Whitefield &c. p* 33.
14 Bissett, J.: *A* LETTER *containing* REMARKS *upon the Late Apology &c. p* 86.
15 Fisher, J.: *Review &c. p* 53.

and was a zealous Seceder, called at Cambuslang on his way to
the Sacrament at Kilmaurs about the end of May 1742, and
wrote 'a long Letter, stuffed with sundry gross Falshoods [*sic*]
anent that work to be handed about among the *Seceders* in
Kirkaldie Linktoun of Abbotshall, Pathhead &c'. In it he
declared that 'Mr *Fisher's* Meeting at *Glasgow is greatly drained,
a great Part of his Auditors having left him*', but these, it was added,
were merely 'a Number of carnal, airy Professors'.[16] In his
Review of Mr Robe's Preface &c. Fisher noted that this apparent
success and the absence of similar results among the Seceders
were causing many to think 'there was no ground for Seceding
from the Established Church'. With partisan polemic, he
attacked the Cambuslang work; only by denigrating that could
he justify himself and his brethren.[17] Hard names were employed
to buttress poor arguments.

George Paton, a seceding bookseller at Linlithgow, wrote in
1744 that the work at Cambuslang 'had been Proven to be an
arrant Delusion of Satan' and said of Whitefield: 'This Stranger
and Hireling, whom Christ's Sheep are commanded to avoid
... is chargeable with dreadful Error, flagrant Enthusiasm,
gross Delusion, and horrid Blasphemies ... filthy Lucre ...
seems to be the Thing he chiefly aims at ... yet, because he is
a fit Tool for suppressing and breaking the Secession, he is
extolled as another Apostle Paul'.[18]

Perhaps the worst of all the many bitter attacks made by the
Seceders against Whitefield and the work at Cambuslang was
made by that implacable and doughty son of thunder, Adam
Gib. The nature of his pamphlet is obvious from its lengthy
title: 'A WARNING against Countenancing the Ministra-
tions of Mr George Whitefield, Published ... June 6, 1742 ...
Wherein are shewn, that *Mr Whitefield* is *no* Minister of *Jesus
Christ*; that his *Call* and *Comming* to *Scotland* are *scandalous*; that

16 Currie, J.: *New Testimony &c. pp* 27, 56.
17 Fisher's biographer says that it is 'Deplorable to find a man like Mr Fisher
calling Mr Whitefield, "a strolling imposter and cheat" ' (Dr John Brown:
Memorial of the Rev Jas Fisher. p 48 *ff*).
18 *Lawfulness & Duty of Separation from Corrupt Ministers and Churches &c.*
Fraser of Brea. Preface, xxvii, xxxvi–xxxvii.

his Practice is *disorderly* and *fertile* of Disorder; that his *whole* Doctrine is, and his Success *must* be *diabolical*; so that People ought to *avoid* him from *Duty* to God, to the Church, to themselves, to Fellow-Men, to Posterity, and to *him*.' Whitefield last and least! Little wonder that Robe described it as 'the most Heaven-daring Paper that hath been published by any set of Men in Britain these hundred years past'.[19] It seems that Gib regretted this outburst in later years, for he counselled a friend: 'Don't read it. When I wrote it, I was warm-blooded, and it would have been much better if I had not written it.'[20] Gib asserted that 'this foreigner' is 'no minister of Christ; his Doctrine is *diabolical*, as proceeding through diabolical *Influence* and applied unto a diabolical *Use*, against the Mediator's, Glory, and the Salvation of Men'.[21]

On 15 July 1742 the Associate Presbytery 'considering the present awful Symptoms of the Lord's Anger . . . in sending *strong Delusions* . . . in the *fond Reception* that *Mr George Whitefield* has met with', issued a call from Dunfermline for a 'Publick Fast' on account of the 'awful work upon the bodies and spirits of men going on at Cambuslang', mentioning in particular the 'bitter outcryings, faintings, severe bodily pains, convulsions, voices, visions and revelations'. Had Ralph Erskine forgotten his letter of 28 September 1739 to John Wesley? The latter had asked for advice about some of his hearers who had been distressed in 'an outward manner'. Quoting from the Scriptural instances of the crowd on the day of Pentecost and the Philippian jailor – so often to be used again as proof-cases by the defenders of the work at Cambuslang! – Erskine wrote: 'We want not instances of this power', and he cited especially sacramental occasions, when congregations sometimes wept and cried aloud 'till their voice be ready to drown out the minister's, that he can scarce be heard'. The real test of the worth of such emotion 'we can only know by the fruits and effects that follow'.[22]

19 Robe, J.: *Kilsyth Narrative.* xv.
20 McKerrow, J.: *History &c. p* 165 *fn.*
21 Gib, A.: *Warning &c. p* 53.   22 Wesley, John: *Journal.* ii *pp* 230-1.

The defenders of the revival appealed often to this empirical test of observable fruit; thus, one wrote: 'Did ever a delusive Spirit make a People forsake Sin? . . . Did ever the Devil of Delusion as you call it, at Cambuslang, turn Drunkards, Swearers, Whoremongers, Liers [sic] &c . . . to become new Creatures?'[23] Laymen rushed into print to defend the revival, especially Andrew Waddell, a soldier. In one pamphlet, directed against the Fast prescribed by the Associate Presbytery, he pointed out the inconsistency of extolling Whitefield to the skies a few months earlier and then denouncing him for 'failing to join with you. Behold how you open and shut the Kingdom of Heaven by your Anathemas as well as if the Pope had sent you his Keys.'[24]

In SATAN'S APE DETECTED &c., addressed to Adam Gib, it is pointed out that to deny that Whitefield was a minister because he was ordained by a diocesan bishop would be to 'depose all the Ministers of our neighbour Church'. Waddell's peroration was not without point: 'God is Love, and are ye like him, when ye are all hatred? Is Love a Duty or not? If it be not, then tear it out of your Bibles: if it be a Duty, then tear Hatred out of your Hearts . . . Are ye sure that God puts the same Value upon your Opinions that ye do?'[25] Another tract written by 'an Old Drumclog Soldier', again with Adam Gib in mind, is full of vituperation and plays on the name Adam with great glee. 'If he had preached as he now hath, about the Time of Drumclog, or Bothwel-Bridge, or Shirreff-Mure, . . . an old Soldier, the Author of this Advertisement, would cut the Lugs out of his Head . . . and burn'd his Tongue with a hot Iron.'[26]

There was warm feeling on both sides, but in the main the friends of the revival, and especially the ministers, preserved a praiseworthy attitude of conciliation. Robe, who with Webster was the foremost apologist and publicist for the work, addressed

---

23 *A Warning & Reproof with Advice &c. p* 4.
24 *Observations in Defence of the Work at Cambuslang &c. p* 4.
25 *Satan's Ape Detected &c. pp* 9, 24.
26 A WARNING. *All the Lovers of Christ to be on their Guard &c. p* v.

himself directly to the Seceders in his *Preface*: 'We pray for you, who despitefully use us. We would lay our Bodies as the Ground and as the Street for you to go over, if it could in the least contribute to remove your Prejudices . . . You declare the Work of God to be a Delusion and the Work of the grand Deceiver. Now, my dear Brethren, for whom I tremble, have you been at due Pains to know the Nature and Circumstances of this Work? Have you taken the Trouble to go to any of these Places, where the Lord hath appeared? Have you ever so much as Written to any of the ministers, to receive Information from them . . .?'[27] This is, at least, a plea for the examined life.

John Currie of Kinglassie, himself a prominent evangelical minister and one-time friend of the Erskines, pleaded for some investigation. In the opening paragraphs of his *New Testimony and Vindication*, he remarked that 'many are of Opinion 'tis washing a *Blackmore* to endeavour the Conviction of *Seceders* . . . yet I question not there are many good and gracious Persons among Seceders'. Noting that Adam Gib and his colleagues had forbidden their hearers either to read or to reason about the revival at Cambuslang, he declared this imprimatur to be but a new Papacy.

Fisher and others had complained about the physical emotion displayed during the revival, but Currie reminded them that he had 'heard such bitter Outcryings at hearing some of the *Seceding Brethren* themselves, before their *Secession,* that not a Word spoken in Sermon could be heard',[28] and he gave yet another *quid pro quo* by pointing out that 'at the last Sacrament in the *Seceding Meeting-House* at *Dunfermline* a woman dy'd suddenly after she had been at the Communion Table . . . but the *Seceders* will not allow her sudden Death to have been any Evidence of the Woman's being under a Delusion'.[29] After quoting from the Westminster Confession, Chapter 26.2, concerning the obligation to hold Communion with all those who in every place call upon the Lord Jesus, Currie asked, 'Are

27 *Kilsyth Narrative. pp* 55–6.
28 Currie, J.: *New Testimony &c. p* 15.
29 *Ibid. p* 23.

there not some among *Episcopals, Anabaptists* and *Independents,* who are not only Saints by Profession but in Reality, and People who call upon the Name of the Lord Jesus?'[30] and then he commended to all the advice of Gamaliel (Acts 5.38, 39) as being 'suitable and wholesome'.

Whitefield's own conduct and spirit under the bitter virulence of this personal attack are beyond all praise; never for a moment was he diverted into controversy or self-justification. One wonders which is the more amazing: the rancour of the attack, or the forgiving spirit in which, at all times, it was received.

Nevertheless, although the leaders of the secession condemned the revival from afar, without any direct investigation, many of their followers were attracted to a closer contact. Out of the 106 cases contained in the M'Culloch manuscripts, nineteen give explicit testimony that they had worshipped with the seceders. Says one: 'I heard some of the North Country Ministers at Corsehill, Of whom I had a great opinion,'[31] and this is echoed by several others. For three years before the revival broke out at Cambuslang, one young woman wrestled with the temptation to join the seceders, often going long distances to hear them 'even to the injuring my bodily health'.[32] She could never feel free to worship with them on Sabbath days for she 'had a Gospel minister at hand'. Another walked 'sometimes seven miles and sometimes to Stirling, which was twelve Miles from the place where I lived'[33] to hear them, and 'chose rather to sit at home, than hear any but them; thinking there were no other sermons right but theirs'.

Often the seceding meetings became Caves of Adullam, frequented by the disgruntled and malcontented. James Jack went for at least a year and 'was never better pleased than when I heard these Seceding Ministers railing upon the Church',[34] although he continued in his vicious habits. The daughter of a Shotts merchant, who went often to hear the

---

30 *Ibid. p* 58.   31 M'C. Mss. i *p* 22 (Janet Jackson).
32 *Ibid.* ii *p* 201 (Isobel Provan).
33 *Ibid.* i *p* 176 (Jean Robe).   34 *Ibid.* i *p* 497.

seceding ministers, came to Cambuslang in March 1742,
seeking to take back an ill report, 'all day resolving that if I saw
any Person there any way misbehaving, I should be sure to
mind that and to tell that when I went home'. Closer acquaintance with preachers and people made her 'quite to alter my
mind'.[35]

Sometimes the very violence of the denunciation drove some
sympathisers with the Secession to Cambuslang. Janet Lennox
had 'left the Kirk altogether'; curiosity led her to Cambuslang,
but, said she: 'I was not touched with what I heard.'[36] When
next she heard Fisher, he 'endeavoured to shew, That no
Revival of Religion was to be expected, or that God would
never return to a people or person in a way of mercy, till they
first humbled themselves'. Such a limitation on God's sovereignty was too much for her: 'This was what I could not agree to,
for I thought that the work must begin in God's part . . . After
this, I went no more back.'[37]

Seceding exclusiveness alienated others; one woman 'did not
find the Seceders way of Praying agreeable, because they
seemd to me to be very narrow in their prayers, and not to
extend them to the whole Israel of God, but to confine them in
a great measure to themselves'. Made very uneasy by the
opposition Fast against the revival, she decided, not without
many qualms of conscience, to go and see for herself. Completely unimpressed, she meditated on the way home on 'the
Lord's way of dealing with his people . . . by the still calm
voice of the Gospel, and could not get my heart brought to a
liking of the work at Camb'.[38] That was to come later.

Many, both laymen and ministers, hoped that the revival
would bring the Seceders and the ministers of the Established
Church together. Whitefield indicated the strength of this
spirit by his account of how when Ralph Erskine 'went up
with me into the pulpit of the Canon-gate church – The people
were ready to shout for joy'.[39] The youthful John Erskine, de-

35 *Ibid.* ii *pp* 183–4 (Agnes Buchanan).   36 *Ibid.* ii *p* 524.
37 *Ibid.* ii *p* 527.   38 *Ibid.* ii *pp* 201–2.
39 *George Whitefield Works.* i *p* 307.

ploring the opposition to the revival by even 'the Lord's Children', related that in *New England*, Presbyterians, Episcopalians, Independents &c have joined Hand in Hand for promoting Religion'. Mr Parsons wrote form New England: 'Never did I see so much Love . . . Old Grudges, it seemed to me, sneaked out of Doors full of Shame!' In his eager enthusiasm he concluded: 'These Things give us Ground ere long to expect a fuller Union among Christians; and that as there is *one Shepherd, so there shall be one Sheepfold* . . .who knows but the present remarkable Revival of Religion may soon be followed by as remarkable an Union among Christians.'[40]

A thirty-eight-year-old Glasgow tailor went to hear both Hamilton at the Barony, and Fisher, to learn wherein they differed, and happened to hear both of them deal with a similar subject, to his great satisfaction. 'I wondered how it came to pass, that Ministers should so exactly agree in their doctrine, while they disagree'd so much otherways.'[41] When the revival broke out at Cambuslang, he concluded that 'surely such a good Man as Fisher would fall in with it, and that the Church Ministers, and the Seceders would come all to unite by means of that work'. Faced with the sharp antithesis between Fisher's denunciations and the experience of a friend who had been greatly helped at Cambuslang, he resolved it only by going, hearing and judging for himself.

One most unusual case is that of a young man, Michael Thomson. Attracted by the preaching of a 'Mountain Minister, *viz* Mr Macmillan', he left home and went to learn a trade in Kilsyth, where Robe had a powerful influence upon him. Returning home, all his friends urged him to forsake the established church and join the 'North Country Ministers'. Going to hear Fisher, he was highly pleased by the sermon, but Fisher, in his closing prayer, petitioned 'that the Lords people might be kept from the Delusion that was now spread abroad in several places', and in this prayer Thomson could not join.[42]

40 Erskine, J.: *Signs of the Times Considered &c. pp* 15–16.
41 M'C. Mss. i *p* 399 (Archibald Bell).   42 *Ibid.* i *p* 482.

Greatly perplexed as to whether he should separate from the established church, Thomson, meditating on the Scriptures, found guidance. In spite of the gross viciousness of the sons of Eli, God did not command the Israelites to forsake worship; Jesus himself had continued in communion with the Jewish Church and preached in the synagogues; He had also advised His disciples to give heed to the religious teachers of the day. Thomson concluded that 'it was better for the People of God to abide together and contend for the truth, than to weaken one another's hands by separation and divisions'. Such illustrations as he found in Scripture made it clear 'that it was unlawfull to separate from this Church, notwithstanding what was wrong in it'. Burdened with a sense of the sins of the land and of the church, he prayed that 'the Lord would heal our woeful backslidings and divisions, and make us all one in him'.[43]

Bound up within the first volume of the M'Culloch manuscripts there is an account, set out in dramatic form, of a conversation between Alexander Bilsland and George Tassie, two of the converts at Cambuslang, and the two seceding ministers, Ebenezer Erskine and James Fisher.

One Thursday night in April 1743 it was made evident at a society meeting for prayer that several 'had done themselves hurt' by hearing those ministers attacking the work at Cambuslang. The following Monday morning the two laymen went to Fisher's house in Glasgow. Obtaining entrance, they recounted their own religious experiences, but Fisher protested that no possible blessing could follow the ministry of men who had joined in settling ministers in parishes against the people's will . . . 'I will not believe any good fruits follow the Ministry of such men as Whitefield, M'Culloch and M'Laurin and others, tho' one that had been in the third heavens would say so.'[44]

Discussion moved briskly to and fro, the laymen by no means getting the worst of the argument. Erskine, who was also present, asked the visitors to 'join with us to fight the battles of the

43 *Ibid.* i *pp* 483–4, 499.
44 *Ibid.* i *pp* 154–68.

Lord', but Bilsland answered: 'We never got any good by you. The worst evil we wish you, is that ye would come back to the Church of Christ.' Erskine went on to criticise Whitefield, and the laymen testified that he had brought good to them; at this Erskine cried (lifting up his hands): 'God save me from Camb: conversions and Mr Wh——ds Doctrine'.[45]

This attitude on the part of the seceders incited some to personal investigation, and others were shocked at the bitter and intolerant invective; many who had been seeking among the seceders for spiritual help under the revival at Cambuslang were led to renew their attachment to the established church and dedicate their new devotion to her welfare. In view of this, and the high hopes expressed by many of the ministers associated with the revival that the 'Glory of the Latter Days' was about to appear, it may well be asked why the revival did not achieve greater results. Why was it halted?

In spite of the lasting benefits that emerged, the hopes and expectations of many were unrealised. Within a few years of 1742, Thomas Gillespie, James Baine (declared by Struthers to be 'In many respects the most remarkable person of all the early fathers to the Relief Church'), Andrew Arrott, brother-in-law to John Willison, and other ministers who participated at Cambuslang, were outside the established church. It looked as if disruptiveness and anarchy were inherent within revivals. Why?

Much of the responsibility for this must be placed firmly on the shoulders of the Moderate party in the church, which was committed unreservedly to support the policy of patronage. To do this, they had, apparently, no qualms about thrusting out some of the godliest ministers and ruining some of the most thriving congregations.

It is not denied that the Moderates contained many men of unblemished character, such as their leader William Robertson; also their love of the liberal arts did much to inspire the culture that was to make Edinburgh the literary capital of Europe. We may lift our eyebrows somewhat sceptically when 'Jupiter'

45 *Ibid.* i *p* 167.

Carlyle claims that the Church contains the best historians philosophers, agriculturalists and so on. The claim is interesting, even imposing – but irrelevant. One of the shrewdest of our modern writers on the subject has concluded: 'It is rather by *what is left out*, whether deliberately or from sheer ignorance, that moderate *preaching* – I doubt very much if it ever had much of a theology – is to be judged.' He goes on to say that their encouragement to husbandry 'shows that they did not live wholly in vain; but it scarcely needed the Incarnation and the Cross to secure in our country an order of officials, who in their leisure time, might promote the cultivation of turnips and a freer use of lime'.[46]

The gravamen of the charge against the Moderates is their acceptance of a thorough-going Erastianism, whereby, for all practical purposes, they converted the Church into a Department of State.[47] This they did by the support given to patronage. Great land-owners, like the Duke of Argyll, maintained tenaciously that this power of presenting an accredited candidate to a congregation was an inviolable piece of property. Thus: 'Setlements would not readily be made against my inclinations. But that is a point I'l never yield, because I take it to be my property, and the right of my family, that none can take from me!'[48] 'Is it not an absurd thing that a tenant or servant who may be removed at a certain term should have a vote in choosing a minister for life to his master?' wrote Sir John Clerk.[49] The Moderate attitude to this claim may be summed up in words found in Dr Wallace's papers: 'I take this grievance to be remediless and that it is in vain to endeavour to have the law repealed . . . I will yeild intirely to the law as it stands.'[50]

In 1735, Francis Hutcheson, the 'father of Moderatism', was aware of the dangers of this system and predicted even greater mischief. Writing in his pamphlet, *Considerations on Patronage addressed to the Gentlemen of Scotland*, he foretells that: 'Instead of

46 Cairns, W. T.: *The Religion of Dr Johnson* – 'Jupiter Carlyle and the Scottish Moderates'. *pp* 86–7, 109.
47 Meikle, H. W.: *Scotland and the French Revolution. pp* 35–40.
48 *Anal.* iii *p* 491. March 1726.   49 *Memoirs – Clerk of Penicuik. p* 248.
50 Laing Mss. ii *pp* 620–9.

studying sobriety of manners, piety, diligence or literature, one or other of which qualities are now necessary to recommend the candidates to the favour of heritors, elders or presbytery, the candidate's sole study will be to stand right in politics, to make his zeal for the *ministry of state* conspicuous; or by all servile compliance with the humour of some great lord who has many churches in his gift, whether the humour be virtuous or vicious, to secure a presentation.'[51]

How justified was this foreboding may be seen from such an epitaph as that on the grave of the Rev Michael M'Culloch, minister of Bothwell (1767–1801).

> Here lies interred beneath this sod
> That sycophantish man of God,
> Who taught an easy way to heaven,
> Which to the rich was always given:
> If he gets in, he'll look and stare
> To find some out that he put there.[52]

Nepotism was inevitable under such conditions. In Glasgow in 1771 there was published *The Patron's A.B.C.*, a lampoon in catechetical form. Thus:

(5) Q. What is the chief end of a modern clergyman?
   A. A modern clergyman's chief end is, to serve the Patron, and his friends, that he may in due time be found worthy to receive and enjoy a benefice, or be advanced to a better place through his favour.

(6) Q. What is a Patron?
   A. A Patron is a Protestant Pope, Christ's vicar, and supreme head of his body the church of England and Scotland; infallible, absolute, incontroulable; of wisdom, which none dare call in question, of power, which none can resist; of holiness, such as becomes the eldest son of the Pope of Rome; of justice, goodness and truth, just as self-interest, or the sollicitation of friends happen at the time to preponderate.

In his *Diary &c.*, George Ridpath opens a window to show

51 McCosh, J.: *Scottish Philosophy &c. pp* 66–7.   52 *Fasti.* iii *p* 231.

us the system at work. In the entry for Monday, 4 June 1759, he sets down his experiences at the General Assembly. 'The company with whom I dined dealt pretty liberally in *Bonum Magnums* after dinner ... Reckonings amounted to 7/6d, a very extravagant sum,[53] and which I scarce should have been led into had I not been making a sort of court to Carlisle [*sic*] who undertook very readily to put a Memorial into Baron Grant's hands relating to the vacant stipend of Hutton.' 'Ridpath sought the patronage of the Crown to settle his brother Philip there.'[54] To be drunk with wine was far more useful than to be filled with the Spirit in securing promotion in the Church!

Expediency characterised much of the Moderate policy and practice. Carlyle tells of an incident in the Assembly of 1766 when a keen battle was fought out over the Schism Overture. Voting had begun when Dr Jardine collapsed and was carried out. The roll-call was stopped and Carlyle left the hall to make enquiries. The surgeon told him that all was over. Writes Carlyle: 'I returned to the house and gave out that there were hopes of his recovery ... the calling of the roll went on',[55] and the ecclesiastical prevaricator exults that his party managed to gain the victory. By 1780 even Carlyle was compelled to acknowledge that this policy had failed: 'Young men of low birth and mean education have discovered that livings may infallibly be obtained by a connection with the most insignificant voter for a member of Parliament.'[56] Edmund Burke declared that 'the clergy of the Church of Scotland ... appeared culpably obsequious to all the measures of Government'.[57] Even the far-sighted Hutcheson was not above manipulation and intrigue when seeking to secure the appointment of Leechman to the chair of theology in Glasgow. M'Laurin was the other candidate, and Hutcheson used his connections to

---

53 Elizabeth Mure wrote: 'A Shillings Reckoning was very high for a night's drinking in 1740'. *Scottish Diaries & Memoirs 1746–1843* (ed J. G. Fyfe), *p* 61 *ff*.
54 *Diary of George Ridpath 1755–61. p* 251.
55 Carlyle, A.: *Autobiography. p* 467.
56 Graham, H. G.: *Scottish Men of Letters &c. p* 99. *fn.*
57 Somerville, T.: *My own Life & Times. p* 251.

inform the Secretary of State for Scotland about those who made themselves 'ridiculous to all men of sense by dangling after Whitefield and M'Culloch'. It seems that the advocates of liberty could not tolerate that a man should be favourable to a revival of religion.[58] Immoderate for Moderation indeed!

This Moderate support for the enforcement of the patrons' rights caused friction and brought loss to almost every parish associated with the revival movement of 1742. After the death of M'Culloch in 1771, Cambuslang had no minister for three years, owing to a disputed settlement. The Duke of Hamilton presented James Meek, but a memorial was submitted to the presbytery saying that this 'was disagreeable to the whole Session and to the great body of the people'. Not a single elder signed the Call in September 1772; in fact, 'Claud Somers, one of the Elders . . . gave in a paper signed by all the Elders and 50 heads of families opposing Meek'.[59]

The presbytery decided not to sustain the presentation of Dr Meek; since five ministers voted for and three against it, the elders must have provided the majority. The General Assembly, on appeal, sustained the call to Meek but had to repeat this twelve months later for no action had been taken. In July 1774, the elders of Cambuslang submitted to the presbytery reasons for their protest. They objected to Meek's doctrine that 'sincerity is the ground of our acceptance with God', and that he had invited people, however enormous their crimes, to the Lord's table, 'if they resolved to do better'; he had also affirmed that 'when faith goes above Reason, it is Credulity'. The presbytery found these objections 'frivolous, absurd and irrelevant', and proceeded to admit Meek as minister of Cambuslang, in spite of protest, on 1 September 1774. The eventual issue was that nine of the elders were placed under the sentence of the lesser excommunication by the presbytery as 'false and malicious Slanderers and defamers' and thereby barred from all sealing ordinances.[60]

58 McCosh, J.: *Scottish Philosophy*. p 65.
59 Hamilton Pres. Recs. 21 July, 27 October 1772.
60 *Ibid*. July 1774, 3 January 1775.

Looking back on this period, Meek's successor, John Robertson, wrote: 'I am convinced the people of Cambuslang were much attached to the establishment, and that if a person had succeeded Mr M'Culloch, in whose orthodoxy and seriousness they had confidence, though he had been a man of inferior abilities, they would thankfully have submitted to his ministry.'[61] Many of the people travelled the seven or eight miles out to the Relief Church at Bellshill, and it has been noted that there was no Secession congregation in Cambuslang itself until 1836, almost a century after the revival.[62]

Let us now turn to Kilsyth. Robe's successor was John Telfer (1754–89). He supported an unpopular presentee, Mr Clark, to Eaglesham, and when his parishioners expressed concern to him, they were told to mind their own business. In his irritation, he offered to preside at Clark's ordination and induction to Eaglesham, and did so with the help of a number of soldiers. The parish of Kilsyth assembled the next day and decided to organise a Relief Church. When Telfer returned home he found 'nearly empty walls to which he might proclaim his triumph; and when he summoned a meeting of session, there was only one elder who honoured his call'.[63] In the parishes of St Ninians, Torpichen and Blantyre, each associated with the awakening of 1742, there was considerable trouble owing to unwelcome settlements.

It was not only congregations that suffered by this high-handed policy; certain individual ministers were either expelled or found themselves so uncomfortable that they were compelled to leave the established church. The outstanding example was Thomas Gillespie of Carnock, who laboured with notable success at both Cambuslang and Kilsyth in 1742. He was the close friend of John Erskine and one of the noblest men of the century. It was his misfortune to become a scapegoat to justify Moderate policy. In 1752 he was expelled from the established church because he was unwilling to take part in a forced settle-

61 Letter in *Edin. Christ. Instructor*. 1831. *p* 554.
62 Small, R.: *History of U.P. Congregations*. ii *p* 131.
63 *The Christian Journal*. 1833. *p* 149; *Fasti*. iii *p* 479.

ment at Inverkeithing. Fifty-two members of Assembly voted for his deposition, whilst 102 others sat silent and did nothing.[64] Nine years later the Relief Presbytery was founded under his leadership. Broad-minded and generous-hearted, this church was the first to state its belief in open communion and also 'to hold communion occasionally with Episcopalians and Independents'. James Baine, who had been minister at Killearn during the days of revival, and was later minister at Paisley, followed his friend Gillespie into the Presbytery of Relief. It will have been noted that the dissident members at Cambuslang and Kilsyth attached themselves to this church rather than to the narrower Seceders. Such men as these would have been an incalculable asset to the established church had they been allowed to remain and keep their consciences free. There were, however, many who were able to stay and who kept alive a spirit of earnestness.

The revival stopped the drift to the Secession and, although Moderate policy served to nullify much that had been accomplished, yet a nucleus of sincere men and women, ministers and laymen, were left behind within their mother church. They preserved the tradition of groups, meeting for prayer and fellowship, and had a direct connection with the events leading up to the Disruption of 1843. We shall conclude this chapter by examining the development of an evangelical remnant.

Among the many hearers of Whitefield during his visits to Scotland were students of divinity, training for their sacred office. Some of the impressions made by the evangelist remained to inspire and guide their future work. For others, it was contact with the revival movement that made them consider afresh the question of vocation, and whether they ought to enter upon the work of the Christian ministry.

George Muir, born at Spott near Dunbar in 1723, began work as a clerk to a Writer to the Signet in Edinburgh. Visiting

64 Dr Robert Wallace in his Mss IRENICUM (Laing Mss ii *p* 97) draws the analogy of 'The Public Executioner who must carry out his orders however unpleasant'.

Cambuslang during the summer of 1742, he determined to devote his whole life to the ministry. This decision was reached after correspondence with friends at Cambuslang. One of these, J.A., a layman, wrote to him on 2 August 1743: 'I have perused yours enclosed to me and some worthy, old, brave Christians here with me have perused it. And after mature deliberation, we do heartily and cheerfully approve of your laudable purpose ... I am glad to hear you counting the cost both of professing and preaching a dear, loving, and yet a despised Jesus ... Mr M'Laurin wants much to see and converse with you when you come west this week.'[65]

Whilst a student at Edinburgh, Muir threw himself into all kinds of religious activities and was well-known among the societies for prayer. On 8 August 1743 he wrote to 'Mr James Aitken, Schoolmaster in Glasgow' – may this be the J.A. mentioned earlier? – about the religious societies in Edinburgh, which were in a flourishing condition. He himself belonged to such a society, many members of which were intending ministers.[66] After finishing his theological course, Muir taught for a time in the school at Carnock. In 1752 he was ordained at Cumnock and exercised a notable ministry there, characterised by a wide catholicity. Mr Belfrage of the Secession Church, Falkirk, and Mr Hervey, rector of Weston Favell, were both intimate with him. One of the most revealing facts about him is found in a letter sent to M'Culloch at Cambuslang on 2 January 1756. Speaking of the state of religion in his parish, he found great comfort 'that a few in this town [four or five] have some time ago, of their own accord, associated together on the Lord's evening for prayer and conference, a thing not known in this village in the memory of man'. They had met at first on the Sabbath evening to be inconspicuous, but now had the courage to meet on a weeknight. 'It is pretty remarkable', wrote Muir, 'that a Seceder was the means of it.' This incomer to the parish had sought out others who were willing to join with him in prayer and had

65 Warrick, J.: *History of Old Cumnock. p* 110.
66 Prince, T.: *Christian History.* 1743. *pp* 271–4.

taken the trouble 'to advise with me in every step he took as to the society'.[67]

When James Baine resigned from the charge of the High Church of Paisley, Muir was called from his country parish to succeed him, being inducted on 30 October 1766. His ministry was notably successful: when cancer developed in his foot, he insisted on being carried to the church in a sedan-chair and spoke from a chair in the pulpit. He died on 20 July 1771, in his forty-eighth year.[68]

It is extremely probable that it was the revival at Cambuslang which brought John Erskine into the ministry. His father was professor of law at Edinburgh University and, in accordance with the family wish, he studied law. His future seemed assured as a lawyer of distinction. Why did he enter the ministry? In a letter from Mr Doddridge dated 11 June 1743, mention is made of the reasons why Erskine intended to study for the ministry; he had sent them to his father and forwarded a copy to the Northampton divine who replied: 'I hope God will abundantly bless your labours for the good of souls.'[69] Bishop Warburton, another of Erskine's correspondents, wrote on 26 September 1743: 'I heartily felicitate you on your choice of the better part', meaning the ministry.[70] Erskine changed his career about twelve months after his association with the revival, and this was probably due, in large measure, to its influence. Every revival has served to furnish new candidates for the ministry.

Others there were who did not seek to enter the ministry but sought for spheres of active Christian service. Laymen had been given greater opportunities for leadership in the revival,

67 Letter in *Edinburgh Christian Instructor*. 1838. pp 211–12.
68 Warrick, in his *History of Old Cumnock*, speaks of several manuscript letters by Muir and others about their observations at Cambuslang in 1742. When Warrick wrote his book in 1899, these manuscript letters were in the possession of Mr Macrae, late teacher at Dalleagles, New Cumnock. Extensive enquiries have failed to locate them, and Mr Macrae's grandchildren are now scattered overseas.
69 Moncrieff-Wellwood, H.: *Life of Erskine, p* 30. *Vide* Doddridge: Letter of 19 February 1743.
70 *Ibid.* pp 53–4.

helping to talk with people in distress, exhorting small groups in various places, taking charge of the increased number of societies for prayer.

Robe, in his *Narrative*, says: 'The Parish of *Baldernock* lying North and West from *Calder* is of all others the most singular and noticeable.' Over ninety people had been awakened by July 1742. For years there had been no minister in the place and they 'yet are without a Pastor . . . The Lord hath honoured their School-master *James Forsyth* to be greatly instrumental in this good Work among them.' As a result of his instruction of the children at school, there were meetings for prayer set up all over the parish.[71] There was a very obvious place for the apostolate of the laity.

On 10 February 1744 two eminent booksellers in Edinburgh, Thomas Lumisden and Jo. Robertson, wrote to Mr Moorhead in New England, telling of a revival in a remote parish in the Highlands. There was no minister, 'but their School-master, who is a pious Man, has travel'd amongst them and instructed them . . . They have formed Societies in sundry places . . . There they pray, sing Psalms and instruct one another. Their School-master goes round them; so that through the Year, he is not a Sabbath of ten at his own House. His Presbytery . . . allows him to explain the Scripture he reads . . . he calls also on the People to give their own Thoughts on sundry Passages of Scripture . . . The Name of this extended Parish is Lochbroom, and the Name of the School-master is Mr Hugh Cameron.'[72]

The eldership had proved itself to be of great service during the revival, but the new desire to serve more zealously and extend the kingdom of God involved many more men than could be given official sanction by admission to the eldership. Many amateur and would-be evangelists had caught a glimpse of the glory of service.

When John Wesley found himself faced by the similar problem of how to harness the sanctified energies of the many who had come to a living faith at his invitation, he gathered the converts into societies, each under the care of a class-leader.

71 *Kilsyth Narrative. pp* 78–80.   72 Prince, T.: *Chr. History.* 1744. *p* 219.

Many a man of humble education found a life-long ministry in this cure of souls. Others, who were somewhat better fitted for a wider ministry, he enrolled into an order of lay-preachers and exhorters, whom he recognised officially. No such *modus vivendi* whereby the enthusiasm of the ardent and gifted layman could be fully utilised was to be found in Scotland. In the Highlands there did arise a body of evangelical laymen, venerated for their godliness, called the 'Men', an influential and extensive brotherhood. Their status was a little more than that of the other laymen, and a little less than that of the minister.[73]

Apart from the 'Men', who were peculiarly a Highland order, the only outlet for laymen was through the Societies for Prayer. There was a deep-rooted distrust of lay-preaching that remained throughout the eighteenth century and beyond. When the brothers Haldane began their unconventional and peripatetic ministrations in the late eighteenth century, there was a storm of anger. All the denominations uttered strong condemnations. One clerical opponent of the novel method admitted: 'It would be a very seasonable service, but I am afraid the difficulties and perils of meeting a set of enthusiasts will prevent it.'[74] 'The whole of this missionary business grows from a democratical root,'[75] complained another. The events of the French Revolution had created another bogey. One can only surmise how far the habit of laymen meeting together regularly for prayer and discussion developed into talk on other themes as the pressures of the Industrial Revolution increased in Scotland. The power of thought and the custom of verbal expression must have served to develop dormant gifts of leadership, just as activity in the class-meetings of Methodism and lay-preaching may be traced in the origins of the Socialist party in nineteenth-century Great Britain.[76]

73 For a full discussion of the 'Men', their rise and development, *Vide* MacInnes: *Evangelical Movement &c. pp* 211–20.
74 Meikle, H. W.: *Scotland and the French Revolution. p* 209.
75 Laing Mss. 500–1.
76 The famous social reformer, Thomas Muir of Huntershill (1765–98), who was tried for sedition and transported to Australia, was an elder in Cadder Church, one of the revival centres near Glasgow.

As an example of how a sturdy love of political liberty was to be found in one who had direct associations with the revival at Cambuslang, William Carlile of Paisley, who was born in 1746, informs us that his mother often visited Cambuslang during the revival; 'she still speaks of it with enthusiasm'.[77] Carlile himself became an elder under Mr Witherspoon at Paisley when only twenty-one years of age, and then served under Dr George Muir, whom we have noticed earlier, and he remained in this office until his death in 1833. He was also a member of a praying society meeting each week.[78] He became a baillie and was well-known as a defender of popular rights, a radical, organising petitions against repressive legislation that prohibited popular assembly. The first man to be titled Provost of Paisley, he became an ardent advocate of many philanthropies, helping popular education and the newly-formed missionary societies.

One of the strangest and most interesting of the laymen who were influenced by the revival movement of 1742 was William Darney, who is referred to in many places in John Wesley's letters. Several of the converts at Cambuslang show tendencies to burst into verse, which turns out usually to be doggerel. Darney too wrote, and published, a collection of 214 hymns,[79] scorned by John Wesley as 'nonsense in verse'. In the preface to No clxii, he says: 'In the Year of our Lord, 1742, after I had begun Preaching, I began to question my Call to the Ministry, altho' I had a clear call in October before.' Nehemiah Curnock conjectures that Darney was converted under the preaching of the Rev James Robe of Kilsyth, and describes him as 'a Scot of Prodigious size, speaking a broad Scottish dialect, "terrible to behold"; about 1742, he appeared suddenly in Rossendale, preaching.'[80]

Soon Darney had established religious societies, named after himself, throughout Yorkshire and Lancashire. He was the main influence behind the conversion of William Grimshaw,

77 *Autobiography of William Carlile.* p 12.   78 *Ibid.* p 20.
79 Wesley, John: *Letters* iii p 31.
80 Wesley, John: *Journal.* iii p 293 *fn.*

the rector of Haworth, meeting him in a quarry by night for conversation. Grimshaw went along to Darney's meetings, where he gave out hymns and engaged in prayer, and was satirised as 'Mad Grimshaw, Scotch Will's Clerk'.

Darney, a man of tireless industry and perseverance, was often assaulted and even imprisoned for preaching. He became one of Wesley's helpers, but was in frequent trouble because of his insistence on preaching Calvinism. John Wesley was determined not to allow this subject to become a ground for public controversy, and said: 'I shall either mend or end him.'[81] But of Darney's apostolic labours throughout the north of England there can be no doubt.[82] Out of the 1742 revival there came those who received the impetus and call for effective service in the ministry, those who fought for public righteousness, and those who had to do the work of evangelists, though in an irregular fashion.

There is one direct link between the revival and the Disruption of 1843. Robert M'Culloch was the only son of the minister of Cambuslang, becoming minister of Dairsie in Fife in 1771, the year his father died. Dairsie manse itself became 'a trysting-place where godly ministers frequently met'.[83] Dr Erskine, Mr Walker, Dr Webster of Edinburgh, and Mr M'Laurin, Dr Gillies and Dr Balfour of Glasgow, were frequent visitors. It was all reminiscent of the manse at Cambuslang.

In March 1776 a daughter Janet was born to M'Culloch, and she eventually married Robert Coutts, minister at Brechin. After two years together he died of consumption and she returned to Dairsie. On 19 February 1811 she wrote to a friend: 'On the Fast Day we had a new miracle of Divine grace, in a Mr Chalmers of Kilmany, a great philosopher, but once an enemy avowedly to the peculiar doctrines of the gospel . . . Oh, I feel interested in him!'[84] From that time there began a cor-

---

81 Wesley, John: *Letters.* iii *p* 30 *fn*; iv *p* 275.
82 Many details about Grimshaw and Darney can be found in *Methodist Heroes in the Haworth Round* (J. W. Laycock).
83 Hetherington, W. M.: *Memoir and Correspondence of Mrs Coutts. p* 13.
84 *Ibid. p* 123.

respondence between Mrs Coutts and Thomas Chalmers that went on until his death; this is not too obvious from Dr Hanna's great biography, but there was undoubtedly a considerable traffic in letters. Until he moved from Kilmany to Glasgow, Chalmers was often at Dairsie manse.

In his letters to her we find indications of the high regard in which he held her. Thus, on 27 January 1815, he wrote: 'Do forgive this presumption in one who is so far behind you in the school of Christ, and who feels himself at the mere threshold of the subject.'[85] On 23 April 1827, he again wrote: 'I never can forget the Christian kindness and encouragement which I enjoyed under the roof of your excellent father . . . Dairsie is one of the most memorable portions in my retrospect of the past; and all the feelings which I had then are undiminished by change of scene or distance of time.'

Mrs Coutts went to live in Edinburgh and became widely known for her generous support of every evangelical cause. During 1827–29 she was greatly attracted by the enthusiasm of Campbell of Row and the excitement created by speaking in tongues. She was completely alienated by the extravagances of Irving and his followers: her close friend and minister, Mr Tait, was, however, deposed from the ministry in 1833 because of his association with the new movement. Mrs Coutts gave unswerving allegiance to Dr Chalmers and his associates in the ten years' conflict preceding 1843, and then gave unstintingly of her means to further the work of the new Free Church. She was the cause of the M'Culloch manuscripts being lodged in the library of the Free Church, now New College, Edinburgh.

On 30 May 1847, Dr Chalmers called to see her and, before going to his home, he named her as one of his dearest and oldest friends. The next morning all Edinburgh was stunned to hear that he had been found dead in his bed. It is interesting to know that Chalmers found his early Christian encouragement in the home where there were so many memories of, and associations with, the work at Cambuslang.

85 *Correspondence of Dr Chalmers.* Edited Hanna. xliv *p* 70.

The Concert for Prayer
and the Missionary Movement

Amongst the various facts set forth in 1751 by M'Culloch as evidence of a work of conversion at Cambuslang was the following:

'The formerly covetous and wordly-minded and selfish, have got a publick spirit, and zealous concern for promoting the kingdom and glory of Christ in the conversion and salvation of souls; and for this end, are careful not only to live inoffensively themselves, but usefully to others, so as all about them may be the better for them: they join cheerfully to their power, and some even beyond it (so that I have sometimes seen it needful, to check some of them for too large quotas or offers) in collections for promoting the interest of religion, or for the relief of these straits, in places near hand or far off: they carefully observe the times fixt in the concert for prayer and joining at such times in earnest pleadings at a throne of grace, for the spreading and success of the gospel, and the outpouring of the Spirit from on high on the churches.'[1] To put it briefly, they were thoroughly missionary-minded!

One cannot read the testimonies gathered together by M'Culloch without being struck by the eager concern expressed for the conversion of others, and the outreachings in prayer and desire to the whole world. The revival had delivered the converts from parochialism! One young man's 'hearts Desire and prayer to God', was '. . . that the Lord may send a Revival of Religion, in the life, and power of it, to all the Corners of the Land'.[2] Sarah Strang, 'Ane Old Widow Woman aged 65',

1 *Kilsyth Narrative.* pp 314–5.   2 M'C. Mss. i p 9 (Wm Baillie).

wrote that she 'would rejoice, if it were possible that the
Whole World should flock in to Christ'.[3] One man habitually
prayed 'that the Lord would revive his work thro' the whole
Land yea thro' the whole Earth. I think I have been much
helped to plead with God, that a Work of Conviction and conversion May spread abroad every where, that there may be ane
ingathering of souls to Jesus Christ.'[4]

When Alexander Bilsland was at the Cambuslang communion
in August 1743, many passages of Scriptures came to his mind,
'Particularly that text in Isaiah 54.5 "Thy Maker is Thy Husband the Lord of Hosts is his Name; the God of the Whole
Earth shall he be called": Upon which my heart was melted
down with love to God; and with difficulty I got My Self
restrained from Shouting aloud for Joy.' He went on: 'What
made Me rejoice most of all at that time, was the last part of
that text "The God of the whole Earth shall he be called",
by which I got a large view of the Extent of the Redeemers
Kingdom to become universal over the Whole Earth: which
prospect was most agreeable and delightful to Me.'[5]

Several people bore witness that freedom in prayer came only
when they ceased to be self-regarding and preoccupied about
their own concerns; like Job, they found that the Lord turned
their captivity when they prayed for their friends – and, in this
case, even their enemies. With fervour in intercession there
went also a forgiving spirit. One account ended: 'I can safely
say in the Sight of the Heart-Searcher that I have no malice,
enmity or ill-will at any person on Earth. I want and heartily
desire that . . . his Kingdom may be advanced all the world
over. On the Monday after the Sacrament at Cambuslang my
heart was so filled with love to Christ and the Souls of others
that I could have been content (if it had been possible) to have
taken all the multitude on the Brae in my arms and to have
carried them all up to Heaven. Oftimes I find myself straitned
when I would pray for blessings to mySelf; but when I begin

3 *Ibid.* i *p* 116.
4 *Ibid.* i *p* 437 (James Tenant).
5 *Ibid.* i *pp* 132-3.

to pray for others, and for the Advancing of the Kingdom of Christ, I get much liberty and enlargement of heart.'[6]

The theme is reiterated: one person finds 'as great concern on my Spirit for the Salvation of others as ever I had for my own';[7] another concludes: 'I bear no grudge or ill-will to any in the world. I pray for all, even for Enemies.'[8] A young man in secret prayer one day found great freedom in praying for revival through the land, 'and the Spreading of the knowledge of Christ thro' the Whole World: I was also helped to pray much for my Commorades'.[9] Marion Callander, a married woman of forty-four years of age, confesses: 'Formerly I had many cares how to gain and gather more and more of the things of the world, and these carking cares were a burden to my Spirit; but . . . Glory to God, he easd and freed my heart of all worldly cares . . . from that time forth my mind was kept stayd on him; and the concerns of his glory and Interest lay nearer to my heart than any concerns of my own: I became concernd for the Salvation of others as much as my own, and prayed as heartily for them as for my Self.'[10]

We may see this new concern for the widening of the Church's reach and the spreading of the Gospel into the whole world as the harbinger of the missionary movement which came to full view at the close of the century. At the same time, this was but the intensifying and developing of an interest that was very much alive before the revival. It was Calvin himself who wrote: 'We should desire to make it at least the subject of our prayers every day that God would gather churches to Himself from all quarters of the world.'[11] Political conditions, notably the control of the sea by Spain until 1588, and the domestic struggle to establish and to preserve the presbyterian way of church life, made any attempts at world-wide evangelisation by the people of Scotland impossible in the 16th century.

Throughout the seventeenth century, the Church of Scotland

6 *Ibid.* i *pp* 195–6 (Agnes Buchanan).
7 *Ibid.* ii *p* 310.   8 *Ibid.* ii *p* 571.
9 *Ibid.* ii *p* 670 (John Parker).
10 *Ibid.* i *p* 577.
11 Calvin, J.: *Institutes.* Book III. Chapter xx. Sections 41–2.

sought to keep in touch with her sons over the seas, expatriate because of persecution, commerce or colonising enterprise. Holland became a gateway to the Continent. In 1647 the General Assembly wrote 'to their countrymen in Poland, Swedland, Denmarke and Hungarie', urging them not to forget the pearl of greatest price in their search for riches far from home. When the ill-fated expeditions sailed for Darien in the last decade of the seventeenth century, ministers were commissioned to go with them so that 'those afar among the pagans might not be left as sheep in a wilderness, without a shepherd; and also, that the light of the Gospel might shine in these dark regions where it never yet shined, and if possible that the poor Heathens might in time be brought to see and walk in this light'.

Ministers went out to serve in India. James Stirling (1631–71), deprived of his charge at Paisley in 1662, sailed for Bombay and died abroad; with him went Patrick Warner (1640–1724) who ministered at Fort St George on the Coromandel coast for three years. He returned to become minister at Irvine, married the daughter of William Guthrie of Fenwick, and acquired the Ayrshire estate of Ardeer in 1707. His daughter Margaret married Robert Wodrow, and his son was one of the officiating elders at the Cambuslang second communion in 1742.[12]

The first organised effort to forward missionary activity beyond the seas was undertaken by the Society in Scotland for Propagating Christian Knowledge. Beginning in a small prayer society of lawyers, and inspired by an Episcopalian minister, James Kirkwood, it is an outstanding example of Christian unity that Presbyterians should agree to work in such close association and harmony with Episcopalians so soon after the exhausting struggle with episcopacy. In 1709 Queen Anne gave the society Letters Patent and, during the years that followed, excellent work was done in organising schools and supplying teachers and libraries to remote, neglected parts of Scotland.

In 1723 there appeared one of the first books published in

12 *Fasti.* iii *pp* 99, 168.

Scotland concerned with the missionary aims and methods; its title was *The History of the Propagation of Christianity and overthrow of Paganism* . . . *the present State of the Heathens is enquired into ; and methods for their Conversion offered.* The author was Robert Millar, minister of the Abbey, Paisley,[13] and there were two volumes. Millar set out what had been done of late years by Protestant missionaries, dealing especially with work in the New England plantations and the Danish mission to Tranquebar. He went on: 'In Scotland, we have had no great Opportunities hitherto for sending Missions to promote Christianity among Heathens in the remote Parts of the World',[14] although he expected that candidates for such work would have excellent instruction in the flourishing universities. Wodrow, who reveals Millar's own son as an *enfant terrible*, would probably have questioned this. Millar also rejoiced in the successful efforts of the S.S.P.C.K. and closed his book with a description of some 'further means to be used for converting the heathen', placing first fervent prayer, and especially 'by joining in solemn days of humiliation and prayer for that end'.

In his Preface, dated 21 October 1723, at Paisley, Millar writes: 'If Christians would serve GOD in Spirit and Truth at home; if they would lay aside their Divisions, Parties and Unchristian Humors; if they would contribute generously, out of their worldly Substance that GOD has given them, for advancing his Glory in the World . . . if Persons of Extensive Knowledge, bright Love and Charity to perishing Souls, and animated with flaming Zeal for the Glory of GOD, would offer themselves as Missionaries, and might be orderly sent into Heathen Countries, especially where they can be encouraged and supported by European Colonies: If these things were done, what a glorious Addition to the Church of CHRIST might we justly expect.'[15] Then there follows that note of apocalyptic consummation, found constantly among the subjects and leaders of the evangelical revivals: 'The Time is coming, when

13 Crawfurd, Geo: *History of the Shire of Renfrew. p* 303.
14 Millar, R.: *History of the Propagation &c.* ii *p* 523.
15 *Ibid.* xvii–xviii.

the Fulness of the Gentiles shall come and all Israel shall be saved. Let us do our Duty.'

Finally Millar reveals his expectation of a religious awakening: 'The Time is coming, and I hope near at Hand, when GOD will do great Things for the Advancement of our Redeemer's Kingdom.'[16] Within less than twenty years Paisley was ringing with the news of revival at Cambuslang and elsewhere, but this scheme for missionary enterprise remained only an aspiration until Carey and the Baptist Missionary Society took action in 1792.

Millar's book was one of the formative influences in the eighteenth century. Pages xxi–xxxvi furnish a list of 468 subscribers: professors, schoolmasters, merchants, lords and ladies, ministers of religion, and students are named. Copies went to all parts – including Nottingham, Derby, Dublin, Belfast, Sheffield, and many other towns, both in England and Scotland. Persons later to be associated with the revivals of 1742 are named: 'Matthew Connel, minister at Kilbride, Hamilton at the Barony, James Rob at Kilsyth, James Warden, student of divinity, and William Warner of Ardeir.' Wodrow sent a copy, with his recommendation, to Dr Cotton Mather at Boston in New England.[17] Later it stirred the heart of Andrew Fuller, the colleague of William Carey.

Part of the Constitution of the S.S.P.C.K. stated that one of the Society's aims was 'to extend their endeavours for the advancement of the Christian religion to heathen nations and for that end to give encouragement to ministers to preach the Gospel among them'. Dr Daniel Williams, a Presbyterian minister in London, died in 1717 and left a sum of money for bursaries at Glasgow University. He also left to the S.S.P.C.K. an estate in Huntingdonshire, which was made transferable to them 'three years after they should send three qualified ministers to infidel and foreign countries'.[18] In 1730 the directors began to correspond with the authorities in New England about

16 *Ibid.* xviii–xx.
17 Wodrow, R.: *Correspondence.* iii *p* 154.
18 Weir, R. W.: *History of the Foreign Missions of the Church of Scotland. p* 9.

appointing missionaries to the Indians, and small boards were organised at Boston, New York and Massachusetts Bay to choose persons qualified for the office of missionaries, to fix the particular places and to disburse funds for advancing work among the Indians. In addition to white missionaries, 'assistants and interpreters were to be chosen'. In 1735 the estate was transferred to the Society, and John Macleod was sent by the Society from Skye to Georgia to minister to the Highland settlers there, but the débacle of the expedition against the Spaniards in 1740 compelled him to leave the colony.

There was then a growing volume of interest in missionary activity in Scotland before the actual awakenings of 1742, but the revivals gave a tremendous impetus to the work. The S.S.P.C.K. provided a rallying-point for the new evangelistic ardour, and received the support, in prayer and gift, of the people associated with Cambuslang. In the brief Memoir prefixed to the posthumous volume of M'Culloch's Sermons we see the minister's own interest in this project. Ever anxious not to let his right hand know what his left hand was doing, he did not succeed in concealing entirely from posterity his benefactions. In 1752 he spent £12 in having 300 copies of a reading primer, the Shorter Catechism and the book of Proverbs, printed and 'dispersed through Scotland and America for the benefit of young people of the poorer sort . . . In 1768 he purchased three hundred Bibles, which cost near £25, and secretly ordered them to be dispersed.' How real was his interest in the S.S.P.C.K. may be understood by his sending a trusted elder to take a personal donation of £200 to Edinburgh, 'with strict charge that he should not tell any person by whom it was sent'.[19] We may take this example by the minister of Cambuslang as being typical of the attitude and actions of others.

In 1742 the S.S.P.C.K. appointed a young man, David Brainerd, to be one of their missionaries to the Indians. When a student at Yale in 1741, he had come under the influence of Jonathan Edwards, and, although he was the best student of his year, he was expelled from the university in February 1742

19 M'Culloch, W.: *Sermons.* Preface *pp* 18–19.

for participating in revival meetings conducted by Gilbert Tennent. All entreaties by several prominent ministers, including Mr Burr, Jonathan Edwards' son-in-law and 'one of the correspondents of the Honourable Society in Scotland',[20] failed to secure his reinstatement. On 19 November 1742, Ebenezer Pemberton, 'Secretary of the Correspondents in New York, New Jersey and Pennsylvania of the Society in Scotland for the Propagation of Christian Knowledge', invited Brainerd to visit New York and discuss work amongst the Indians, and a week later, on 25 November 1742, he was commissioned to this task. For five years he persisted in labours abundant, and died of tuberculosis on 9 October 1747 at the age of twenty-nine. His *Diary* has been one of the greatest inspirations behind missionary enterprise: John Wesley, William Carey and Henry Martyn acknowledge gladly their immense debt to his saintly life as revealed in his diary. Gillies, in his weekly newspaper to his parishioners in Glasgow in November 1750, tells them of 'Mr David Brainerd, lately deceas'd'.[21]

The Cambuslang revival aroused a deeper interest in the work of overseas missions; it also brought together into a warm and living fellowship many ministers and laymen of varying points of view. A new and remarkable catholicity was begun in the revival and continued afterwards. Perhaps the most abiding result of Whitefield's visits to Scotland was the revelation of the breadth of his religious sympathies and the impact which this made upon his friends.

Speaking of Whitefield's fourteen visits, Butler says: 'Their predominant influence was in breaking down party zeal and sectarian bigotry . . . one who rose above all party shibboleths, and who would preach anywhere if he only felt a new opportunity presenting itself of doing good. It is pleasant, too, to recall that pulpits in the Church of Scotland were open to him, when those in England were closed against him.'[22] Thomas Somerville, in the late eighteenth century, pays great tribute to

20 Edwards, J.: *Works* (*ed* S. E. Dwight). cxvii.
21 Gillies, J.: *Exhortations &c.* 1750. i *p* 94.
22 Butler, D.: *John Wesley & George Whitefield in Scotland. p* 61.

'the conversation and preaching of the celebrated George Whitefield as a major cause of the extirpation of narrow prejudices ... and the more rapid progress of a catholic spirit'.[23]

It is evident that there were those within the established church who were ready to follow Whitefield's example. On 8 October 1741, Willison wrote to a friend, giving his opinion of Whitefield: 'I see the man to be all of a Piece, his Life and Conversation, to be a transcript of his Sermons ... so eminent for Humility in the Midst of Applause ... God, by owning him so wonderfully, is pleased to give a Rebuke to our intemperate Biggotry and party Zeal ... Many with us are for preferring Ministers according to the Party they are of, but commend me to a pious Christ exalting and Soul winning Minister, whatever be his Denomination; such are Ministers of Christ's sending.' Ogilvie of Aberdeen writes in similar strain: 'His attachment to no party but to Christ, appears to me a peculiar excellency in him.'[24] On 16 June 1742, Mrs Whitefield, writing from Edinburgh to John Cennick, shows that a similar spirit was to be found amongst the ministers of the Church of Scotland: 'My husband *publicly declared here*, that he was a member of the *Church of England*, and a curate thereof; and, yet, he was permitted to *receive* and *assist at the Lord's Supper* in the churches at Edinburgh.'[25]

Even a casual acquaintance with Whitefield's many letters shows how great was this roving evangelist in his breadth of vision and magnanimity. Writing to Gilbert Tennent on 2 February 1742, he says: 'What a pity it is, that we should fall out in the way to heaven!'[26] To a friend in New York on 26 February 1742, he defines his attitude: 'How can I act consistently, unless I receive and love all the children of GOD ... of whatever denomination they may be? I talk freely with the Messrs W[esley]s though we widely differ in a certain point.'[27] When he received news of the Fast organised by the Seceders

23 Somerville, T.: *My Own Life & Times*. pp 65–6.
24 *Glasgow Weekly History*. No 13 pp 4–8.
25 Tyerman, L.: *Life of George Whitefield*. ii p 5.
26 *George Whitefield Works*. i p 363.
27 *Ibid*. i p 372.

against himself and the work at Cambuslang, he merely comments: 'to what lengths may prejudice carry even good men? From giving way to the first risings of bigotry and a party spirit, good LORD deliver us!' Faced by Adam Gib's intemperate railings in that 'bitter pamphlet', Whitefield declares, echoing St Ignatius when he anticipated being ground into fine flour by the wild beasts at his approaching martyrdom: 'Now I begin to be a disciple of JESUS CHRIST.'[28] Never a word of retaliation!

This same attitude persisted to characterise the evangelical ministers who were associated with the Cambuslang revival. In his paper, *The Glasgow Weekly History*, M'Culloch prints a letter written on 12 February 1742 by the Welsh evangelist, Howell Harris, to a religious society in London. It is a remarkable expression of a passion for oecumenicity. He calls on the Dissenters to acknowledge that God has a few faithful even in 'this benighted Church'. Then, to members of the established church, he declares that there are many 'precious lambs of Christ among the various Denominations'. 'I think that it is contrary to the Gospel of Christ, so to join any Party, as not to be free to join with all other Parties of Believers . . . all ministers . . . of every perswasion, should meet to relate their own Experiences to each other . . . and to lend their Pulpits to each other alternately . . . bearing a publick Testimony against the selfish Spirit of Party-Zeal . . . and all . . . willing to communicate together.'[29]

Henry Davidson of Galashiels, the last survivor of the Representing Brethren, 'the twelve apostles' who defended the use and teaching of *The Marrow of Modern Divinity*, wrote on 23 August 1742: 'The associate presbytery are raging against Mr Whitefield and the work of God in the west. Have not they and the Lord's children in this land been for many years crying for the return of the departed Spirit and now that he is not returned in a way of their own devising, it must be all delusion . . . What lengths will party-spirit carry even good men!'[30]

28 *Ibid.* i *pp* 411, 413.   29 *Glasgow Weekly History.* No 14 *pp* 5-6.
30 Davidson, H.: *Letters to Christian Friends. pp* 61-2.

Alexander Webster of the Tolbooth, Edinburgh, wrote to defend the revival at which he had often been present. In his peroration he says: 'The warm opposition by several GOOD MEN may teach us it is a dangerous Thing to censure without proper Enquiry. It may serve likewise as a Solemn Warning against a Party-Spirit.' It could also serve as an incentive to make men long eagerly for the land above . . . 'Where are no Wranglings, no Strivings about Matters of Faith . . . Where Perfect Light will lay a Foundation for perfect Harmony and Love'. Webster comes to a close: 'It is with peculiar Pleasure that I often think of this happy Meeting of ALL the scattered Flock of Christ . . . And have not the least Doubt but that my good Friend Ebenezer, shall then enter into the everlasting Mansions with many glorified Saints whom the ASSOCIATE PRESBYTERY have now given over as the Property of Satan.'[31] Speaking of this generous magnanimity as 'golden words', Dean Stanley said: 'This is Moderation, if ever there was such on earth . . . words which no mere enthusiast could have conceived or penned.'[32]

There was a sincere reluctance on the part of many of the friends of the revival to enter into controversy at all. The Rev William Gusthart of Edinburgh, Dean of the Chapel Royal, wrote to M'Culloch on 4 April 1743, informing him that 18 February had been observed in Edinburgh as a commemoration of the outbreak of revival at Cambuslang. He turns to discuss M'Culloch's accounts of the awakened, and suggests that only the most remarkable cases should be published, a few at a time. 'I pray you never mention the Seceders; there's nothing will convince them, till God himself do it; and they'll be sure to snarle, and make returns, which will hinder you from much better work. I was sorry when Mr Robe was obliged to enter into such warfare; he was better employed. The devil wants to divert us from our better work! Let us be easy, God's work will appear to be his own, contradict it who will.'[33]

31 Webster, A.: *Divine Influence &c. pp* 52–3.
32 Stanley, A. P.: *The Church of Scotland. pp* 137–8.
33 *Edinburgh Christ. Instructor.* 1839. *pp* 338–9.

In 1748 an attempt was made by an Overture to prohibit or discourage Whitefield from preaching in Scottish parish churches; this afforded the evangelical ministers associated with the Cambuslang revival, especially John Gillies and John Erskine, an opportunity of stating publicly their advocacy of that catholic spirit which had found embodiment in the visiting clergyman who was being condemned.[34] Mr Millar, minister in Hamilton, who was married to the daughter of that consistent adversary of M'Culloch, Hamilton of Westburn, spoke at the Synod of Glasgow and Ayr of 'a celebrated Stranger whose Character was at best dubious'. Two ministers of the Presbytery of Glasgow had even invited him to their pulpits, and Millar urged that such a thing should be prohibited.

Gillies told the Synod that he 'did not repent of it; The Synod might inflict what Censure they pleased'; Erskine, ever the lawyer, demanded that a Libel be given. The opposition to Whitefield dwelt on 'that chimerical Scheme, his Georgia Orphan-house'. Where was the evidence that the money collected had been rightly applied? As for his preaching, it was *Vox, et praeterea nihil*. To this it was answered that to approve such an Overture would close the door against all ministerial communion with other churches ... 'Shall I refuse to cultivate Union and Friendship with those whom God has received, because in lesser Points their sentiments differ from mine? ... If Bp Butler, Bp Sherlock, or Bp Secker were in Scotland, I should welcome them to my Pulpit ... Mr Rutherford, as firm a Presbyterian as any of us, was of that Mind, else he would not have employed a Bp Usher to preach for him.'[35] The motion was lost by twenty-seven to thirteen in favour of an amendment, which left the matter as it had been before.

John Gillies welcomed John Wesley as his guest and preacher in the College Church in 1753, the first visit made by Wesley to the West of Scotland. He helped Gillies with his book, the

34 *A fair and impartial* ACCOUNT *of the* DEBATE *in the Synod of Glasgow and Air* [sic] *Sixth October 1748, anent employing Mr Whitefield.* This was written by John Erskine. (*Vide Life &c. p* 134.)
35 *Ibid. pp* 8–9.

Historical Collections, and brought in, not without opposition, the innovation of singing hymns at the close of the service. Commenting in his diary on this invitation, Wesley exclaims: 'Surely with God nothing is impossible! Who would have believed, five and twenty years ago, either that the minister would have desired it or that I should have consented to preach in a Scotch kirk?[36] ... the behaviour of the worshippers was beyond anything I ever saw but in our congregation.' Later, John Gillies himself preached in the Methodist meeting-house.[37] At a later visit to Gillies in 1757, Wesley organised praying societies and advised them to meet with Mr Gillies every week; by 1759 Wesley met with about forty members of such societies.

This gracious and generous friendship shown by Gillies to Wesley was also to be seen in the attitude of other friends to the 1742 revival. In 1761, Wesley dined with Ogilvie at Aberdeen: 'a more open-hearted friendly man I know not that I ever saw'. So warm was the welcome given to him on this occasion, and on later visits, that he doubted his ability 'to bear all this sunshine!'[38] Wesley himself was not afraid to express the widest tolerance. Thus, he wrote to John Newton (9 April 1765), 'Is Thomas à Kempis, Mr de Renty, Gregory Lopez gone to hell? Believe it who can.'[39] John Newton later spoke generous words defining his own outlook. In a letter (29 March 1781) he declared: 'My hearers are made up of all sorts ... My endeavour is to persuade them to love one another . . . Accordingly Churchmen and Dissenters, Calvinists and Arminians, Methodists and Moravians, now and then I believe, Papists and Quakers, sit quietly to hear me ... whether a *surplice* or a *band* be the fittest distinction of a minister ... whether water-baptism should be administered by a spoonful or tub-full, or in a river, in any river, or in Jordan (as Constantine thought), are to me points of no great importance ... If a man loves

36 Wesley, J.: *Journal.* iv *pp* 62–4. Also Whitehead, *Life of Wesley.* ii *pp* 272–3.
37 Wesley, J.: *Letters.* v *p* 59.
38 Wesley, J.: *Journal.* iv *p* 451; v *p* 14.
39 Wesley, J.: *Letters.* iv *p* 293.

Jesus, I will love him, whatever hard name he may be called by . . . His differing from me will not always prove him to be wrong, except I am infallible myself.'[40]

This spirit of tolerance concerning the denominational affiliations of like-minded men made possible the later co-operation which was to be so characteristic a feature of the beginnings of the missionary movement in the latter years of the eighteenth century. We may best trace this development through the growth of the ideal and practice of the Concert for Prayer, a direct link between the revival at Cambuslang and the enterprise that began with the sailing of William Carey to India.

On 12 January 1748, Jonathan Edwards, after first preaching to his people a series of sermons in its favour, published at Boston, New England, his book *An HUMBLE ATTEMPT to Promote Explicit Agreement and Visible Union of GOD'S PEOPLE IN EXTRAORDINARY PRAYER for the revival of Religion and the Advancement of Christ's Kingdom on earth.*[41] (Lengthy as is this title, it is an abbreviation of the original title with its 187 words.) The complete title made explicit the fact that the book was occasioned by a certain 'CONCERT for prayer' entered into by many ministers and others in Scotland and Great Britain. For some time M'Culloch and Edwards had been in frequent correspondence. In Section 3 he pointed out that in October 1744 a number of ministers in Scotland engaged themselves to unite in prayer that God would 'revive true religion in all parts of Christendom . . . and fill the whole earth with his glory'.[42] They pledged themselves to try to persuade others to join with them and to devise some method that would ensure success.

The arrangement made was to be binding for the 'two years next following'; some time on Saturday evening and Sabbath morning was to be devoted to this purpose each week, 'and more solemnly, the first Tuesday of each quarter (beginning with the first Tuesday of November) . . . either the whole day,

40 Newton, J.: *Works.* vi *pp* 98–9.
41 Edwards, J.: *Works.* ii *p* 423 ff.
42 *Ibid.* ii *p* 440.

or part of the day, as persons find themselves disposed, or think their circumstances will allow: the time to be spent either in private praying societies, or in public meetings, or alone in secret'. Saturday evening and Sabbath mornings were specially chosen because of their nearness to 'the time of dispensing gospel ordinances throughout the christian world'.[43] Such an agreed union would help to animate and encourage God's people everywhere, knowing that multitudes of their fellow-christians in so many distant places were at the same time engaged by agreement in the same holy exercise.

Edwards notes that the way in which the Concert was arrived at was not through the press, but by personal conversations and private correspondence. Great numbers in Scotland and England and some in North America had agreed to unite in this method. The Scottish praying societies had given it their whole-hearted support, and he cites Edinburgh as having 'thirty societies of young people there newly erected, some of which consisted of upwards of thirty members'. There were also forty-five societies in Glasgow.

One of the leaders among the Scottish ministers was John M'Laurin (1693-1754) of the north-west parish of Glasgow – 'scarcely less intellectual than Butler, he is as spiritual as Leighton'.[44] Before the Cambuslang revival, he had kept up a frequent correspondence with the New England ministers, Cooper, Prince and Jonathan Edwards, and 'when he received their accounts, he spread them among his acquaintances', writes his son-in-law, John Gillies, whom he 'met once a week ... to receive and communicate religious intelligence'. When societies for prayer multiplied in Glasgow, M'Laurin organised a monthly general meeting to supervise the expanding work, consisting of a member from each society with a minister as chairman. Gillies goes on: 'He was the chief contriver and promoter of the concert for prayer.' The youthful John Erskine was one of M'Laurin's most intimate friends.

The two-year arrangement had ended 'last November'

43 *Ibid.* ii *pp* 440–1.
44 *Works of the Rev John M'Laurin* (ed Goold). *pp* xvii *et passim*.

(1747). Several Scottish ministers had subscribed a printed memorial, 'signed by twelve clergymen of that country', inviting still more to unite in prayer. Five hundred copies of this had been sent to New England, and Edwards inserts a copy in full as Section IV of his book.[45] The new proposal was that the Concert for Prayer should be renewed, this time for seven years. This memorial is dated 26 August 1746. Edwards concludes his *Humble Attempt* by pointing out that the contemporary charge of novelty is ill-founded, and cites examples of such schemes in London in 1712 and in Scotland in 1732 and 1735. He also says of these Scottish ministers, whose proposal he is endorsing, that they 'are no separatists or schismatics . . . but are quiet, peaceable members and ministers of Scotland . . . they concealed their names from what perhaps may be called an excess of modesty'.[46]

Edwards does not mention that probably the idea was in part inspired by himself. In the closing paragraphs of his book, *Some Thoughts concerning the Present Revival &c.*, published in 1742 and read widely in Scotland, he recommends that ministers might make a draft of a covenant with God. 'Suppose the matter be fully proposed and explained to the people, and, after sufficient opportunity for consideration, they be led . . . particularly to subscribe the covenant. Suppose also all appear together on a day of prayer and fasting, publicly to own it before God in his house.' Here he gives the example of the 1596 General Assembly which was inspired to dedicate itself to concerted prayer and repentance by the bold and stirring words of John Davidson.

Robe in the Preface to his *Sermons* says: 'This concert was first set on foot, spread, and carried on, without printing any thing about it for some time, in the way of private, friendly correspondence, by letters in 1744. Afterwards some account of it was published in *The Christian Monthly History for 1745, No 1*.'[47] We may gather some idea of how this was done by a letter,

45 Edwards, J.: *Works.* ii *pp* 443–4.
46 *Ibid.* ii *pp* 535–8.
47 Quoted in Gillies: *Historical Collections.* ii *p* 399.

dated 22 December 1744,[48] written by 'Robert Wightman Esq, an Edinburgh merchant and Dean of Guild in that city', to M'Culloch at Cambuslang.

Erskine of Grange had informed Wightman of the proposed Concert for Prayer, and he mentioned the weekly and quarterly periods to be set aside exactly as Edwards later cites them. Wightman approved the idea, with some modifications, for he had never before joined in any fellowship meetings. 'I have long thought ostentation in religion a dangerous thing, and indeed inconsistent with it. I am thoroughly conscious, how strong a bias there is, towards displaying one's self in every thing.' This new proposal wins his support, however: 'It is very much to my taste, on that very account that it is a secret one, and therefore if you please, let me creep in amongst you at the throne of grace, without being enlisted in Mr Robe's list . . .' Wightman considered that such a company of supplicants, united although far apart and unknown to each other, resembled the heavenly host who stand before the throne of God. His one regret was that no precise hour had been decided upon for prayer on Saturday evenings and Sunday mornings.

On 28 June 1751, Edwards wrote to John Erskine: 'What if you, dear Sir, and other ministers in Scotland . . . should now take occasion to inform ministers in the Netherlands of it [the Concert for Prayer] and move them to come into it and join with us in our united and extraordinary prayers for an universal revival of religion.'[49]

Erskine of Grange had informed Robe of the work of John and Charles Wesley, and the minister of Kilsyth recommended to him that the two brothers should be invited to join the Concert for Prayer. John Wesley replied to Erskine of Grange on 16 March 1745, thanking him for the transcript from Robe's letter which he had sent. 'It shows a truly Christian spirit. I should be glad to have also the note you mention touching the proposal for prayer and praise. Might it not be practicable to have the concurrence of Mr Edwards in New England, if not

48 *Edin. Christ. Instr.* 1839. *pp* 339–40.
49 Edwards J.: *Works. p* cxxxii.

of Mr Tennent also, herein? It is evidently one work with what we have seen here. Why should we not all praise God with one heart?'[50] Robe was able later to write of the Wesleys that 'they have acceded'.[51] So it was that an English Episcopalian recommended to Scottish Presbyterians the inclusion of an American Independent within the comprehension of united intercession![52]

As we have already noted, the sponsors of the Concert for Prayer in Scotland, amongst whom were undoubtedly M'Laurin of Glasgow, Robe of Kilsyth and M'Culloch of Cambuslang,[53] got in touch with Jonathan Edwards as Wesley advised. Throughout the years they kept up a correspondence with him, and none more than their youthful associate, John Erskine. When Edwards, the great American divine, was ejected from his Northampton charge, Erskine, M'Laurin and M'Culloch organised financial support for him from among Scottish ministerial friends, and offered to use their good offices to secure a charge for him within the Church of Scotland, if he would consent to come.[54] Henry Davidson, the minister of the Church of Scotland at Galashiels, wrote to W. H(ogg), merchant in Edinburgh, on 14 January 1751: 'You will receive eight guineas for the worthy man's use as he and his family are brought into straits for the sake of the truth. I request you to mention my name to no mortal.'[55]

Fittingly enough, it is through the agency of John Erskine, by then an old man, that the Concert for Prayer achieved what may be accounted its greatest success. First we must retrace our steps.

Amongst the many who were powerfully influenced by the preaching of Whitefield was a young Yorkshireman, John

50 Wesley, J.: *Letters.* ii *p* 33.
51 Whitehead, J.: *Life of Wesley.* ii *p* 195.
52 Wesley had read Edwards' narrative when walking to Oxford, 9 October 1738 (*Journal.* ii *pp* 83–4), and had reprinted it in 1744 (Green, R.: *Wesley Bibliography. p* 31).
53 Cambuslang Session Records, October 1749, show the Session planning to meet, 'the last Fryday [*sic*] of every Month . . . a dyet for prayer'.
54 M'Laurin J.: *Works.* xlvii–lv. Edwards J.: *Works.* clxiii.
55 Davidson, H.: *Letters. p* 124.

Fawcett, born near Bradford in January 1740. He became the
Baptist minister first at Wainsgate, and then at Hebden
Bridge near Halifax, and 'was regarded as the first man of his
denomination in that part of the country'.[56] Fawcett ranks,
along with John Nelson, the Methodist stonemason, William
Grimshaw, incumbent of Haworth, and Henry Venn, vicar of
Huddersfield, among the leading Yorkshire evangelicals of the
eighteenth century.

About the year 1768, Fawcett baptised a sixteen-year-old
boy from Halifax, John Sutcliff, who became the Baptist pastor
at Olney, within the Northamptonshire Association, in July
1775.[57] Under the preaching of Dan Taylor, another native of
Halifax, and the close friend of both Fawcett and Sutcliff, the
English Midlands were aroused. 'His presence and preaching
set every Leicestershire meeting he entered on fire . . . Fresh
churches of this Baptist faith sprang up everywhere . . . he
stirred thought and discussion by this dangerous new doctrine
of grace.'[58] These churches were grouped into Associations and
the 'Northampton' stretched from St Albans to Lincoln. It had
been launched in 1764 by six village ministers, Calvinists, but
'not as hide-bound and circumscribed in outlook as is sometimes
imagined'.[59] From their records for almost twenty years (1764–
84) we learn that days of prayer were often held.

One of the ministers in this Northamptonshire Association
was Andrew Fuller, born near Ely on 6 February 1745.
Brought to despair through the arid theology of his minister,
he so hungered after forgiveness and peace that he determined
'to run all hazards, like Esther, even though I should perish in
the attempt'.[60] When Andrew Fuller found grace by personal
venturing of his all on Christ, 'whether He would have me or
no', he himself began to proclaim Christ as a gift to others,
calling men to come, rather than dwelling on the 'decrees' of

56 *D.N.B.* viii *pp* 257–8.
57 Sermon preached at the funeral of Sutcliff by Andrew Fuller (Fuller:
  Works. iv *pp* 314 *ff.*).
58 Carey, S. P.: *William Carey.* *p* 9.
59 Payne, E. A.: *The Prayer Call of 1784.* *p* 3.
60 Fuller: *Works* – Memoir. i, *p* xvi.

God. 'Fullerism' became a subject for heated argument between Particular and General Baptists throughout the land.

Into Fuller's hands there came a copy of the book written by Robert Millar of Paisley; as his diary entry reveals, '30th August 1780 – I found my soul drawn out in love to poor souls while reading Millar's Account of Elliott's labours among the North American Indians and their effects on those poor, barbarous savages'.[61] In October 1783, Fuller, after much heart-searching, moved to Kettering, and was brought into more intimate contact with Sutcliff of Olney and Ryland of Northampton. In April 1784 there reached the Northampton-shire Baptist leaders, in a parcel of books from Dr John Erskine of Edinburgh, a copy of Jonathan Edwards' *Humble Attempt to Promote Explicit Agreement and Visible Union of God's People in Extraordinary Prayer* – a stirring call to prayer.

Upon the motion of John Sutcliff, the Associations, meeting at Nottingham 'in the spring of 1784, agreed to set apart an hour of the evening of the first Monday in every month for social prayer for the success of the Gospel and to invite Christians of other denominations to unite with them in it'.[62] Dr Payne, the distinguished Baptist scholar, notes that the dates were 2 and 3 June, and adds that Fuller's sermon on this occasion was printed, and to it was added *Persuasives to a General Union in Extraordinary Prayer for the Revival and Extent of Real Religion.*

In the *Persuasives*, under seven headings, Fuller urged his readers to review Christ's readiness to hear and answer prayer, to consider the past, to contemplate the needy present, to consider what God had promised to do for his Church in time to come – even the uttermost parts of the earth were to become the kingdom of Christ! Fuller pointed out that 'regard for our countrymen, connections and friends should inspire us, and what is asked for is so small ... As to the *times* that are proposed, nothing can be less burdensome than *once a month* – but what did I say? *Burdensome?* God forbid that any employment of this

61 *Ibid.* i *p* xl.
62 *Ibid.* iv *p* 326.

sort should ever prove a burden! It is hoped it will be attended to as a *privilege* rather than merely as a duty.'[63] Fuller concluded that, whatever was the immediate and apparent issue, the work would not be in vain . . . 'Our petitions may prove like seed in the earth, that shall not perish, though it may not spring up in our days . . . what if we should be the sowers and our posterity the reapers! Shall we think much at this?'

How much nearer and greater were the results of this *Call* than ever these good men could have imagined! Fifty years later Dr F. A. Cox, seeking for 'the primary cause of the missionary excitement in Carey's mind' and its influence among Carey's ministerial brethren, found it in this *Call to Prayer* of 1784.[64]

In 1785 a circular letter, entitled 'Causes of Declension in Religion and Means of Revival',[65] was addressed to the churches of the Northamptonshire Association. One part stated that 'it affords us not a little satisfaction to hear in what manner the *monthly prayer meetings*, which were proposed in our letter of last year, have been carried on'. Many had been stirred up to wrestle in prayer for revival, and this was considered as more than balancing the failure to increase membership. 'It was resolved, without any hesitation, to continue the meetings of prayer on the first Monday evening in every kalendar month.'

This decision was renewed in 1787 at Leicester; the adjoining Warwickshire Association also decided to join in the scheme. The movement spread to the Independent churches and the Baptist churches in Yorkshire too. Sutcliff decided to fan the growing interest into a stronger flame by reissuing Jonathan Edwards' *Humble Attempt*, and it was reprinted at Northampton in May 1789, and sold at ninepence a copy. In his preface, Sutcliff pleaded: 'O for thousands upon thousands, divided into small bands in their respective cities, towns, villages and neighbourhoods, all met at the same time, and in pursuit of the same end, offering up their united prayers.'[66]

63 *Ibid.* v *p* 530. 64 Cox, F. A.: *History of the Baptist Missionary Society.* i *p* 10.
65 Fuller, A: *Works.* iv *p* 566.
66 Payne, E. A.: *The Prayer Call of 1784. pp* 6–7.

On 27 April 1791, Andrew Fuller preached to a ministers' meeting from Haggai 1.2, pointing out that too often the Church indulged 'in a kind of prudent caution (as we call it)', which magnified difficulties and thwarted great and good work for the cause of Christ. 'Perhaps the work requires *expense*; and Covetousness says, Wait a little longer . . . Perhaps it requires *concurrence*; and we wait for every body to be of a mind . . . The apostles executed their commission with assiduity and fidelity; but . . . we seem to sit down half contented that the greater part of the world should still remain in ignorance . . . We pray for the conversion and salvation of the world, and yet *neglect the ordinary means* by which those ends have been used to be accomplished . . . Ought we not then at least to try . . . to convey more of the good news of salvation to the world around us ?'[67]

One man there was who was willing to live out this creed and pay the price which such an enterprise demanded. On 5 October 1783, William Carey, 'a poor journeyman shoemaker', was baptised in the river Nene at Northampton, near to Dr Doddridge's meeting-house. Entering the ministry in 1786, he suggested to his ministerial brethren that the command to teach all nations might be obligatory upon even them, only to hear: 'Young man, sit down, sit down, you are a miserable enthusiast . . . When God pleases to convert the heathen, He will do it without your aid or mine . . . certainly nothing can be done before another Pentecost.'[68]

Carey had, however, been fired by the New Testament and Captain Cook's log-books, especially that explorer's opinion about the impossibility of any Christian mission to Tahiti. Cook wrote: 'It is very unlikely that any measure of this kind should ever be seriously thought of, for it can neither serve the purpose of public ambition nor private avarice; and, without such inducements, I may pronounce that it will *never* be undertaken.'[69] But there was one man eager to rub out Cook's 'never' – and ready at that very moment!

67 Fuller, A: *Works*. iv p 39 ff.   68 Smith, G.: *Life of William Carey*. p 29.
69 Carey, S. P.: *William Carey*. p 43.

In 1792, Carey published *An Enquiry into the Obligations of Christians to use Means for the Conversion of the Heathens &c., in which the Religious State of the Different Nations of the World, the Success of Former Undertakings, and the Practicability of Further Undertakings, are considered by WILLIAM CAREY.* Thomas Potts, a Birmingham manufacturer, subsidised the publication with £10, and it was sold for 1s 6d, any profits 'to go to the proposed mission'. It was suggested that a society be formed of 'persons whose hearts are in the work', and the method was that they should tithe their incomes to support missionary work at home and abroad.

That same year, on 30 May, Carey preached his memorable sermon at Nottingham from Isaiah 54.2, 3, its theme being, 'Attempt great things for God; Expect great things from God' – 'two plain, practical, pungent, quotable watchwords', as Dr Clifford described them.[70] After the *Persuasives* and the years of prayer, at long last there followed a 'Plan'. The next day Fuller proposed 'that a Plan be prepared . . . for forming a Baptist Society for Propagating the Gospel among the Heathens'. On Tuesday, 2 October 1792, at Kettering, in the hospitable back-parlour of Mrs Wallis, twelve ministers and two other people launched the modern missionary movements on I.O.U.s for £13 2 6d, collected in Andrew Fuller's snuff-box, and added this to their consecrated faith in God's purpose and power. The venture could not have been started apart from the zeal and urgency that issued from almost a decade of concerted prayer.

In the 1784 *Call to Prayer*, Sutcliff had written that those who engage in this activity ought not to confine their prayers to their own churches or denomination. 'Let the whole interest of the Redeemer be affectionately remembered; and the spread of the Gospel to the most distant parts of the habitable globe be the object of your most earnest requests. We shall rejoice if any other Christian societies of our own or other denominations will join with us, and we do now invite them most cordially to join heart and hand in the attempt.' As they hoped, so it happened. Very soon after the formation of the Baptist Mis-

70 *Ibid. p* 84.

sionary Society, other societies were brought into being, and the greatest Christian adventure of the modern world had begun.

On 12 May 1786, in New York, 'a Proposal submitted to the consideration of God's people of Every Denomination' had urged 'that they agree to meet at the throne of grace every Sabbath morning, in their closets, sometime between the hours of seven and nine o'clock, to unite in prayer for the outpouring of the Holy Spirit and the spread of the Gospel in its purity and power throughout the world . . . Much need not be said to engage those whose hearts are right with God, to join in this Concert for Prayer.' It was then noted that 'the universal spread of the gospel of Christ in due time . . . is a matter of express and frequent promise in the sacred oracles'. Prayer and mission were closely linked together.

After pointing out that 'the Concert for Prayer . . . is not a new thing', . . . the writer asked, 'Who then will join in this duty, so peculiarly necessary in our day?' This proposal was reprinted at Glasgow on 23 March 1787, and prefixed to the 1790 edition of Robe's *Narrative &c. pp* xi–xii.

The missionary impulse was felt in Scotland during the last decade of the eighteenth century,[71] and found its leadership in the venerable figure of Dr John Erskine who, years before, had been stirred by the revival movement of 1742. His well-known intervention in the debate at the General Assembly of 1796 – 'Moderator, rax me that Bible' – has been questioned by some critics, since it is not mentioned in Heron's very full account of that debate, but the former Principal of New College, the late Professor Hugh Watt, was well satisfied with its veracity.[72] If the story should be apocryphal, the spirit it reveals is authentic enough. An Overture had been brought in, asking the General

71 John Mill, in January 1797, speaks of this new interest in overseas missions and the foundation of the London Missionary Society. 'Ministers not only of Presbyterians but Episcopalians, Anabaptists, etc, laying aside all bigotry and blind zeal for parties, met together in one Church at London . . . great collections were made in money for carrying on the design' – Mill, J.: *Diary. p* 107.
72 *Records, S.C.H.S.* lx *p* 1.

Assembly 'to consider of the most effective method by which
the Church of Scotland may contribute to the diffusion of the
Gospel over the world'. There was a controversial debate,
which contained much innuendo from opponents of the idea of
mission, who compared missionary societies to revolutionary
groups. The aged 'Jupiter' Carlyle commented that this was
the first time he had ever heard such a proposal during his fifty
years' membership of the Assembly. Opposing it, he declared:
'As clergymen let us pray that Christ's Kingdom may come in,
as we are assured, it shall come in the course of providence.'[73]

The opportunity was lost at that time, but there were some
who were not content merely to pray and to substitute devotion
for decisive action. In February 1796, the Scottish Missionary
Society was formed in Edinburgh (one had already been
started in Glasgow), and on 24 April of that year, Dr John
Erskine, its first president, preached a sermon on its behalf.
Within a month the Society received £700. While Carlyle was
talking pious platitude, Erskine and his colleagues were working and giving.

One of the greatest of the early missionaries was Claudius
Buchanan; one Anglican historian asserts that the present-day
Indian Church owes its existence to the championship of
Buchanan in the formative years of planting the Gospel in
India.[74]

Buchanan was born at Cambuslang on 12 March 1766, and
so would be christened by the venerable M'Culloch, then
seventy-five years of age; his father was the teacher at the local
school, and his mother was the daughter of Claudius Somers,
one of the converts in the 1742 revival at Cambuslang and
later elder and treasurer. The father had been helped to faith
by a letter from M'Culloch, and this letter was sent by Buchanan's mother to him in his own time of spiritual distress.[75]
Claudius Buchanan had been 'adopted' by his grandfather and
lived with him, and he had earnestly encouraged his grandson

73 Heron, R.: *Proceedings of the 1796 Assembly.* p 38.
74 Campbell, J. M.: *Christian History in the Making.* pp 85–8.
75 Pearson, H.: *Life of Buchanan.* i p 39.

to enter the ministry; but the youth forgot the promise of boy-hood and, leaving home for London, sank into dissipation. His mother, when he eventually wrote to tell her of his concern about religion, directed him to see John Newton who helped him to faith.

Henry Thornton, one of the Clapham Sect, lent to Buchanan the money to go to Cambridge, and he became a minister of the Anglican Church. In 1797, Buchanan went as a chaplain to the East India Company in Calcutta, where he played the major role in constituting Fort William College, and securing the appointment of William Carey as Professor of Bengali there. He provided from his own private purse the money to endow bursaries in the British universities in order to stimulate interest in things Indian. Also he paid for three years the salary of an Armenian, Lassar, who had been born in Macao, in order that he might give his assistance to the Serampore trio (Carey, Marshman and Ward) who were translating the Scriptures into Chinese. The translation was crude and little used, al-though it was of some help in preparing the way for a later version.[76]

How William M'Culloch would have rejoiced to see Buchanan, once held in his arms and part of the spiritual fruit of the revival days of 1742, building the kingdom of God in India and seeking to send the good news into China. From Cambuslang to Cathay!

76 *Ibid.* i *pp* 320–1; Latourette, K. S.: *A History of Christian Missions in China, pp* 210–11.

BIBLIOGRAPHY

[A] EIGHTEENTH CENTURY (AND EARLIER)

1 MANUSCRIPTS

M'Culloch Manuscripts, 2 vols.

Laing Manuscripts Division, ii 97[6], 471, 620[29], 500–1.

Register of the Presbytery of Hamilton. From 17 November 1719 to 10 June 1778.

Register of the Presbytery of Glasgow. From 1 May 1723 to 15 December 1761.

Kilsyth Kirk Session Records. From 26 April 1713 to 2 February 1761.

Minutes of the Kirk Session of Cambuslang & Treasurers' Accounts. Vol 1, 1658–1724, 1749–74, 1779–88; Vol 2, 1731–48.

2 PAMPHLETS

Samson's Riddle, or a Bunch of Bitter Wormwood . . . by a poor weelewisher and companion in tribulation. c 1678. Holland.

The Christian Sanctuary or ROOM for Returning Sinners with a Compassionate Saviour. By Thomas Whitaker. 1717. Edinburgh. 86 *pp.*

A Sermon against the Idolatrous Worship of the Church of Rome, Preached in the New-Church of Glasgow, the Fifth of November, 1725. William M'Culloch. 1726. Glasgow. 48 *pp.*

Considerations on Patronage, addressed to the Gentlemen of Scotland. F. Hutcheson. 1735. London.

Considerations in the Time of Adversity. A sermon by Ninian Niving, 19 December 1729 (Rosebery Pamphlets).

The Wonderful Scotch Prophecy, as revealed . . . to John Porter. 1737. Glasgow.

Fifty and two DIRECTIONS . . . by Mr John Welch of Irongray. Reprinted 1740. Glasgow.

New Testimony and Vindication. J. Currie. 1743. 64 *pp.*

A Short ACCOUNT of God's Dealings with the Reverend Mr George Whitefield, A.B. By George Whitefield. 1741. Edinburgh. 52 *pp.*

A Letter from W.D. to his friend in the Gorbels [sic] *of Glasgow.* 1741.

A Short Narrative of the Extraordinary Work at Cambuslang, in a Letter to a Friend. 8 May 1712. Glasgow. 32 *pp.*

A True ACCOUNT of the Wonderful CONVERSIONS at Cambuslang &c . . . from a GENTLEMAN in the Gorbals . . . to his FRIEND at Greenock. 1742. Glasgow. 8 *pp.*

The Wonderful Narrative, or a Faithful ACCOUNT of the FRENCH PROPHETS etc by ANTI-ENTHUSIASTICUS. 1742. Glasgow. Printed and sold by Robert Foulis. *pp* i–xv, 1–88.

The DECLARATION of the True Presbyterians within the Kingdom of Scotland concerning Mr George Whitefield and the WORK at Cambuslang. 1742. Glasgow. 32 *pp.*

An APOLOGY for the Presbyterians of Scotland who are Hearers of the Reverend Mr George Whitefield &c. 1742. Edinburgh. 40 *pp.*

A LETTER containing REMARKS upon a Late Apology for the Presbyterians Etc. By John Bisset. 1741. 112 *pp.*

ROBE, James: *A faithful NARRATIVE of the Extraordinary Work of the SPIRIT OF GOD at Kilsyth and other Congregations in the Neighbourhood, with a Preface wherein there is an Address to the Brethren of the Associate Presbytery, anent their late Act for a Publick FAST.* 1789. Glasgow. Also in 1742 edition. Glasgow. 318 *pp.*

A Short ACCOUNT of the Remarkable CONVERSIONS at Cambuslang in a Letter from a Gentleman in the West Country to his Friend at Edinburgh. 1742. Glasgow. 16 *pp.*

SATAN'S APE DETECTED: or some OBSERVATIONS on a Scandalous Pamphlet against Mr Whitefield, and the Clergy of this Church, to disparage the Work at Cambuslang, &c . . . Written by Mr ADAM GIB, Minister of the Associate Congregation at Edinburgh. By ANDREW WADDELL, Soldier in Dumbarton Castle. 1742. Glasgow. 24 *pp.*

OBSERVATIONS in Defence of the Work at Cambuslang against the Malicious Spirit of the ACT of the Associate Presbytery Anent their Late Fast . . . Written by a Soldier. 1742. Glasgow. 8 *pp.*

A Warning and Reproof, with ADVICE . . . to those who have spoken, and do speak Calumniously and with Bitterness against the Work of the Spirit of God, at Cambuslang, Kilsyth and Calder . . . By the Author of the Warm and Serious Adress [sic]. 1742. Glasgow. 24 *pp.*

A WARNING to all the Lovers of Christ in Scotland to be upon their GUARD AGAINST The Spreading Contagion broken out from Mr Adam Gib, &c. Done by an Old Drumclog Soldier, who was Author of the Warm Address. Edinburgh. September 1742. 38 *pp.*

Signs of the Times Considered, or the high PROBABILITY, that the present APPEARANCES in New England, and the West of SCOTLAND are a PRELUDE of the Glorious Things promised to the CHURCH in the latter Ages. Edinburgh. October 1742. By John Erskine. 36 *pp.*

A REVIEW of the Preface to a Narrative of the Extraordinary Work at Kilsyth, &c. written by the Rev Mr James Robe. By Rev James Fisher. Glasgow. 1742. 68 *pp.*

DIVINE INFLUENCE the True Spring of the Extraordinary WORK at CAMBUSLANG, &c . . . in a LETTER from Mr Alexander WEBSTER . . . to a Gentleman in the Country. The Second Edition with a PREFACE . . . in answer to the Reverend Mr Fisher's Review. 1742. Edinburgh. 64 *pp.*

A WARNING against Countenancing the Ministrations of Mr George Whitefield &c. By Adam Gib. Edinburgh. 1742. 65 *pp.*

ACT of the Associate Presbytery anent a PUBLICK FAST &c. 1742. 8 *pp.*

LETTER from A. Webster to Ralph Erskine Concerning Fraud and Falsehood Discovered. Edinburgh. 1743. 20 *pp.*

A CONFERENCE BETWIXT A CONFORMIST . . . AND: A NON-CONFORMIST . . . Anent hearing Mr George Whitefield preach &c. Edinburgh. 1741. 28 *pp.*

Preface to Fraser of Brea's The Lawfulness and Duty of Separation from Corrupt Ministers and Churches, &c. Printed 1744 by George Paton, Linlithgow.

A Fair and Impartial ACCOUNT of the DEBATE in the Synod of Glasgow and Air [sic], anent employing Mr Whitefield. 6 October 1748. Edinburgh. By John Erskine.

A Letter from a Layman to a Lay Deacon of the Kirk of Scotland, Containing the Reasons of his Dissenting from the PRESBYTERIAN and joining the EPISCOPAL Communion, &c. MDCCXLIX. A Defence and vindication of his Action by D—— I——. 52 *pp.* Edinburgh (Duncan Innes).

A Short ACCOUNT of the Rise and Continued Progress of a remarkable Work of Grace in the United Netherlands in several LETTERS from the Reverend Mr Hugh Kennedy, Minister of the Gospel in the Scots Congregation in Roterdam [sic]. 1750–52. Printed London.

The Balm of Gilead. John Willison. (Fifth edition.) 1758.

The PATRON'S ABC &c. Glasgow. 1771. 60 *pp.*

The Judicial Testimony of the Associate Presbytery, issued December 1736. Glasgow. 1779.

An ENQUIRY into the Obligations of Christians to use means for the Conversion of the Heathens &c. By William Carey. 1792. Leicester. 87 *pp.*

An *ACCOUNT of the Proceedings and Debate in the General Assembly of the Church of Scotland, 27th May 1796, on the Overtures respecting the propagation of the Gospel among the Heathen.* 1796. Edinburgh.

An Address to Christians on the Revival of Religion. 1797.

3 PERIODICALS

The Scots Magazine. 1739–50.

The Glasgow Weekly History &c. (*ed* W. M'Culloch.) 1741–2. Glasgow.

The Christian Monthly History (*ed* J. Robe). From November 1743. Edinburgh.

The Christian History (*ed* T. Prince Junr). 1743–4. Boston. N.E.

An Exhortation to the Inhabitants of the South Parish of Glasgow, and the Hearers in the C O L L E G E - K I R K (*ed* J. Gillies). September 1750–51. Glasgow.

4 DIARIES AND LETTERS

Scottish Diaries and Memoirs 1550–1746. Ed J. G. Fyfe. 1928. Stirling.

Scottish Diaries and Memoirs 1746–1843. Ed J. G. Fyfe. 1942. Stirling.

Boston, Thomas, Memoirs &c of. Ed G. H. Morrison. 1899. Edinburgh.

Buchanan, Dugald, The Diary of, 1836. Edinburgh.

Carlile, William, Autobiography of, 1746–1829. 1863. Paisley.

Carlyle, Alexander, Autobiography of. Ed J. H. Burton. Third edition. 1861. Edinburgh.

Clerk of Penicuik, Sir John, Memoirs of, 1676–1755. Ed J. M. Gray. S.H.S. XIII. 1892. Edinburgh.

Cockburn, Henry T.: *Memorials of His Time.* 1856. Edinburgh.

Cuningham of Campvere, Thomas, The Journal of, 1640–54. Ed E. J. Courthope. S.H.S. XI. Third series. 1928. Edinburgh.

Davidson, Henry: *Letters to Christian Friends.* 1811. Edinburgh.

Doddridge, The Diary and Correspondence of Philip. Ed J. D. Humphreys. 1830. London.

Early Methodist Preachers. 6 vols *Ed*, with an Introductory Essay by Thomas Jackson. 1866. London.

Elchies, Letters of Patrick Grant, Lord. Ed H. D. Macwilliam. Aberdeen. 1927.

Erskine of Carnock, The Journal of the Hon John, 1683–7. Ed W. MacLeod. S.H.S. XIV. 1893. Edinburgh.

Erskine, The Life and Diary of the Rev Ebenezer. Ed D. Fraser. 1831. Edinburgh.

Erskine, The Life and Diary of the Rev Ralph. Ed D. Fraser. 1834. Edinburgh.

Halyburton, Memoirs of the Life of Thomas. n.d. Edinburgh.

Hog, Memoir of the Rev James, of Carnock. Ed Prof Bruce. Edinburgh. 1798.

Hog, Memoirs of Mrs William Veitch, Mr Thomas, &c. Edinburgh. 1846.

Mill, The Diary of the Rev John, 1740–1803. Ed G. Goudie. S.H.S. v. 1889. Edinburgh.

Ridpath, The Diary of George, 1755–1761. Ed J. Balfour Paul. S.H.S. II Third series. 1922. Edinburgh.

Somerville, T.: *My Own Life and Times: 1741–1814,* 1861. Edinburgh.

Wesley, The Journal of John. Standard edition. Ed N. Curnock. 1909. London.

Wesley, The Letters of John. Standard edition. 1931. London.

Whitefield Journals. (Banner of Truth Trust. 1960.)

Whitefield, Memoir of the Life of the Rev George. By J. Gillies. 1772. London.

Whitefield, A Select Collection of Letters of the late Reverend George, 1772. London.

Wodrow, The Correspondence of Robert. Ed T. M'Crie. 3 vols. Wodrow Society. 1842. Edinburgh.

5 COLLECTED WORKS

Edwards, Jonathan: The Works of. 1817. London.

Erskine, Ebenezer, Works of. Ed D. Fraser. 1826. London.

Erskine, Ralph: Works of. 1821. London.

Fuller, Andrew: The Complete Works of. Ed A. G. Fuller. 1831–2. London.

Knox, John: Works of. Ed D. Laing. 1895 edition. Edinburgh.

Newton, John: Works of. 1808. London.

6 ANNALS

Acts of the General Assembly 1638–1842. Pub Church Law Society. 1843. Edinburgh.

Glasgow Burgh Records, Vol V (1718–38); Vol VI (1739–59). Ed Renwick. 1909. Glasgow.

Morren, N.: *Annals of the General Assembly of the Church of Scotland.* 1739–52. 1838. Edinburgh; 1752–66. 1840. Edinburgh.

Wodrow, Robert: *Analecta.* 4 vols. Maitland Club edition. 1842. Glasgow.

Register of the Privy Council of Scotland. Vol XI (Third series). 1685–6. Ed Henry Paton. 1929. Edinburgh.

7 OTHER WORKS

Burnet, Gilbert: *History of My Own Time. Ed* Airey. 2 vols. 1897. Oxford.

Darney, William: *A Collection of Hymns.* 1751. Leedes [*sic*].

Darney, William: *The Fundamental Doctrines which are contained in the Holy Scriptures.* 1755. Glasgow.

Defoe, Daniel: *Memoirs of the Church of Scotland.* 1844 edition. Perth.

Defoe, Daniel: *A Tour Through the Whole ISLAND OF GREAT BRITAIN &c.* Vol IV. (Seventh edition.) 1769. London.

Doddridge, Philip: *Sermons on Regeneration.* 1842. London.

Durham, James: *The Dying Man's TESTAMENT to the Church of Scotland, or A Treatise concerning Scandal.* 1659. Edinburgh.

Erskine, Ralph: *Faith no Fancy.* 1745. Edinburgh.

Fleming, Robert: *The Fulfilling of Scripture.* 1669. Rotterdam.

Gillies, John: *Historical Collections, relating to the Remarkable Periods of the Success of the Gospel, &c.* Vol II. 1754. Glasgow.

Gillies, John: *APPENDIX to the Historical Collections &c.* 1761. Issued in thirty parts. Glasgow.

Guthrie, William: *A Short Treatise of the Christian's Great Interest.* 1724 edition. Edinburgh; also 1828 edition, preface by Thomas Chalmers.

Hamilton, Janet: *Poems of Purpose, &c.* 1870 edition. Glasgow.

Hamilton, William: *Description of the Sheriffdom of Lanarkshire and Renfrew.* Compiled about 1710. 1831. Glasgow.

Knox, The Liturgy of John. Ed G. W. Sprott. 1901. Edinburgh.

M'Culloch, William: *Sermons on Several Subjects. Ed* R. M'Culloch. 1793. Glasgow.

Marrow of Modern Divinity, The. Ed C. G. M'Crie. 1902. Glasgow.

Millar, Robert: *The History of the Propagation of Christianity . . . the present State of the Heathens is enquired into; and Methods for their Conversion offered.* 2 vols. 1723. Edinburgh.

Moncrieff-Wellwood, H.: *An Account of the Life and writings of John Erskine.* 1818. Edinburgh.

New Testament in Scots, The. Ed T. G. Law. S.T.S. XLVI. 1901. Edinburgh.

Old Statistical Account, The. Ed Sinclair. Vol V. 1793. Edinburgh.

Pearson, H.: *Memoirs of the Life and Writings of the Rev Claudius Buchanan.* 1819. Third edition. London.

Scougal, Henry: *The Life of God &c* to which is added a sermon preached at the Author's Funeral by George Garden. 1747. Edinburgh.

Symson, A. (edited): *Register of the Synod of Galloway 1664–1671.* 1856. Kirkcudbright.

Vincent, T.: *An Explicatory Catechism.* 1867 edition. Edinburgh.
Walker, P.: *Six Saints of the Covenant.* Ed D. H. Fleming. 2 vols. 1901. London.
Whitehead, J.: *The Life of the Rev John Wesley.* 2 vols. 1796. London.
Wodrow, R.: *History of the Sufferings of the Church of Scotland.* Vol II. 1721–2. Edinburgh.
Woodward, J.: *Account of the Rise of the Religious Societies.* 1701. Third edition. London.

[B] LATER WORKS

I HISTORIES
Brown, P. Hume: *The History of Scotland to the Present Time.* Vol III. 1911. Cambridge.
Burton, J. Hill: *The History of Scotland.* Vol VIII. Second edition. 1873. Edinburgh.
Campbell, A. J.: *Two Centuries of the Church of Scotland, 1707–1929.* 1930. Paisley.
Cunningham, J.: *The Church History of Scotland.* Vol II. 1859. Edinburgh.
Hutchison, M.: *The Reformed Presbyterian Church in Scotland, 1686–1876.* 1893. Paisley.
Lindsay, T. M.: *The History of the Reformation.* Vol I. 1906. Edinburgh.
M'Kerrow, J.: *The History of the Secession Church.* 1841 edition. Edinburgh.
Stanley, A. P.: *Lectures on the History of the Church of Scotland.* 1872. London.
Steven, W.: *The History of the Scottish Church, Rotterdam.* 1832. Edinburgh.
Struthers, G.: *The History of the Rise, Progress and Principles of the Relief Church.* 1843. Glasgow.
Thomson, A.: *Historical Sketch of the Origins of the Secession Church.* 1848. Edinburgh.

2 BIOGRAPHIES
Apostle of the North, The. J. Kennedy. 1866. London.
Bourignon, Antoinette. A. R. MacEwen. 1910. London.
Brainerd, David: Flagellant on Horseback. R. E. Day. 1950. Philadelphia.
Buchanan, Reminiscences of the Life and Labours of Dugald. A. Sinclair. 1875. Edinburgh.

Cameronian, Apostle, A. H. M. B. Reid. 1896. Paisley.

Coutts, Memoirs and Correspondence of Mrs. W. M. Hetherington. 1854. Edinburgh.

Doddridge, Philip. Ed G. F. Nuttall. 1951. London.

John Fergusson, 1727–1750. Jas. Fergusson. 1948. London.

Fisher, Memorial of the Rev James. J. Brown (U.P. Fathers). 1849. Edinburgh.

Howell Harris, The Early Life of. Richard Bennett. 1962.

John Hepburn and the Hebronites. W. Macmillan. 1934. London.

Knox, The Life of John. T. M'Crie. 1855. Edinburgh.

Peden, Alexander, The Prophet of the Covenant. J. C. Johnstone. 1902. Glasgow.

The Wesley Family. A Clarke. Vol II. 1823. London.

Whitefield, The Life and Travels of George. J. P. Gledstone. 1871. London.

Whitefield, The Life of the Rev George. L. Tyerman. 2 vols. 1876. London.

Lives of the U.P. Fathers, Ebenezer Erskine, William Wilson and Thomas Gillespie. 1849. Edinburgh.

3 MISSIONARY

Campbell, J. M.: *Christian History in the Making.* 1946. London.

Carey, S. P.: *William Carey.* 1934. London.

M'Kichan, D.: *The Missionary Ideal in the Scottish Churches.* 1927. London.

Latourette, K. S.: *A History of Christian Missions in China.* 1929. London.

Payne, E. A.: *The Prayer Call of 1784.* 1941. London.

Smith, G.: *The Life of William Carey.* 1887. London.

Walker, F. D.: *William Carey.* 1926. London.

Weir, R. W.: *A History of the Foreign Missions of the Church of Scotland.* 1900. Edinburgh.

4 ANNALS AND REFERENCE

Dictionary of National Biography, The, 1885–1901. London.

Fasti Ecclesiae Scoticanae. Ed Hew Scott. 1915 edition. Edinburgh.

M'Kelvie, W.: *Annals and Statistics of the United Presbyterian Church.* 1875. Edinburgh.

Small, R.: *History of the Congregations of the United Presbyterian Church, 1733–1900.* 2 vols. 1904. Edinburgh.

The New Statistical Account. Vols V, VI. 1845. Edinburgh.

5 OTHER WORKS

Agnew, A.: *History of the Hereditary Sheriffs of Galloway.* 1864. Edinburgh.

Anton, P.: *Kilsyth, a Parish History.* 1893. Glasgow.

Brown, J. T. T.: *Cambuslang, a Sketch of the Place and the People, earlier than the nineteenth century.* 1884. Glasgow.

Butler, D.: *Wesley and Whitefield in Scotland.* 1898. Edinburgh.

Butler, D.: *Henry Scougal and the Oxford Methodists.* 1899. Edinburgh.

Cairns, J.: *Unbelief in the Eighteenth Century.* 1881. Edinburgh.

Cairns, W. T.: *The Religion of Dr Johnson and other Essays.* 1946. Oxford.

Cameron, J.: *The History of the Buchanite Delusion.* 1904. Dumfries.

Chalmers, The Correspondence of Dr. Ed W. Hanna. 1853. Edinburgh.

Couper, W. J.: *Scottish Revivals.* 1918. Dundee.

Couper, W. J.: *The Edinburgh Periodical Press.* 1908. Stirling.

Cowan, A.: *The Influence of the Scottish Church in Christendom.* 1896. London.

Cowan, R. M. W.: *The Newspaper in Scotland.* 1946. Glasgow.

Crawfurd, G.: *History of the Shire of Renfrew.* 1782. Paisley.

Davies, G. C. B.: *The Early Cornish Evangelicals 1735–1760.* 1951. London.

Eyre-Todd, G.: *The History of Glasgow.* Vol III. 1931. Glasgow.

Findlay, J. T.: *The Secession in the North.* 1898. Aberdeen.

Fraser, J.: *The Humorous Chap-books of Scotland.* 1873. New York.

Graham, H. G.: *The Social Life of Scotland in the Eighteenth Century.* 1901. London.

Graham, H. G.: *Scottish Men of Letters in the Eighteenth Century.* 1901. London.

Greyfriars Church, Glasgow, Historical Sketch of, 1872. Glasgow.

Hamilton, G.: *The House of Hamilton.* 1933. Edinburgh.

Harrison, A. W.: *The Evangelical Revival and Christian Reunion.* 1942. London.

Harvey, W.: *Scottish Chapbook Literature.* 1903. Paisley.

Henderson, H. F.: *The Religious Controversies of Scotland.* 1905. Edinburgh.

Kennedy, J.: *The Days of the Fathers in Ross-shire.* 1861. Edinburgh.

Knox, R. A.: *Enthusiasm: A Chapter in the History of Religion, with Special Reference to the Seventeenth and Eighteenth Centuries.* 1950. Oxford.

Laycock, J. W.: *Methodist Heroes in the Great Haworth Round, 1734–1784.* 1909. Keighley.

Lee, J. R.: *Greyfriars, Glasgow, 1738–1938.* 1938. Glasgow.

M'Cosh, J.: *The Scottish Philosophy . . . from Hutcheson to Hamilton.* 1875. London.

Macfarlan, D.: *The Revivals of the Eighteenth Century, particularly at Cambuslang &c.* n.d. (1845?) Edinburgh.

M'Giffert, A. C.: *Protestant Thought before Kant.* 1911. London.

MacInnes, J.: *The Evangelical Movement in the Highlands of Scotland 1688-1800.* 1951. Aberdeen.

Mackenzie, W.: *The History of Galloway.* Vol II. 1841. Kirkcudbright.

Meikle, H. W.: *Scotland and the French Revolution.* 1912. Glasgow.

Millar, J. H.: *Scottish Prose in the Seventeenth and Eighteenth Centuries.* 1912. Glasgow.

Miller, J.: *History of Dunbar.* 1830. Dunbar.

Murray, E. G.: *The Old School of Cardross.* 1949. Glasgow.

Notestein, W.: *The Scot in History.* 1946. London.

Pagan, J.: *The History of Glasgow.* 1847. Glasgow.

Porter, W. H.: *Cambuslang and its Ministers.* 1897. Edinburgh.

Provand, W. S.: *Puritanism in the Scottish Church.* 1923. Paisley.

Reid, H. M. B.: *The Divinity Professors in the University of Glasgow 1640-1903.* 1923. Glasgow.

Smellie, A.: *Men of the Covenant.* 1911. London.

Söderblom, N.: *The Living God.* 1933. London.

Strang, John: *Glasgow and its Clubs.* 1856. London and Glasgow.

Train, J.: *The Buchanites from First to Last.* 1846. Edinburgh.

Walker, J.: *The Theology and Theologians of Scotland.* 1872. Edinburgh.

Warrick, J.: *The History of Old Cumnock.* 1899. Paisley.

Wearmouth, R. F.: *Methodism and the Common People of the Eighteenth Century.* 1945. London.

Webster, J. M.: *History of Carnock.* 1938. Edinburgh.

Wilson, J. A.: *A History of Cambuslang.* 1929. Glasgow.

6 ARTICLES, LETTERS ETC IN PERIODICALS

Records of the Scottish Church History Society, especially 'Psychology of the Cambuslang Revival'. S. Mechie (x. *pp* 171-85).

Records of the Glasgow Bibliographical Society.

The Christian Repository, 1819.

The Edinburgh Christian Instructor, 1828, 1831, 1838, 1839.

The United Presbyterian Magazine, 1899.

The Original Secession Magazine, 1878, 1934.

The Evangelical Quarterly, 1944, 1947.

INDEX

Warner, Margaret, 213
  Patrick, 213
  William, 215
Warrick (historian), 204 *fn*
Warwickshire Association, 230
Watson, Thomas, his *Body of Divinity*,
  76
Watt, Hugh, 233
Webster, Alexander, 7, 83, 85, 115,
  118, 120, 137, 145, 146, 150, 152,
  153 *fn*, 157, 168, 178 *fn*, 190, 208,
  220
Weekly History, The, 92–3, 132, 142
Welsh, John, 36, 55, 65, 158
Wesley, Charles, 3, 58, 61, 99, 226
  John, 3, 15 *fn*, 22, 53, 58, 61, 99,
    161, 189, 205, 207, 208, 217,
    218, 221–2, 226, 227
  Susanna, 99
Westburn, 45, 144, 164–5, 221
Wester-Weems, 188
West Linton, 31
Westminster Assembly (1644–8), 19, 59
  Confession, 187, 191
Weston Favell, 203
White, Hugh, 156
  John, 146
Whitefield, George, 3, 7, 25 *fn*, 53, 98,
  105, 145, 157 *fn*, 160, 175, 178 *fn*,
  200, 202
  helps to publish *Memoirs of
    Halyburton*, 15 *fn*
  first visit to Scotland (1741), 81, 92,
    101–2
  abused by Scottish landowner, 87;
    by *Scots Magazine*, 89–90; by
    Cameronians, 164–5
  influenced by book written by
    Henry Scougal, 99–100
  comes into touch with M'Culloch
    of Cambuslang, 102, 111–12
  visits Dundee, 110
  his work in London described,
    113–14
  visits Cambuslang during Revival
    (1742), 114–22
  visits Kilsyth, 130
  visit to Scotland (1748), 166
  opposed by the Seceders (Associate
    Presbytery), 183–91, 193, 195–6
  Overture to hinder his preaching in
    Scottish Parish Churches, 221
  results of visits to Scotland, 217–19
Whitefield, Mrs, 218
Whithorn, 34, 37
Wightman, Robert, 140, 226
Wigtown, 34, 35, 36, 39
William III (King), 9, 11, 46, 68, 138
Williams, Daniel, 215
Willison, John, 7, 26, 81, 85, 110–11,
  115, 128, 132, 157, 161, 186, 196,
  218
Wilson, Gabriel, 27
  Margaret, 36
  William, 26
Wishart (18th-century minister), 16
  William, 100
Witherspoon, John, 207
Wodrow, Robert, 16, 17, 24, 39, 43,
  46, 59, 60, 67, 68, 79, 87, 138, 151,
  213, 214, 215
Woodward, Josiah, 59, 60, 61
Wycliffe, John, 62

Yale, 217
Young, James, 110

Zinzendorf, Count, 58

BOOKS VALUED BY CAMBUSLANG REVIVAL CONVERTS

Alarm to the Unconverted (Alleine), 78
Body of Divinity (Thos Watson), 76, 84, 85
Catechisms (Crawford and Vincent), 78, 84, 85
Christian's Great Interest (Wm Guthrie), 85–7
Life of Elizabeth Waste (West), 85
Poems (Craig), 84
Sincere Convert (Thos Shepard), 84
Trial of a Saving Interest in Christ, see *Christian's Great Interest*

Some Other Banner of Truth Trust Titles

THE PURITAN HOPE

Iain Murray

Views on the future prospects of the Christian Church in history have differed drastically during the various periods of her life since Pentecost. In certain eras of darkness and chaos Christians have anticipated no future save that to be ushered in by the imminent Second Advent of Christ, while at other times conviction has gripped the Church that the gospel in which she believes is yet to be a world-transforming power. It was owing to the Puritans that the latter outlook became dominant in British Christianity for over two hundred years. How this occurred and how widespread was the influence of their hope is the subject of this volume.

After tracing some of the salient features of the Puritan revival age, the author goes on to show how their witness reverberated through the succeeding centuries. As late as 1874 John Richard Green could write: 'The whole history of English progress since the Restoration, on its moral and spiritual sides, has been the history of Puritanism.' And beyond Britain, first in North America, then in India and Africa, the confidence which stemmed from the theology of the Puritan school inspired the greatest missionary advance since the apostolic era.

312 pages, illustrated, £1·20

SOME PAPERBACK TITLES

An Alarm to the Unconverted *Joseph Alleine* 160*pp*, 22*p*
The Best Books *W. J. Grier* 176*pp*, 22*p*
The Bible Tells Us So *R. B. Kuiper* 144*pp*, 25*p*
The Christian's Great Interest *William Guthrie* 208*pp*, 25*p*
The Christian View of Man *J. Gresham Machen* 254*pp*, 25*p*
Five English Reformers *J. C. Ryle* 160*pp*, 17*p*
For a Testimony *Bruce F. Hunt* 160*pp*, 25*p*
Genesis 3 *Edward J. Young* 176*pp*, 25*p*
*God-Centred Evangelism *R. B. Kuiper* 240*pp*, 30*p*
Hebrews *G. B. Wilson* 192*pp*, 30*p*
Letters of John Newton 192*pp*, 22*p*
The Momentous Event *W. J. Grier* 128*pp*, 25*p*
Precious Remedies Against Satan's Devices *Thomas Brooks* 272*pp*, 37*p*
Profiting from the Word *A. W. Pink* 128*pp*, 25*p*
The Rare Jewel of Christian Contentment *Jeremiah Burroughs* 240*pp*, 22*p*
Reformation Today *K. Runia* 160*pp*, 25*p*
Romans *Geoffrey Wilson* 256*pp*, 30*p*
*The Sovereignty of God *A. W. Pink* 160*pp*, 25*p*
*Summary of Christian Doctrine *Louis Berkhof* 192*pp*, 17*p*
Today's Gospel *Walter Chantry* 96*pp*, 20*p*
Warnings to the Churches *J. C. Ryle* 176*pp*, 25*p*

Not for sale to the U.S.A. or Canada

SOME OTHER TITLES

An All-Round Ministry *C. H. Spurgeon* 418*pp*, 75*p*

The Beatitudes *Thomas Watson* 320*pp*, £1·20

A Body of Divinity *Thomas Watson* 328*pp*, 75*p*

Charity and Its Fruits *Jonathan Edwards* 372*pp*, £1·05

*The Child's Story Bible *Catherine Vos* 732*pp*, £2·10

George Whitefield *Arnold Dallimore* 624*pp*, £2·10

*The Glorious Body of Christ *R. B. Kuiper* 392*pp*, £1·05

*The History of Christian Doctrines *Louis Berkhof* 296*pp*, £1·25

The Interpretation of Prophecy *Patrick Fairbairn* 546*pp*, £1·25

John G. Paton: Missionary to the New Hebrides 528*pp*, £1·05

The Log College *Archibald Alexander* 256*pp*, £1·05

The Lord's Prayer *Thomas Watson* 320*pp*, 75*p*

The Office and Work of the Holy Spirit *James Buchanan* 296*pp*, £1·05

Robert Murray M'Cheyne: Memoir and Remains *Andrew A. Bonar* 664*pp*, £1·25

*Romans: Atonement and Justification *D. M. Lloyd-Jones* 272*pp*, £1·25

Spurgeon: the Early Years 570*pp*, £1·25

*Systematic Theology *Louis Berkhof* 784*pp*, £2·10

Thoughts on Religious Experience *Archibald Alexander* 368*pp*, £1·05

For free illustrated catalogue write to

THE BANNER OF TRUTH TRUST

78b Chiltern Street London WIM IPS